CHILDREN'S LEARNING IN SCHOOL

C000284240

edited by
Victor Lee
at The Open University

Hodder & Stoughton

LONDON SYDNEY AUCKLAND TORONTO
in association with The Open University

This reader forms part of The Open University course E271 *Curriculum and Learning*. For further information on the course, write to School of Education (E271), The Open University, Walton Hall, Milton Keynes MK7 6AA.

This reader is one part of an Open University integrated teaching system and the selection is therefore related to other material available to students. It is designed to evoke the critical understanding of students. Opinions expressed in it are not necessarily those of the course team or of the University.

The E271 course team is against the use of sexist language and gender stereotyping. We have tried to avoid the use of sexist language in this reader but some examples may remain from the original articles, and for this we apologise.

British Library Cataloguing in Publication Data
Lee, Victor
    Children's learning in school. – (Curriculum and learning)
    I. Learning by children
    I. Title   II. Series
    155.413

    ISBN 0–340–54007–9

First published 1990

© 1990 The Open University

All rights reserved. No part of this publication may be reproduced or transmitted in any form or by any means, electronic or mechanical, including photocopy, recording, or any information storage and retrieval system, without permission in writing from the publisher or under licence from the Copyright Licensing Agency Limited. Further details of such licences (for reprographic reproduction) may be obtained from the Copyright Licensing Agency Limited, of 33–34 Alfred Place, London WC1E 7DP.

Typeset by Wearside Tradespools, Fulwell, Sunderland.
Printed for the educational publishing division of Hodder and Stoughton Ltd, Mill Road, Dunton Green, Sevenoaks, Kent by Clays Ltd., St Ives plc.

CONTENTS

ACKNOWLEDGMENTS

The publishers would like to thank the following for permission to reproduce material in this volume:

Neville Bennett for 'Implementing cooperative groupwork in classrooms' by Neville Bennett and Elizabeth Dunne; Bristol Classical Press for 'Instrumental Enrichment' by Bob Burden and Anton Florek from M J Coles and W D Robinson (eds) *Teaching Thinking* (1989); The British Psychological Society/T N Carraher for 'Mathematics in the Streets and in Schools' by Terezinha Nunes Carraher, David Carraher and Analucia Dias Schliemann from *British Journal of Development Psychology* Vol 3, 1985; Lawrence Erlbaum Associates Inc. for 'The tension between theories of learning and instruction in mathematics' by Paul Cobb from *Educational Psychologist* Vol 23, 1988; Falmer Press for 'What is behavioural approach to teaching?' by Kevin Wheldall and Frank Merrett from N Hastings and J Ackwieso (eds) *New Directions in Educational Psychology* Vol 2, 1987; Willliam Heinemann Ltd for 'The application of intelligences' by Howard Gardner from *Frames of Mind* (1984); The Menninger Clinic for 'The stages of intellectual development of the child' by Jean Piaget from the *Bulletin of the Menninger Clinic* Vol 26, pp 102–128, copyright 1962, The Menninger Foundation; Methuen and Co for 'Communication and Control' by Derek Edwards and Neil Mercer from *Common Knowledge: The development of understanding in the classroom* (1987); Nafferton Books for 'The Story of Stories – an enquiry into Children's thought' by Michael Armstrong from *Curriculum* Vol 4, 1983; Open University Press for 'Children's Ideas and the Learning of Science' from Driver, Guesne and Tiberghien (eds) *Children's Ideas In Science* (1985) and 'Practical Work in Science – a task-based approach?' by Richard Gott and Judith Mashiter from Woolnough (ed) *Practical Science* (1990); Plenum Publishing Corporation for 'The joint socialisation of development by young children and adults' by Barbara Rogoff from M L Lewis and S Feinman (eds) *Social Influences and Behaviour*; TESOL for 'Orality and Literacy: From the *Savage Mind* to *Ways With Words*' by James Paul Gee from *TESOL Quarterly* Vol 20, pp 719–746, copyright 1986; John Wiley and Sons, Inc. for 'Computer-based learning: the social dimensions' by Paul Light and Agnes Blaye from Hugh Foot, Michelle Morgan and Rosalyn Shute (eds) *Children Helping Children*.

Every effort has been made to trace and acknowledge ownership of copyright. The publishers will be glad to make suitable arrangements with any copyright holders whom it has not been possible to contact.

GENERAL INTRODUCTION

VICTOR LEE

This collection of readings is the second of four volumes compiled to accompany Open University course *Curriculum and Learning* (E271). Each volume is independent, this Reader being concerned with learning. Although it is designed with the needs of students of the above course in mind, it is also intended to serve a wider audience and stand as a source book of ideas for anyone interested in learning.

Any selection of readings concerned with learning has to be not just selective, but highly selective. The twentieth century has seen the spawning of more than a fair share of articles and books on learning. Ideas that seem elegant to one generation seem less compelling to the next. In this Reader there is an attempt to represent current issues and debates without being limited to them. So, it is true to say that the current popularity of constructivist viewpoints is reflected throughout the text in the extracts of such people as Rosalind Driver and her colleagues, and Paul Cobb. However, there was a time when behaviourism, for instance, held sway, and the Wheldhall and Merrett extract is in this tradition.

The three main areas treated in this Reader are learning theories (part 1), learning contexts (part 2) and learning in action (part 3). These divisions are not intended as watertight compartments but as loose groupings reflecting the structure of the *learning* part of the course with which the Reader is associated. The Rosalind Driver chapter, for example, is included under *Learning Theories*, while the Cobb chapter is used in *Learning in Action* where the subject areas of mathematics, science, thinking skills and English come into their own.

The importance of *context* on learning has come to be realised more and more in recent years, and the whole of part 2 is devoted to it. The treatment here is broad, ranging from an evaluation of the importance of collaborative learning with computers to a consideration of mathematics as practised in the streets and in schools.

Two of the 'ideologies' behind this volume are the attempts to bring together the concerns of psychology and curriculum, and the desire to combine theory and practice.

This book of readings, like the course itself, is a collaborative effort. I am grateful to those colleagues and consultants who have proposed readings and helped in the production of this volume.

part one
LEARNING THEORIES

INTRODUCTION

VICTOR LEE

The general trend in this Reader is a gradual shift away from articles rooted in psychology to those concerned with curriculum. But I hasten to add that this is a general trend. Even more, perhaps, it is a question of emphasis, because one of the main thrusts of the book as a whole is to stress the inter-relation between psychology and curriculum, and how, in these instances, the one informs the other. That said, it remains true that the emphasis in part 1 is on the psychological.

The very title of chapter 1.1, *The Application of Intelligences*, raises the question that lurks behind any learning theory: what is intelligence? Learning ability has often been defined as intelligence and vice versa. Howard Gardner tries to get beyond the old IQ definition of intelligence to intelligence as cultivated and applied in different domains and curricula. The plural form, 'intelligences', is a clue to Howard Gardner's theory of multiple intelligences rather than a single, monolithic idea. In his nativist way he regards an individual as being 'blessed' with strong intellectual abilities. Such abilities can be identified early and can be changed. He argues that these intelligences should be assessed in different ways at different ages, and discusses the significance of his view of intelligences in educational planning.

The second extract is in the behaviourist tradition, a tradition that has seen better days, but still lives on. Kevin Wheldall and Frank Merrett conveniently sum up the major assumptions behind a behavioural approach, such as its concern with the observable and its belief that behaviour is learned. The rest of chapter 1.2 deals with case studies of the application of the behavioural approach, one concerning a nursery class, the other a top junior class.

Jean Piaget has long been a major figure in any consideration of learning, and chapter 1.3 concerns his 'stage' theory of intellectual development. He offers a very different interpretation of intelligence from the 'intelligences' of Howard Gardner, seeing it develop over four stages: the sensori-motor stage, the pre-operational, the stage of concrete operations, and the stage of formal operations. His contribution has been major, and could be termed as constructivist, although most would not identify him as a mainstream constructivist.

A more central constructivist viewpoint lies behind the extract by Rosalind Driver and her colleagues on how children construe the world. She examines the personal nature, coherence and stability of children's ideas in relation to science, and discusses the value of taking account of such ideas when it comes to such tasks as planning learning activities. Her account stresses that teaching comes into the middle of things in the sense that children are not blank slates but are products of their experience and do not respond to teaching in a neutral way.

The key word in the last extract in part 1 is *interaction*. Barbara Rogoff concentrates on the relationships between child and caregiver in the *joint* socialisation of the child. At the same time she stresses that the children themselves are *active* partners in the process. The child must be seen in the context of its social world. Biology and culture are inseparable, as she puts it, twin aspects of the one context for socialising the child. *Guided participation* is the answer as she sees it, and this involves a bridging process between what children know and what is new to them. The importance it attaches to context makes it a fitting link with the chapters in part 2.

1.1 THE APPLICATION OF INTELLIGENCES

HOWARD GARDNER

Intelligences should be thought of as entities at a certain level of generality, broader than highly specific computational mechanisms (like line detection) while narrower than the most general capacities, like analysis, synthesis, or a sense of self (if any of these can be shown to exist apart from combinations of specific intelligences). Yet it is in the very nature of intelligences that each operates according to its own procedures and has its own biological bases. It is thus a mistake to try to compare intelligences on all particulars; each must be thought of as its own system with its own rules. Here a biological analogy may be useful. Even though the eye, the heart, and the kidneys are all bodily organs, it is a mistake to try to compare these organs in every particular: the same restraint should be observed in the case of intelligences.

Intelligences are not to be thought of in evaluative terms. While the word *intelligence* has in our culture a positive connotation, there is no reason to think that an intelligence must necessarily be put to good purposes. In fact, one can use one's logical-mathematical, linguistic, or personal intelligences for highly nefarious purposes.

Intelligences are best thought of apart from particular programmes of action. Of course, intelligences are most readily observed when they are being exploited to carry out one or another programme of action. Yet the possession of an intelligence is most accurately thought of as *a potential*: an individual in possession of an intelligence can be said to have no circumstance that prevents him from using that intelligence. Whether he chooses to do so (and to what end he may put that intelligence) fall outside the purview of this [chapter]. [. . .]

In the study of skills and abilities, it is customary to honour a distinction between *know-how* (tacit knowledge of how to execute something) and *know-that* (propositional knowledge about the actual set of procedures involved in execution). Thus, many of us know how to ride a bicycle but lack the propositional knowledge of how that behaviour is carried out. In contrast, many of us have propositional knowledge about how to make a soufflé without knowing how to carry this task through to successful completion. While I hesitate to glorify this rough-and-ready distinction, it is helpful to think of the various intelligences chiefly as *sets of know-how* – procedures for doing things. In fact, a concern with propositional knowledge about intelligences seems to be a particular option followed in some cultures, while of little or no interest in many others.

[. . .]

Source: *Frames of Mind* (Heinemann, 1984, pp. 68, 385–92).

ASSESSING INTELLECTUAL PROFILES

A first point is that intelligences should not be assessed in the same ways at different ages. The methods used with an infant or a preschooler ought to be tailored to the particular ways of knowing that typify these individuals and may be different from those employed with older individuals. My own belief is that one could assess an individual's intellectual potentials quite early in life, perhaps even in infancy. At that time, intellectual strengths and weaknesses would emerge most readily if individuals were given the opportunity to learn to recognise certain patterns and were tested on their capacities to remember these from one day to the next. Thus, an individual with strong abilities in the spatial realm should learn to recognise target patterns quite quickly when exposed to them, to appreciate their identity even when their arrangement in space has been altered, and to notice slight deviations from them when they are presented on subsequent trials or subsequent days. Similarly, one could assess pattern-recognition abilities in other intellectual domains (like language or number) as well as the ability to learn motor patterns and to revise and transform them in adaptive ways. My own hunch about strong intellectual abilities is that an individual so blessed does not merely have an easy time learning new patterns; he in fact learns them so readily that *it is virtually impossible for him to forget them*. The simple melodies continue to play on in his mind, the sentences linger there, the spatial or gestural configurations are readily brought to the fore, although they may not have been tapped for a while.

Even if such intellectual profiles could be drawn up in the first year or two of life, I have little doubt that profiles at that early date can be readily shifted. In fact, that is what early neural and functional plasticity is all about. A principal reason for early assessment is to allow an individual to proceed as rapidly as seems warranted in those intellectual channels where he is talented, even as it affords an opportunity to bolster those intellectual endowments that seem relatively modest.

At a somewhat later age (all the way up through the preschool years!) it should prove possible to secure a contextually rich and reliable assessment of an individual's intellectual profile. The preferred route for assessment at this age is to involve children in activities which they themselves are likely to find motivating: they can then advance with little direct tutelage through the steps involved in mastering a particular problem or task. Puzzles, games, and other challenges couched in the symbol system of a single intelligence (or of a pair of intelligences) are particularly promising means for assessing the relevant intelligence.

Involvement with such inherently engrossing materials provides an ideal opportunity to observe intelligences at work and to monitor their advances over a finite period of time. If one could watch a child as he learns to build various constructions out of blocks, one would receive insight into his skills in the areas of spatial and kinaesthetic intelligence: similarly, the child's capacities to relate a set of stories would reveal facets of his linguistic promise, even as his capacity to operate a simple machine would illuminate kinaesthetic and logical-mathematical skills. Such involvements in rich and provocative environments are also most likely to elicit 'markers' – those signs of early giftedness that are readily noticed by adults expert in a particular intellectual domain. The future musician may be marked by perfect pitch; the child gifted in personal matters, by his intuitions about the motives of others; the budding scientist, by his ability to pose provocative questions and then follow them up with appropriate ones.

Note how this approach to assessment differs from that employed in traditional intelligence testing. In the conventional test, the child is confronted by an adult who fires at him a rapid series of questions. The child is expected to give a single answer (or, when somewhat older, to write down his answer or to select it from a set of choices). A premium is placed on linguistic facility, on certain logical-mathematical abilities, and on a kind of social skill at negotiating the situation with an elder in one's presence. These factors can all intrude when one is trying to assess another kind of intelligence – say, musical, bodily-kinaesthetic, or spatial. By removing the experimenter and his paraphernalia from the assessing situation – or, at least, by placing them firmly in the background – and by substituting the actual elements and symbols of the particular realm under consideration, it should prove possible to obtain a more veridical picture of the child's current intellectual abilities – and of his intellectual potential.

Proceeding from some ideas originally put forth by the Soviet psychologist Vygotsky, it should be possible to devise tests suitable for individuals who have had little or no prior experience with the particular material or symbolic elements in question, and to see how rapidly they can progress in a given area in a limited period of time. Such a mission places a particularly strong burden on the tester to locate problems that are intrinsically engaging and serve as 'crystallising experiences' for young and naïve but possibly talented individuals. In the present study of intelligences, I have noted some of the experiences that proved catalytic for particular individuals in particular domains: watching folk pageants, for the future dancer; looking at recurrent alternating visual patterns, for the young mathematician; learning long and intricate rhymes, for the future poet.

Naturally the specific experiences favoured for the assessment of intellectual potential will differ, given the age, the sophistication, and the cultural background of the individual. Thus, when monitoring the spatial realm, one might hide an object from the one-year-old, pose a jigsaw puzzle to the six-year-old, or provide the pre-adolescent with a Rubik's cube. Analogously, in the musical realm, one might vary a lullaby for the two-year-old, provide the eight-year-old with a computer on which he can compose simple melodies, or analyse a fugue with an adolescent. In any case, the general idea of finding intriguing puzzles and allowing children to 'take off' with them seems to offer a far more valid way of assessing profiles of individuals than the current favourites world-wide: standard measures designed to be given within a half-hour with the aid of paper and pencil.

My own guess is that it should be possible to gain a reasonably accurate picture of an individual's intellectual profile – be he three or thirteen – in the course of a month or so, while that individual is involved in regular classroom activities. The total time spent might be five to ten hours of observing – a long time given current standards of intelligence testing, but a very short time in terms of the life of that student. Such a profile should indicate which lines are already launched in an individual, which lines show a decided potential for development, which are more modestly endowed or entail some genuine obstacles (such as tone-deafness, meagre visual imagery, or clumsiness).

EDUCATING INTELLIGENCES

Now comes the decisive but delicate step in the educational planning process. Given the curricular ends that one has in mind for an individual, and the individual's own intellectual profiles, a decision must be made about which educational regimen to follow. First of all, there must be a general strategic decision: does one play from strength, does one bolster weakness, or does one attempt to work along both tracks at the same time? Naturally this decision must be made in terms of the resources available, as well as of the overall goals of both the society and the individuals most directly involved.

Assuming room for developing more than a single faculty along a single track, decisions of a far more focused sort must be made as well. In the case of each individual, those charged with educational planning must decide which means can best be mobilised to help that individual attain a desired competence, skill, or role. In the case of the highly talented individual, it may be necessary (and sufficient) to enable him to work directly with an acknowledged master, in a kind of apprenticeship relation; it should also be possible to provide him with materials that he can explore (and with which he can advance) on his own. In the case of the individual with meagre abilities, or even frank pathologies, it will probably be necessary to devise special prostheses: machinery, mechanisms, or other means whereby the information or skills can be presented to him in such a way as to exploit the intellectual capacities he has, while circumventing (to as large an extent as possible) his intellectual frailties. In the case of the individual who does not fall at either extreme of the bell-shaped curve, there will presumably be a larger set of procedures and curricula from which one can draw, always acknowledging the limits of resources and the competing demands on the student's and the teacher's time.

Surprisingly little work has been done by educational psychologists in charting the general principles that may govern progress through an intellectual domain. (This lack may be due in part to a lack of concern with particular domains – as opposed to general learning; in part, to extensive concern with just how a *specific* task is mastered.) Of various efforts in this direction, I find most suggestive the work by the Soviet school of psychology – such followers of Lev Vygotsky as V. V. Davydov, D. Elkonin, and A. K. Markova. These researchers believe that at each age children exhibit a different set of interests: thus, during infancy, the dominant activity involves emotional contact; at age two, the child is absorbed in manipulation of objects; at ages three to seven, role play and other kinds of symbolic activity come to the fore; during the ages of seven to eleven, the feature activity is formal study in school; and in adolescence, the youth pursues a combination of intimate personal relations and career-oriented exploration. Any educational programme should keep these biases in mind; though, of course, the specific profile of interests may differ significantly across cultures.

Working within these broad parameters, the educator searches for *genetic primary examples*. These are problems or lessons that can be handled by the novice but, at the same time, harbour within them the most relevant abstractions within that domain. Mastery of a genetic primary example serves as an indication that an individual can successfully negotiate the succeeding steps within the field. For the educator, the challenge consists in planning the steps – the hurdles that the child must overcome so that he can progress satisfactorily through the domain, until he reaches the next phase and the next genetic primary example. If the kind of analysis put forth by Soviet psychologists could be merged with the approach being developed here, it might be possible to chart an optimal path of educational progress in each of the intellectual domains with which I have been concerned. Such an analysis would reveal the path or the set of paths to be negotiated by normal children as well as by those with special gifts or particular difficulties.

Given a wide range of cultural goals, and an even greater variety of intellectual profiles, the challenge of obtaining a match between student and method may seem overwhelming. In fact, however, students have managed to learn even when lessons are in no way tailored for them, presumably because most curricula are redundant, and because the students themselves possess an array of intellectual strengths and strategies on which they can draw. A 'matching system' should help ensure that a student can rapidly and smoothly master what needs to be mastered, and thus to proceed further along both optional and optimal paths of development.

Of course, the idea of matching individuals with particular subject matters and/or styles of teaching is familiar and has implicitly guided much instruction since Classical times. It is therefore disappointing to note that attempts to document significant improvements as a result of matching students with appropriate teaching techniques have not met with much success.

Educational scholars none the less cling to the vision of the optimal match between student and material. In my own view, this tenacity is legitimate: after all, the science of educational psychology is still young; and in the wake of superior conceptualisations and finer measures, the practice of matching the individual learner's profile to the materials and modes of instruction may still be validated. Moreover, if one adopts M.I. [multiple intelligences] theory, the options for such matches increase: as I have already noted, it is possible that the intelligences can function both as subject matters in themselves and as the preferred means for inculcating diverse subject matter.

Carrying out relevant research is a task for the future. The most I can do here is to sketch some expectations. In the case of learning to program a computer, for example, it seems plausible that a number of intellectual competences may prove relevant. Logical-mathematical intelligence seems central, because programming depends upon the deployment of strict procedures to solve a problem or attain a goal in a finite number of steps. Writing the program requires that the steps be clear, precise, and organised in a strictly logical order. Linguistic intelligence is also relevant, at least so long as manuals and computer languages make use of ordinary language. The metaphor of the program as a story (complete with subplots) may also help certain budding programmers with a linguistic bent. The intuitions that individuals have about particular domains may well help them in learning to program. Thus, an individual with a strong musical bent might best be introduced to programming by attempting to program a simple musical piece (or to master the use of a program that composes). An individual with strong spatial abilities might be initiated through some form of computer graphics – and he might also be aided in the task of programming through the use of a flow chart or some other spatial diagram. Personal intelligences can play important roles. The extensive planning of steps and goals carried out by the individual as he engages in programming relies on intrapersonal forms of thinking, even as the cooperation needed for carrying out a complex task or for learning new computational skills may rely on an individual's ability to work with a team. Kinaesthetic intelligence may play a role in working with the computer itself, facilitate skill at the terminal, and be exploited in those cases where the subject matter of a program involves use of the body (programming a dance or a sequence of football plays).

Parallel lines of reasoning can be invoked in analysing the task of learning to read. Particularly in the case of individuals who have initial difficulty in learning to read text, it may make sense to begin with an introduction to some other symbolic systems – for example, those used for musical notation, map-making, or mathematics. Moreover, individuals with pronounced reading disabilities sometimes must resort to unusual measures of learning – for example, mastering the letters through tactile-kinaesthetic exploration. The particular subject matter may also play an important role in improving reading comprehension: an individual who knows something about a field, or is interested in increasing his knowledge base, may find reading easier and will also be more highly motivated to read. Whether the actual process of reading involves, in significant measure, intelligences other than linguistic ones is problematic. However, in view of the various reading systems already invented by human beings (such as pictographic systems) and the kinds likely to be devised in the future (logical-mathematical systems for use with computers), it seems clear that one's facility in reading will depend on more than one's linguistic capacities.

Even as computers offer a useful way to think about the marshalling of intelligences to master educational goals, the potential utility of computers in the process of matching individuals to modes of instruction is substantial. While effecting a match between a student's intellectual profile and the instructional goals can be a highly demanding task for even the most gifted instructor, the relevant kinds of information could be readily handled by a computer that can, in a fraction of a second, suggest alternative pedagogical programs or routes. More important, the computer can be a vital facilitator in the actual process of instruction, helping individuals to negotiate sequences at their preferred pace by using a variety of educational techniques. I should point out, however, that the computer cannot assume certain roles of an interpersonal sort and seems less relevant for certain intellectual domains (say, kinaesthetic) than for others (logical-mathematical). There is the risk that the electronic computer – a product of Western thinking and technology – may prove most useful for perpetuating just those forms of intelligence that led to its devising in the first place. It is also possible, however, that extensions of the computer – including robots – might eventually be developed which would facilitate learning and mastery in the full gamut of intellectual domains.

While it is desirable to consider the fine points of the learning process, it is important for the planner or policy-maker not to lose sight of his overall educational agenda. Ultimately, the educational plans that are pursued need to be orchestrated across various interest groups of the society so that they can, taken together, help the society to achieve its larger goals. Individual profiles must be considered in the light of goals pursued by the wider society; and sometimes, in fact, individuals with gifts in certain directions must nonetheless be guided along other, less favoured paths, simply because the needs of the culture are particularly urgent in that realm at that time. The synthetic ability entailed in this form of decision-making involves its own blend of intelligences – if not a special form of intelligence. It is important that a society find some way of training, and then using, those abilities that permit a vision of a large and complex whole.

WHAT IS THE BEHAVIOURAL APPROACH TO TEACHING?

1.2

KEVIN WHELDALL AND FRANK MERRETT

Problems of classroom behaviour and motivation are [...] endemic in education. Teachers consistently cite difficulties in these two areas as their main classroom concerns and traditionally they have been dealt with in the same way, that is, by punitive methods. Both unacceptable or troublesome behaviour and idleness or lack of interest represent threats to the teacher's role which he or she commonly seeks to excise or avoid by aversive means. One consequence of this may be the daily litany of desist commands heard in many classrooms: 'Sit down, Sarah. Talking again, Barry. Leave Brendon alone, Nigel – get on with your own work. Something of interest outside, Mary? Eyes on your work please,' and so on, endlessly. [...] Teachers the world over spend a considerable proportion of their teaching time reprimanding children for troublesome and/or non-work-related behaviours and hardly ever comment approvingly on appropriate behaviour (Merrett and Wheldall, 1986a). Moreover as our surveys in both primary and secondary schools [...] clearly show, teachers are mostly concerned with high frequency but relatively trivial troublesome behaviours such as 'talking out of turn' and 'hindering other children'. These are the behaviours which help to cause teacher stress as they occur with monotonous regularity and call for immediate action which usually takes the form of reprimands and sanctions. In this chapter we will consider an alternative approach to such problems based on behavioural psychology: the behavioural approach to teaching. We will describe the basic operating principles and then illustrate the effectiveness of this approach with demonstration studies of its application with both younger and older children in schools.

The behavioural approach to teaching refers to the application(s) of behavioural psychology to promote good classroom practice by, almost exclusively, positive methods. In this chapter we shall concentrate primarily on its use with the social behaviour of children since it is generally accepted that good social behaviour in the classroom is necessary for academic learning to take place. The application of behavioural psychology is sometimes referred to as *behaviour modification*.

Behaviour modification is a generic term referring to the applied use of behavioural psychology to bring about changes in human behaviour by workers in the helping professions (clinical and educational psychologists, social workers,

Source: *New Directions in Educational Psychology*, Hastings, N. and Ackwieso, J. (eds), Vol. 2: *Behaviour and Motivation* (Falmer Press, 1987), pp. 167–190. First published under the title 'What is the Behavioural Approach to Teaching?'

teachers and so on). Based on the operant conditioning model of B. F. Skinner, its central tenet holds that all behaviour is primarily learned and maintained as a result of an individual's interactions with his environment, which includes other individuals, and is hence susceptible to change by exerting control over features of that environment. Behaviour change may be achieved by manipulating the consequences following behaviour, in line with the 'law of effect'. Simply stated, this means that, within any particular context, whether a behaviour is repeated or not depends upon the consequences following it.

Behaviour modification has proved an effective technique for teaching more appropriate behaviour and reducing the frequency of inappropriate behaviour, with a variety of populations in many different settings. Such techniques have been found to be efficient and effective procedures for instituting and maintaining more appropriate behaviours but have not been without their critics who have questioned the ethics of such procedures. In reply to criticisms that behaviour modification is repressive and constitutes 'mind control', its advocates have claimed that it is ethically neutral, can be used for good or evil, by devil or saint, and merely formalises and enhances the natural learning processes of the everyday world. Unhappily the term 'behaviour modification' has acquired an unfortunate public image. Hence, in the rest of this paper we employ the currently preferred term, 'behavioural approaches' or 'Positive Teaching'.

In our book *Positive Teaching* (Wheldall and Merrett, 1984), we defined the behavioural approach to teaching in terms of five key principles. These are as follows:

1 *Teaching is concerned with the observable.* Teachers using the behavioural approach concern themselves with what a child actually does rather than speculating about unconscious motives or processes which may be thought to underlie behaviour. The only evidence we have about what people can do or will do and about what they believe comes to us by observing their behaviour. Consequently, careful definition and observation of behaviour are central to the behavioural approach. Frequently, people propose explanations for behaviour which are not reasons at all. These are 'explanatory fictions' and some examples are innate aggression, language acquisition device and, dare we say it, dyslexia. To say that a child is often out of his seat *because* he is hyperactive is, quite simply, circular and gets us nowhere fast; hyperactive is just another way of describing the same behaviour. It does nothing to explain it.

2 *Almost all classroom behaviour is learned.* This is not to decry genetic inheritance nor to assume that anybody can be taught to do anything given time. Genetic inheritance sets the limits for what an individual can learn, but behaviour is still the result of learning. Certainly this applies to the sort of behaviour that parents and teachers are chiefly concerned with, for example, knowing how to respond politely to others and being able to carry out academic tasks like reading. Of course, children learn bad behaviour as well as good behaviour, a fact which parents and teachers are less ready to accept. The good news is that bad behaviour can be unlearned and new, more appropriate, behaviour learned in its place.

3 *Learning involves change in behaviour.* The only way that we know (that we can know) that learning has taken place is by observing a change in the child's behaviour. Teachers should not be satisfied with vague statements such as, 'Gemma has a better attitude towards school now'. Evidence is needed that she now attends on time, answers more questions, completes her homework or whatever. These are all clear examples of behaviours which can, if necessary, be counted and compared.

4 *Behaviour change depends mainly upon consequence.* This means that children (and adults and other animals, for that matter) learn on the basis of tending to repeat behaviours which are followed by consequences which they find desirable or rewarding whereas they tend not to repeat behaviours, the consequences of which they find aversive or punishing. The emphasis should be upon desirable consequences following appropriate behaviour. It has been shown repeatedly that rewarding good behaviour is more effective than punishing undesirable behaviour.

5 *Behaviours are also influenced by the contexts within which they occur.* In any situation some behaviours are more appropriate than others. If a child's behaviour is appropriate for a particular circumstance then it is likely to be rewarded by the people (adults or peers) who are around. If it is inappropriate to the situation it is less likely to be rewarded and may even be punished. As a result children rapidly learn not only how to perform certain behaviours but also when and where they are appropriate. Similarly, certain behaviours are more likely in some situations rather than others simply because there is more opportunity to engage in them. There is far more chance to chatter and to interfere with others when seated in classroom table groups than when in rows, for example, whilst young children are more likely to push and jostle when crowded together around the teacher than when spread out. It is important to emphasise that it is necessary to consider classroom ecological variables and setting events for behaviour as well as consequences.

This is what is meant by the behavioural approach to teaching. The main assumption is that children's behaviour is primarily learned and maintained as a result of their interactions with their environment, which includes other children and teachers. Consequently, children's behaviour can be changed by altering certain features of that environment. As we have said, the key environmental features are events which immediately precede or follow behaviour. This means that classroom behaviours followed by consequences which the pupils find rewarding will tend to increase in frequency. Similarly, certain changes in behaviour may be brought about merely by changing the classroom setting (for example, seating arrangements or classroom rules). The five points set out above may be seen as the essential features of the behavioural approach to teaching.

If we believe that teaching is concerned with helping children to learn new skills and gain new information, and if we believe also that learning implies a change or changes in behaviour, then it follows logically that teaching is about changing children's behaviour, whether we are talking about the acquisition of appropriate social skills or the learning of new academic information. Moreover, if teaching is about changing behaviour then the role of the teacher is, quite simply, to bring about changes in the behaviour of the children in his or her class.

The basic model embodying the crucial elements of the behavioural approach is known as the three term analysis of behaviour or the ABC model. It provides a basis for the analysis of, and intervention in, any particular teaching situation. 'A' refers to the antecedent conditions, i.e., the context in which a behaviour occurs or what is happening in that environment prior to a behaviour occurring. 'B' refers to the behaviour itself, i.e. what a child is actually doing in real physical terms (not what you think he is doing as a result of inferences from his behaviour). 'C' refers to the consequences of the behaviour, i.e., what happens to the child after the behaviour. Let us look at these three elements again in a little more detail, beginning with behaviour.

Behaviour. We have already said that a child's behaviour refers to what she is actually doing and we attempt to say what a child is doing in as precise a way as possible. If we observe a child building a tower with bricks, we would not write down 'creative play' since another observer or someone else reading our notes might interpret 'creative play' differently. It is too vague and imprecise. We would record that the child constructed a tower of four bricks. To say that it is 'creative' and/or that it is 'play' is to interpret, is prone to inaccuracy and vagueness and is unlikely to be useful. Similarly, if a teacher tells us that Jason is always 'messing about' in class, we have to ask the teacher to define the behaviour more clearly. What you regard as 'messing about' may not be what he regards as 'messing about'. Moreover, if we use a vague definition there is no guarantee that it is the same sort of behaviour we are categorising in this way two days running. So we would ask the teacher to list any of Jason's behaviours which he finds objectionable and then to define them as precisely as possible. A behaviour which is frequently found at the top of many teachers' lists is 'talking out of turn'. If we define this as 'any talking by a child when the teacher has requested the class to get on with set work in silence', then we are moving closer towards an objective definition. The more objective our definition, the easier it is for two observers to agree that a certain behaviour has occurred and the easier it is to count instances of such behaviour. Counting instances of behaviour can be an extremely useful, if not essential, component of the behavioural approach to teaching.

Precise definition of behaviour also helps us to avoid the danger of over-interpretation and giving explanatory fictions as causes of behaviour. These are generally unhelpful and give a veneer or gloss of 'scientific' explanation. For example, if Darren keeps hitting other children his teacher may describe him as being 'aggressive', but if we ask her how she knows this, she may reply 'He keeps hitting other children'. The word 'aggressive' is simply a label for a child who frequently hits other children but is sometimes used as if it were an explanation of this behaviour.

Consequences. As we said earlier, this refers to the fact that we tend to repeat behaviours which bring us what we want and to refrain from repeating behaviours leading to occurrences which we want to avoid. This appears to be a characteristic of all animals but we differ from animals, and also from each other, in terms of what we seek out and what we seek to avoid. In common with other animals, we tend to seek out food and will repeat behaviours which have led to the provision of food when we are deprived of it. Moreover, many, if not most of us, will work for money. Similarly, the majority of people find praise and approval rewarding and tend to behave in a way which is likely to be followed by praise or approval. On the other hand, perhaps few of us go out of our way to collect train numbers and, thankfully and more seriously, even fewer seek out and behave in a way likely to secure the 'reward' of drugs such as heroin. A major concern within the behavioural approach to teaching is with the identification of things and events which children find rewarding and to structure the teaching environment so as to make access to these rewards dependent upon behaviour which the teacher wants to encourage in his class.

In simple, everyday language consequences may be described as 'rewarding' or 'punishing'. Rewarding consequences, which we call positive reinforcers, are events which we seek out or 'go for', whilst we try to avoid punishing consequences; neutral consequences are events which affect us neither way. Behaviours followed by positive reinforcers are likely to increase in frequency. Behaviours followed by punishers tend to decrease in frequency whilst neutral consequences have no effect. In the behavioural approach to teaching, infrequent but desired behaviours (for example, getting on with the set work quietly) are made more frequent by arranging for positive reinforcers, such as teacher attention and approval, to follow their occurrence. Undesired behaviours may be decreased in frequency by ensuring that positive reinforcers do *not* follow their occurrence, i.e., a neutral consequence is arranged. Occasionally it may be necessary to follow undesired behaviours with punishers (for example, a stern 'telling off') in an attempt to reduce the frequency of behaviour rapidly, but there are many problems associated with this procedure. Contrary to popular belief, punishment plays only a minor and infrequent role in the behavioural approach, not least because what we believe to be punishing could, in fact, be reinforcing to the child. For example, the child who receives little attention from adults may behave in ways which result in adult disapproval. This child may prefer disapproval to being ignored and will continue to behave like this because adult attention is positively reinforcing. This is known as attention-seeking behaviour.

We should note that terminating a punishing consequence is also reinforcing and can be, and often is, used to increase desired behaviours. This is known as negative reinforcement. Again this has problems associated with its use since the child may rapidly learn other, more effective, ways of avoiding the negative consequence than you had in mind. For example, a teacher may continually use sarcasm and ridicule with his pupils. He ceases only when they behave as he wishes. Another way of avoiding this unpleasant consequence, however, other than by doing as the teacher wishes, is to stay away from school.

Finally one can punish by removing or terminating positive consequences (for example, by taking away a child's sweets). This is known as *response cost* but again there are similar problems associated with this approach. The following diagram shows the relationships between these various consequences and their effects.

Antecedents. Antecedent events or conditions, i.e., events which precede behaviour, may also influence its occurrence. They can serve to prompt a certain behaviour. Consider the situation when a teacher leaves the room and his class is left alone. For some classes this occurrence will have become a cue for noisy, disruptive behaviour since there is no-one around to reprimand the children. When the teacher does return the noisy disruptive behaviour will cease. We can see that a specific antecedent condition has control over this particular behaviour which is derived from association with certain consequences. Let us take another example which highlights how this might occur.

The teacher asks a child a question in class (antecedent stimulus), the child gives a silly answer (the behaviour), and his classmates laugh (the consequence). If this consequence is positively reinforcing, we may expect the child to produce silly answers upon subsequent similar occasions. He will probably be less likely to do so, however, when his classmates are not there. The presence of his peers has become a stimulus for his misbehaviour. This example gives some of the idea behind the need to consider the context in which behaviours occur. The relationships between A, B, and C, the antecedent conditions, the behaviours and the consequences are known as the contingencies of reinforcement. Another important consideration which we must bear in mind, however, is the frequency of reinforcement.

	To Increase Behaviour(s)	**To Decrease Behaviour(s)**
Delivery of	'Good things', i.e., rewarding with smiles, sweets, toys, praise, etc. Technical term: *Positive reinforcement*	'Bad things' i.e., punishing with smacks, frowns, reprimands, etc. Technical term: *Punishment*
Removal of	'Bad things' i.e., allowing escape from pain, noise, nagging, threats, etc. Technical term: *Negative reinforcement*	'Good things' i.e., losing privileges, house points, money, opportunities to earn 'good things'; etc. Technical term: *Response Cost*

Table 1   *Changing behaviour*

When we want to teach a child to do something new, or to encourage him to behave in a certain way more frequently than he normally does, it is important that we ensure that he is positively reinforced every time he behaves as we want him to. This normally leads to rapid learning and is known as continuous reinforcement. When he has learned the new behaviour and/or is behaving as we want him to do regularly, then we may maintain this behaviour more economically by reducing the frequency of reinforcement. Another important reason for wanting to reduce the frequency is that the child may become less responsive if the positive reinforcer becomes too easily available. Consequently, once a child is regularly behaving in a desired way we can best maintain that behaviour by ensuring that he is now reinforced only intermittently. Intermittent reinforcement can be arranged so that a child is reinforced every so often (i.e., in terms of time) or, alternatively, after so many occurrences of the behaviour. These different ways of organising the frequency of reinforcement are known as reinforcement schedules.

Following this summary of basic behavioural theory, we can now turn to a consideration of what the behavioural approach to teaching is all about. With some children the behaviour that concerns us has not yet been learned, with others the behaviour is learned but does not occur frequently enough whilst other children frequently behave in inappropriate ways. The behavioural approach to teaching is about changing the frequencies of behaviour. It can be used to teach new skills or to increase or decrease existing rates of behaviour. It is important to emphasise that the behavioural approach to teaching is primarily concerned with increasing the frequency of desirable behaviour in the classroom.

The effectiveness of the behavioural approach to teaching in the normal classroom has been demonstrated in a wide variety of experimental studies. Our own studies have demonstrated how to bring about changes in the problem behaviour of single children, small groups and even whole classes of children from a wide range of educational populations (Merrett, 1986; Wheldall and Merrett, 1984). More importantly, we have shown teachers how to encourage and increase the kinds of behaviour they want to see children in their classes engaged in and which are of educational benefit to them.

The methods advocated are all firmly based on behavioural principles and have all been carefully and rigorously tried and tested in work with teachers. Simple and straightforward interventions by teachers using positive methods can bring about dramatic results in terms of improved classroom atmosphere and the quantity and quality of work produced. Both antecedents and consequences can be engineered to good effect. Moreover, these methods, illustrated in the case studies below, have been shown to yield more satisfying and rewarding classroom experiences for both teachers and children.

CASE STUDIES IN THE BEHAVIOURAL APPROACH TO TEACHING

The behavioural approach can be applied in the management of classroom social behaviour in an endless variety of ways, calling for imagination, inventiveness and initiative on the part of teachers. There is no single prescriptive nostrum. The behavioural approach to teaching requires the consistent application of basic principles to unique and personal classroom problems. Behavioural methods work with all ages and in all subject areas; their operationalisation, however, necessarily changes from situation to situation. Moreover, demonstrations of the effectiveness of behavioural interventions differ in terms of the formality with which they are carried out and evaluated. The rigorous designs beloved of researchers cut less ice with practical teachers for whom simple 'suck it and see' methods are enough. Both forms of demonstration study are necessary. First, let us consider a study which is little more than an anecdote, but which nevertheless proved a very rewarding lesson for the teacher, nursery assistant and parents involved.

HELPING AN INDIVIDUAL CHILD IN A NURSERY CLASS

In the nursery class in our Centre for Child Study, the two staff were concerned about a four-year-old boy, whom we will refer to as Gavin. Gavin came from a caring, professional family, but in comparison with the other children in the nursery, he seemed to our staff to be 'rather immature'. Pressed to be more specific, the nursery teacher and nursery assistant described how he very rarely played with the other children, never initiated interactions and, in fact, did not seem to do very much for himself at all. He behaved, they said, in some ways more like a two-year-old than a four-year-old and was 'babied' by his parents.

Casual observation certainly confirmed the worries of the nursery staff. Gavin spent most of his time standing on the fringe of the nursery action, watching or daydreaming, with his thumb in his mouth. Both nursery class staff employ positive methods and are au fait with our behavioural approach but they reported that praise seemed to have little effect on Gavin. It certainly did not seem to encourage him to participate more. Consequently, we suggested that a more powerful form of reward might be necessary in the form of tokens. The usual sort of star chart is not appropriate for young children and so the 'snake' programme was suggested. A long snake was drawn for him on a stiff card, divided up into a number of sections. It was explained to Gavin, in simple terms, that whenever he completed an activity, he would be allowed to colour in one of the segments of his snake. When his snake was complete he would receive a prize, a small model vehicle which, in common with most small boys, he was very keen to have.

It is only fair to add that our staff were not, at this stage, totally convinced that this scheme would work for Gavin. Nevertheless, they enthusiastically put the scheme into operation and began by suggesting activities to him, for example, painting a picture or building a Lego model. Gavin, to his credit, responded to these suggestions and consequently earned his points and the right to colour succeeding segments of the snake. Later on, the staff asked him what he wanted to do next, as a prompt, and he continued to be rewarded every time he completed an activity. Finally, he began gradually to initiate activities himself, pausing only to tell the staff that he had finished and to colour another segment.

Gavin's progress was remarkable and by the end of the first week he had completed his snake and was delighted to receive his prize, a model tractor. Another snake programme was immediately initiated, at his request. No formal data were collected apart from the implicit recording of completed activities in the colouring-in of the snake. This visual record of progress confirmed casual observations of Gavin's increased activity level. Instead of almost literally 'doing nothing' Gavin was now clearly seen to be engaging in several different activities every morning, to the satisfaction of the nursery staff. An unplanned bonus for the staff came from Gavin's parents, who had been told about the programme and who had been encouraged to praise Gavin for his progress on the snake. Shortly after the programme began they reported improvements in his social behaviour at home. He rapidly began to change from being a passive child with little interest in his world to a far more active individual with a lively curiosity. In spite of being more active he began to sleep *less* and was not nearly so sluggish as he had previously been. As Gavin was approaching the age to begin formal schooling these were important developments.

A 'GAME' APPROACH TO IMPROVE THE BEHAVIOUR OF A TOP JUNIOR CLASS

The informal report above illustrates how in some situations hard data collection is not essential. The changes were sufficiently large and obvious to impress both nursery staff and parents. In the next example, however, more objective data collection was carried out in the context of a study carefully designed to demonstrate the effectiveness of a behavioural intervention with primary aged pupils.

Ways of maintaining control in an unruly classroom are many and various, but the key principle using the behavioural approach is basically to praise the good and try to ignore the bad. Becker, Madsen, Arnold and Thomas (1967) and Madsen, Becker and Thomas (1968) in classic studies on this, compared 'rules, praise and ignoring': i.e., set a series of simple, positively phrased rules which are made known to the class, for example, 'we sit quietly while working'; ignore all behaviour contravening these rules where possible; catch the children being good and reinforce them. They compared various combinations of these three basic procedures. The first condition, rules only, had little effect in reducing undesirable behaviour. The results were still inconsistent when 'ignoring' was added. But the third combination in which praise was added to 'rules' and 'ignoring' was shown to be a highly effective procedure for maintaining classroom control. Hence they concluded that 'praise for appropriate behaviour was probably the key teacher behaviour in achieving effective classroom management'.

Similarly, an experiment by Thomas, Becker and Armstrong (1969) showed how 'good' teachers who normally maintain a well ordered classroom by ignoring inappropriate behaviours and by consistently reinforcing appropriate behaviours, can, by altering these contingencies, produce dramatic deterioration in classroom behaviour. In one study disruptive behaviour was raised from the normal low level of around eight to nine per cent to over forty per cent accompanied by an appreciable rise in noise level. This was 'achieved' by the teacher frequently expressing disapproval for inappropriate behaviours. Thus it has been shown experimentally that whilst reinforcing (by expressing approval of) desirable behaviours leads to increased good behaviour, attending to inappropriate behaviour, even by expressing disapproval, may increase the very behaviours it is attempting to reduce. It has similarly been shown that increasing the number of 'sit down' commands increases the amount of out-of-seat behaviour, whilst praising for in-seat behaviour reduces out-of-seat behaviour.

In our own study demonstrating one approach to behavioural classroom management, we wanted to devise a positive approach which the children would actually find enjoyable. Consequently, rather than concentrating on trying to eliminate undesirable behaviours, which is known to be ineffective, we decided to concentrate on the behaviour we wanted, i.e., getting on with school work or 'studying behaviour' and to try to raise the frequency of what was, in the class we studied, relatively infrequent behaviour. As we make clear in our original paper reporting this study (Merrett and Wheldall, 1978), the approach was not totally original, being based on several other studies employing 'game' strategies, but it was highly successful.

The subject was a young, relatively inexperienced, female teacher, who was having a lot of trouble in controlling her class of thirty intellectually below average 10–11 year olds attending a state primary school. Classroom seating was arranged around four tables and we decided to make use of this in our intervention strategy.

However, initially we needed more specific and accurate information about the children's behaviour in the classroom. A cassette-tape was prepared to give a clear 'ping' on a 'variable interval' schedule of sixty seconds, i.e., at irregular intervals but on average once per minute. On hearing the sound the teacher would look at one of the four tables of children, indicated in random order on a pre-prepared sheet, and note the behaviour of the target child for that table by ticking the appropriate column. The target child was chosen afresh for each observation session on a random basis and thus all children in the class were observed during the study. Every time she heard the 'ping' the teacher had to glance at the schedule to see which table was next and record the behaviour of the target child by ticking appropriately. She could do this whilst working at her desk and, with experience, whilst walking around the room advising individuals and commenting on their work. The reliability of the teacher's results was checked from time to time by the experimenter using an identical record sheet and the same target children, and there was found to be very high agreement.

After several weeks of practice, 'baseline' data was collected, i.e., data collected prior to the teacher being given any instruction in behavioural methods (she also had no prior knowledge of the behavioural approach). By averaging over sessions we calculated that the children were 'on-task', i.e., quietly getting on with their work, only forty-four per cent of the time. The teacher was then given some basic instruction in the behavioural approach and an intervention strategy was suggested to her. She readily agreed since she was well aware of the rather 'chaotic' state of her classroom.

Briefly, the children were told the rules of a 'game' which were: we stay in our seats whilst working; we get on quietly with our work; we try not to interrupt. Whilst the game was in progress, the cassette would be switched on and every time the 'ping' sounded the teacher would look at one of the tables. If everyone on the table was keeping the rules, then each child on the table would score a house point.

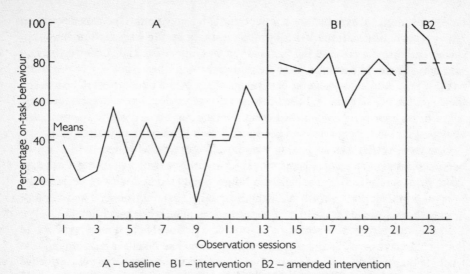

A – baseline   BI – intervention   B2 – amended intervention

Figure 1 *Average on-task behaviour of the class over the three phases of the study*

(They were assured that all tables would get equal turns but that the order would be random.) Each time a team point was given it was accompanied by verbal praise. This procedure lasted for five weeks when an amendment was announced. In future points would be awarded on only fifty per cent of the signals (pings), again on a random basis. The pings continued to serve the teacher as a signal for observing and recording the behaviour of the target children as well as a signal for reinforcement.

The results were remarkable and immediate, as figure 1 shows. From the baseline on-task behaviour of only 44 per cent, it rose to 77 per cent following the intervention. Moreover, when the amendment to the schedule of reinforcement was made, after five weeks, the on-task behaviour rose even higher to between 80 and 100 per cent. Interestingly the quality of 'off-task' behaviour also changed. Whereas before the intervention disruptiveness was mainly shown in loud talking and quite a lot of movement around the room, after intervention off-task behaviour consisted mainly of passive inattention, daydreaming, watching other children and so on.

A purely subjective estimate of the classroom after the intervention was of great improvement in terms of orderliness and quiet during classroom work periods. An attempt was also made to measure academic output both before and after intervention. For example, samples of written work taken from the class during the collection of baseline data showed a mean output of approximately five written words per minute. During one of the first intervention sessions this had improved to a mean of approximately thirteen written words. However the number of spelling errors, despite the big increase in output, had hardly changed.

Comment was invited from the teacher once the project was completed. She used the term 'harrowing' to describe her problems with class control in her first (probationary) year. The recording of baseline data had proved 'tedious and time-consuming' at first but she thought that it became easier and less distracting after practice. She said she 'felt silly' about putting up the wall chart of rules, but she agreed that the effect of the intervention was immediate and very effective and said that she would continue using behavioural techniques especially in providing positive reinforcement for good behaviour. Some of the children were also asked their opinion of the game. Of the thirteen who responded, twelve were approving. All of those approving commented upon the fact that the quietness that prevailed enabled them to concentrate and get on with their work without interruption.

One issue which was surprising was the effectiveness of house points. It had been supposed that some stronger back-up reinforcement would be needed to make the game effective. Perhaps the house points worked so well because the intervention took place shortly after the system had been introduced and because it, in turn, was backed up by the award of badges to be worn in school. [. . .]

In this chapter we have attempted to outline a positive, behavioural approach to improving classroom discipline. The central focus has been on encouraging the types of behaviour which teachers consider to be most appropriate for effective learning to take place. What should be taught and in what order and how it should be taught are decisions for teachers to make as expert and professional educationists. The behavioural approach to teaching provides the means for achieving whatever teachers decide is in the best interests of their pupils.

REFERENCES

Becker, W. C., Madsen, C., Arnold, C. R. and Thomas, D. (1967) 'The contingent use of teacher attention and praise in reducing classroom behaviour problems', *Journal of Special Education*, 1, pp. 287–307.

Madsen, C. H., Becker, W. C. and Thomas, D. R. (1968) 'Rules, praise and ignoring: Elements of elementary classroom control', *Journal of Applied Behaviour Analysis*, 1, pp. 139–50.

Merrett, F. (1986) *Encouragement Works Better Than Punishment*, (second edition) Birmingham, Positive Products.

Merrett, F. and Wheldall, K. (1978) 'Playing the game: A behavioural approach to classroom management', *Educational Review*, 30, pp. 391–400.

Thomas, D. R., Becker, W. C. and Armstrong, M. (1969) 'Production and elimination of disruptive classroom behaviour by systematically varying teacher's behaviour', *Journal of Applied Behaviour Analysis*, 1, pp. 35–45.

Wheldall, K. and Merrett, F. (1984) *Positive Teaching: The Behavioural Approach*, London, Allen and Unwin.

The Stages of the Intellectual Development of the Child

Jean Piaget

A consideration of the stages of the development of intelligence should be preceded by asking the question, What is intelligence? Unfortunately, we find ourselves confronted by a great number of definitions. For Claparède, intelligence is an adaptation to new situations. When a situation is new, when there are no reflexes, when there are no habits to rely on, then the subject is obliged to search for something new. That is to say, Claparède defines intelligence as groping, as feeling one's way, trial-and-error behaviour. We find this trial-and-error behaviour in all levels of intelligence, even at the superior level, in the form of hypothesis testing. As far as I am concerned, this definition is too vague, because trial and error occurs in the formation of habits, and also in the earliest established reflexes: when a newborn baby learns to suck.

Karl Bühler defines intelligence as an act of immediate comprehension: that is to say, an insight. Bühler's definition is also very precise, but it seems to be too narrow. I know that when a mathematician solves a problem, he or she ends by having an insight, but up to that moment he or she feels, or gropes for, his or her way; and to say that the trial-and-error behaviour is not intelligent and that intelligence starts only when he or she finds the solution to the problem, seems a very narrow definition. I would, therefore, propose to define intelligence not by a static criterion, as in previous definitions, but by the direction that intelligence follows in its evolution, and then I would define intelligence as a form of equilibration, or forms of equilibration, towards which all cognitive functions lead.

But I must first define equilibration. Equilibration in my vocabulary is not an exact and automatic balance, as it would be in *Gestalt* theory; I define equilibration principally as a compensation for an external disturbance.

When there is an external disturbance, the subject succeeds in compensating for this by an activity. The maximum equilibration is thus the maximum of the activity, and not a state of rest. It is a mobile equilibrium, and not an immobile one. So equilibration is defined as compensation; compensation is the annulling of a transformation by an inverse transformation. The compensation which intervenes in equilibration implies the fundamental idea of reversibility, and this reversibility is precisely what characterises the operations of the intelligence. An operation is an

Source: *Bulletin of the Menninger Clinic*, 1962, Vol. 26, pp. 120–8. Also in P. Barnes, J. Oates, J. Chapman, V. Lee and P. Czerniewska (eds), *Personality, Development and Learning* (Hodder & Stoughton, 1984), pp. 31–8.

internalised action, but it is also a reversible action. But an operation is never isolated; it is always subordinated to other operations; it is part of a more inclusive structure. Consequently, we define intelligence in terms of operations, coordination of operations.

Take, for example, an operation like addition: addition is a material action, the action of reuniting. On the other hand, it is a reversible action, because addition may be compensated by subtraction. Yet addition leads to a structure of a whole. In the case of numbers, it will be the structure that the mathematicians call a 'group'. In the case of addition of classes which intervene in the logical structure it will be a more simple structure that we will call a grouping, and so on.

Consequently, the study of the stages of intelligence is first a study of the formation of operational structures. I shall define every stage by a structure of a whole, with the possibility of its integration into succeeding stages, just as it was prepared by preceding stages. Thus, I shall distinguish four great stages, or four great periods, in the development of intelligence: first, the sensori-motor period before the appearance of language; second, the period from about two to seven years of age, the pre-operational period which precedes real operations; third, the period from 7 to 12 years of age, a period of concrete operations (which refers to concrete objects); and finally after 12 years of age, the period of formal operations, or propositional operations.

SENSORI-MOTOR STAGE

Before language develops, there is behaviour that we can call intelligent. For example, when a baby of 12 months or more wants an object which is too far from him, but which rests on a carpet or blanket, and he pulls it to get to the object, this behaviour is an act of intelligence. The child uses an intermediary, a means to get to his goal. Also, getting to an object by means of pulling a string when the object is tied to the string, or when the child uses a stick to get the object, are acts of intelligence. They demonstrate in the sensori-motor period a certain number of stages, which go from simple reflexes, from the formation of the first habits, up to the coordination of means and goals.

Remarkable in this sensori-motor stage of intelligence is that there are already structures. Sensori-motor intelligence rests mainly on actions, on movements and perceptions without language, but these actions are co-ordinated in a relatively stable way. They are co-ordinated under what we may call schemata of action. These schemata can be generalised in actions and are applicable to new situations. For example, pulling a carpet to bring an object within reach constitutes a schema which can be generalised to other situations when another object rests on a support. In other words, a schema supposes an incorporation of new situations into the previous schemata, a sort of continuous assimilation of new objects or new situations to the actions already schematised. For example, I presented to one of my children an object completely new to him – a box of cigarettes, which is not a usual toy for a baby. The child took the object, looked at it, put it in his mouth, shook it, then took it with one hand and hit it with the other hand, then rubbed it on the edge of the crib, then shook it again, and gave the impression of trying to see if there was noise. This behaviour is a way of exploring the object, of trying to understand it by assimilating it to schemata already known. The child behaves in this situation as he will later in Binet's famous vocabulary test, when he defines by usage, saying, for instance, that a spoon is for eating, and so on.

But in the presence of a new object, even without knowing how to talk, the child knows how to assimilate, to incorporate this new object into each of his already developed schemata which function as practical concepts. Here is a structuring of intelligence. Most important in this structuring is the base, the point of departure of all subsequent operational constructions. At the sensori-motor level, the child constructs the schema of the permanent object.

The knowledge of the permanent object starts at this point. The child is not convinced at the beginning that when an object disappears from view, he can find it again. One can verify by tests that object permanence is not yet developed at this stage. But there is there the beginning of a subsequent fundamental idea which starts being constructed at the sensori-motor level. This is also true of the construction of the ideas of space, of time, of causality. What is being done at the sensori-motor level concerning all the foregoing ideas will constitute · the substructure of the subsequent, fully achieved ideas of permanent objects, of space, of time, of causality.

In the formation of these substructures at the sensori-motor level, it is very interesting to note the beginning of a *reversibility*, not in thought, since there is not yet representation in thought, but in action itself. For example, the formation of the conception of space at the sensori-motor stage leads to an amazing decentration if one compares the conception of space at the first weeks of the development with that at 1½–2 years of age. In the beginning there is not one space which contains all the objects, including the child's body itself; there is a multitude of spaces which are not coordinated: there are the buccal space, the tactilokinaesthetic space, the visual and auditory spaces; each is separate and each is centred essentially on the body of the subject and on actions. After a few months, however, after a kind of Copernican evolution, there is a total reversal, a decentration such that space becomes homogenous, a one-and-only space that envelops the others. Then space becomes a container that envelops all objects, including the body itself; and after that, space is mainly coordinated in a structure, a coordination of positions and displacements, and these constitute what the geometricians call a 'group'; that is to say, precisely a reversible system. One may move from A to B, and may come back from B to A; there is the possibility of returning, of reversibility. There is also the possibility of making detours and combinations which give a clue to what the subsequent operations will be when thought will supersede the action itself.

PRE-OPERATIONAL STAGE

From 1½–2 years of age, a fundamental transformation in the evolution of intelligence takes place in the appearance of symbolic functions. Every action of intelligence consists in manipulating significations (or meanings) and whenever (or wherever) there are significations, there are on the one hand the 'significants' and on the other the 'significates'. This is true in the sensori-motor level, but the only significants that intervene there are perceptual signs or signals (as in conditioning) which are undifferentiated in regard to the significate; for example, a perceptual cue, like distance, which will be a cue for the size of the distant object, or the apparent size of an object, which will be the cue for the distance of the object. There, perhaps, both indices are different aspects of the same reality, but they are not yet differentiated significants. At the age of 1½–2 years a new class of significants arises, and these significants are differentiated in regard to their significates. These differentiations can be called symbolic function. The appearance of symbols in a children's game is an example of the appearance of new significants. At the sensori-motor level the games are nothing but exercises; now they become symbolic play, a play of fiction; these games consist in representing something by means of something else. Another example is the beginning of delayed imitation, an imitation that takes place not in the presence of the original object but in its absence, and which consequently constitutes a kind of symbolisation or mental image.

At the same time that symbols appear, the child acquires language; that is to say, there is the acquisition of another phase of differentiated significants, verbal signals, or collective signals. This symbolic function then brings great flexibility into the field of intelligence. Intelligence up to this point refers to the immediate space which surrounds the child and to the present perceptual situation; thanks to language, and to the symbolic functions, it becomes possible to invoke objects which are not present perceptually, to reconstruct the past, or to make projects, plans for the future, to think of objects not present but very distant in space – in short, to span spatio-temporal distances much greater than before.

But this new stage, the stage of representation of thought which is superimposed on the sensori-motor stage, is not a simple extension of what was referred to at the previous level. Before being able to prolong, one must in fact reconstruct, because behaviour in words is a different thing from representing something in thought. When a child knows how to move around in his house or garden by following the different successive cues around him, it does not mean that he is capable of representing or reproducing the total configuration of his house or his garden. To be able to represent, to reproduce something, one must be capable of reconstructing this group of displacements, but at a new level, that of the representation of the thought.

I recently made an amusing test with Nel Szeminska. We took children of 4–5 years of age who went to school by themselves and came back home by themselves, and asked them if they could trace the way to school and back for us, not in design, which would be too difficult, but like a construction game, with concrete objects.

We found that they were not capable of representation; there was a kind of motor-memory, but it was not yet a representation of a whole – the group of displacements had not yet been reconstructed on the plan of the representation of thought. In other words, the operations were not yet formed. These are representations which are internalised actions; but actions still centred on the body itself, on the activity itself. These representations do not allow the objective combinations, the decentrated combinations that the operations would. The actions are centred on the body. I used to call this egocentrism; but it is better thought of as lack of reversibility of action.

At this level, the most certain sign of the absence of operations which appear at the next stage is the absence of the knowledge of conservation. In fact, an operation refers to the transformation of reality. The transformation is not of the whole, however; something constant is always untransformed. If you pour a liquid from one glass to another there is transformation; the liquid changes form, but its liquid property stays constant. So at the pre-operational level, it is significant from the point of view of the operations of intelligence that the child has not yet a knowledge of conservation. For example, in the case of liquid, when the child pours it from one bottle to the other, he thinks that the quantity of the liquid has changed. When the level of the liquid changes, the child thinks the quantity has changed – there is more or less in the second glass than in the first. And if you ask the child where the larger quantity came from, he does not answer this question. What is important for the child is that perceptually it is not the same thing any more. We find this absence of conservation in all object properties, in the length, surface, quantity, and weight of things.

This absence of conservation indicates essentially that at this stage the child reasons from the configuration. Confronted with a transformation, he does not reason from the transformation itself; he starts from the initial configuration, then sees the final configuration, compares the two but forgets the transformation, because he does not know how to reason about it. At this stage the child is still reasoning on the basis of what he sees because there is no conservation. He is able to master this problem only when the operations are formed and these operations, which we have already sensed at the sensori-motor level, are not formed until around 7–8 years of age. At that age the elementary problems of conservation are solved, because the child reasons on the basis of the transformation *per se*, and this requires a manipulation of the operation. The ability to pass from one stage to the other and be able to come back to the point of departure to manipulate the reversible operations, which appears at around 7–8 years of age, is limited when compared with the operations of the superior level only in the sense that they are concrete. That is to say, the child can manipulate the operations only when he manipulates the object concretely.

STAGE OF CONCRETE-OPERATIONS

The first operations of the manipulation of objects, the concrete-operations, deal with logical classes and with logical relations, or the number. But these operations do not deal yet with propositions, or hypotheses, which do not appear until the last stage.

Let me exemplify these concrete-operations: the simplest operation is concerned with classifying objects according to their similarity and their difference. This is accomplished by including the subclasses within larger and more general classes, a process that implies inclusion. This classification, which seems very simple at first, is not acquired until around 7–8 years of age. Before that, at the pre-operational level, we do not find logical inclusion. For example, if you show a child at the pre-operational level a bouquet of flowers of which one half is daisies and the other half other flowers and you ask him if in this bouquet there are more flowers or more daisies, you are confronted with this answer, which seems extraordinary until it is analysed: the child cannot tell you whether there are more flowers than daisies; either he reasons on the basis of the whole or of the part. He cannot understand that the part is complementary to the rest, and he says there are more daisies than flowers, or as many daisies as flowers, without understanding this inclusion of the subclass, the daisies, in the class of flowers. It is only around 7–8 years of age that a child is capable of solving a problem of inclusion.

Another system of operation that appears around 7–8 years of age is the operation of serialising; that is, to arrange objects according to their size, or their progressive weight. It is also a structure of the whole, like the classification which rests on concrete operations, since it consists of manipulating concrete-objects. At this level there is also the construction of numbers, which is, too, a synthesis of classification and seriation. In numbers, as in classes, we have inclusion, and also a serial order, as in serialising. These elementary operations constitute structures of wholes. There is no class without classification; there is not symmetric relation without serialisation; there is not a number independent of the series of numbers. But the structures of these wholes are simple structures, groupings in the case of classes and relations, which are already groups in the case of numbers, but very elementary structures compared to subsequent structures.

STAGE OF FORMAL-OPERATIONS

The last stage of development of intelligence is the stage of formal-operations or propositional-operations. At about 11–12 years of age we see great progress; the child becomes capable of reasoning not only on the basis of objects, but also on the basis of hypotheses, or of propositions.

An example which neatly shows the difference between reasoning on the basis of propositions and reasoning on the basis of concrete-objects comes from Burt's tests. Burt asked children of different ages to compare the colours of the hair of three girls: Edith is fairer than Susan, Edith is darker than Lilly; who is the darkest of the three? In this question there is seriation, not of concrete-objects, but of verbal statements which supposes a more complicated mental manipulation. This problem is rarely solved before the age of 12.

Here a new class of operations appears which is superimposed on the operations of logical class and number, and these operations are the propositional-operations. Here, compared to the previous stage, are fundamental changes. It is not simply that these operations refer to language, and then to operations with concrete-objects, but that these operations have much richer structures.

The first novelty is a combinative structure; like mathematical structures, it is a structure of a system which is superimposed on the structure of simple classifications or seriations which are not themselves systems, because they do not involve a combinative system. A combinative system permits the grouping in flexible combinations of each element of the system with any other element of that system. The logic of propositions supposes such a combinative system. If children of different ages are shown a number of coloured disks and asked to combine each colour with each other two by two, or three by three, we find these combinative operations are not accessible to the child at the stage of concrete-operations. The child is capable of some combination, but not of all the possible combinations. After the age of 12, the child can find a method to make all the possible combinations. At the same time he acquires both the logic of mathematics and the logic of propositions, which also supposes a method of combining.

A second novelty in the operations of propositions is the appearance of a structure which constitutes a group of four transformations. Hitherto there were two reversibilities: reversibility by inversion, which consists of annulling, or cancelling; and reversibility which we call reciprocity, leading not to cancellation, but to another combination. Reciprocity is what we find in the field of a relation. If A equals B, by reciprocity B equals A. If A is smaller than B, by reciprocity B is larger than A. At the level of propositional operations a new system envelops these two forms of reversibility. Here the structure combines inversion and reversibility in one single but larger and more complicated structure. It allows the acquisition of a series of fundamental operational schemata for the development of intelligence, which schemata are not possible before the constitution of this structure.

It is around the age of 12 that the child, for example, starts to understand in mathematics the knowledge of proportions, and becomes capable of reasoning by using two systems of reference at the same time. For example, if you advance the position of a board and a car moving in opposite directions, in order to understand the movement of the board in relation to the movement of the car and to other movement, you need a system of four transformations. The same is true in regard to proportions, to problems in mathematics or physics, or to other logical problems.

The four principal stages of the development of intelligence of the child progress from one stage to the other by the construction of new operational structures, and these structures constitute the fundamental instrument of the intelligence of the adult.

Children's Ideas and the Learning of Science

1.4

Rosalind Driver, Edith Guesne and Andrée Tiberghien

Two 11-year-old boys, Tim and Ricky, are studying the way a spring extends as they add ball-bearings to a polystyrene cup which is hanging from it (see figure 2). Ricky is intent on adding ball-bearings one at a time and measuring the new length of the spring after each addition. Tim is watching him, then interrupts: 'Wait. What happens if we lift it up?'

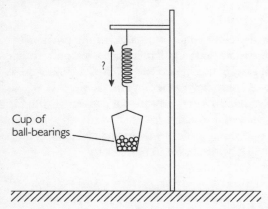

Cup of ball-bearings

Figure 2 *Extending a spring by loading a cup of ball-bearings*

He unclamps the spring, raises it higher up the stand, and measures its length again. Apparently satisfied that the length is the same as before he continues with the experiment. Later, when he is asked the reason for doing this, Tim picks up two marbles, holds one up higher than the other and explains:

> this is farther up and gravity is pulling it down harder the farther away. The higher it gets the more effect gravity will have on it because if you just stood over there and someone dropped a pebble on him, it would just sting him, it wouldn't hurt him. But if I dropped it from an aeroplane it would be accelerating faster and faster and when it hit someone on the head it would kill him.

Source: Rosalind Driver, Edith Guesne and Andrée Tiberghien (eds) *Children's Ideas in Science* (Open University Press, 1985), pp. 1–9.

Tim's idea about weight increasing as objects are lifted higher from the Earth's surface is not an irrational one as his argument indicates (although from a scientist's point of view he seems to be referring here to gravitational potential energy).

Like Tim, many children come to science classes with ideas and interpretations concerning the phenomena that they are studying even when they have received no systematic instruction in these subjects whatsoever. Children form these ideas and interpretations as a result of everyday experiences in all aspects of their lives: through practical physical activities, talking with other people around them and through the media.

This [chapter] documents the conceptions that have been uncovered in children aged 10–16, in different physical domains, and indicates the importance of these for teachers and others concerned with science education.

WHAT CAN BE SAID ABOUT THESE IDEAS?

Do the ideas that children possess represent coherent models of the phenomena that are frequently presented in classroom settings? Experienced teachers realise that students do have their own ideas about phenomena, even if at times these 'ideas' may seem incoherent at least from the teacher's point of view. It is also recognised that such ideas often persist even when they are not consistent with the experimental results or the explanation of a teacher. In other words, they may be stable ideas. These characteristics of children's ideas – their personal nature, their coherence and their stability – will now be discussed in more detail.

THESE IDEAS ARE PERSONAL

When children in a class write about the same experiment they can give various diverse interpretations of it. Each one has 'seen' and interpreted the experiment in his or her own way. Our own behaviour is similar; when we read a text or discuss a topic with another person, we may or may not modify our own point of view. The extent to which we do modify our thinking depends at least as much on the ideas we have to start with as on what is written or said. A number of people attending the same lecture or reading the same book, even a scientific text, will not necessarily get from it and retain the same points.

Individuals internalise their experience in a way which is at least partially their own; they construct their own meanings. These personal 'ideas' influence the manner in which information is acquired. This personal manner of approaching phenomena is also found in the way in which scientific knowledge is generated. Most philosophers of science accept that hypotheses or theories do not represent so-called 'objective' data but that they are constructions or products of the human imagination. In this way of thinking, observations of events are influenced by the theoretical frameworks of the observer. The observations children make and their interpretations of them are also influenced by their ideas and expectations.[1]

The fact that these ideas, whether of a child or a scientist, are personal does not necessarily mean that they may not be shared by many people (just as in the history of the sciences, it has happened that different scientists have independently developed and used the same theoretical framework). [. . .] Students, even those in different countries, may have the same ideas, or the same interpretations of similar events.

A CHILD'S INDIVIDUAL IDEAS MAY SEEM INCOHERENT

What teacher has not been struck by the different and at times contradictory interpretations of phenomena that have been proposed by individuals in a class? Even if students are confronted with what appear to be contradictions to the teacher, they will not necessarily recognise them. In addition, [. . .] the same child may have different conceptions of a particular type of phenomenon, sometimes using different arguments leading to opposite predictions in situations which are equivalent from a scientist's point of view, and even switching from one sort of explanation to another for the same phenomenon. [. . .] Why these contradictions? The need for coherence, and the criteria for coherence, as perceived by a student are not the same as those of the scientist: the student does not possess any unique model unifying a range of phenomena that the scientist considers as equivalent. Nor does the student necessarily see the need for a coherent view, since *ad hoc* interpretations and predictions about natural events may appear to work quite well in practice.

THESE IDEAS ARE STABLE

It is often noticed that even after being taught, students have not modified their ideas in spite of attempts by a teacher to challenge them by offering counter-evidence. [. . .] Students may ignore counter-evidence, or interpret it in terms of their prior ideas. Although students' notions may be persistent, as we have already argued, this does not mean that the student has a completely coherent model of the phenomena presented, at least in the scientist's sense of the word coherent. The students' interpretations and conceptions are often contradictory, but none the less stable.

How do these ideas affect the learning process? A possible model

Students' minds are not blank slates able to receive instruction in a neutral way; on the contrary, students approach experiences presented in science classes with previously acquired notions and these influence what is learnt from new experiences in a number of ways. These include the observations made of events, the interpretations offered for such observations and the strategies students use to acquire new information, including reading from texts and experimentation.

The child, even when very young, has ideas about things, and these ideas play a role in the learning experience. Many different authors such as Ausubel, Piaget and Wallon, have incorporated this notion as an integral part of their theory. What children are capable of learning depends, at least in part, on 'what they have in their heads', as well as on the learning context in which they find themselves.

A model introduced by cognitive scientists fits well with what we now know of the interaction between the child's different ideas and the manner in which these ideas evolve with teaching. This model is based on the hypothesis that information is stored in memory in various forms and that everything we say and do depends on the elements or groups of elements of this stored information. Such elements or groups of elements have been called 'schemes'.* A scheme may concern an individual's knowledge about a specific phenomenon (for example, the sensation of cold elicited by a metallic object), or a more complex reasoning structure(for example, the association of one variable with another that leads some children to anticipate that 'the brighter the light bulb, the larger the shadow will be'). Thus, the term 'scheme' denotes the diverse things that are stored and interrelated in memory. These 'schemes' also influence the way a person may behave and interact with the environment, and in turn may be influenced by feedback from the environment.

We will illustrate the idea of 'scheme' using as an example a person's notion of a high school.[2] This scheme may incorporate relationships between events or situations that compromise it and which are themselves schemes. Some of these represent physical features, e.g. one or more buildings, stairways, corridors, rooms, a playing field; or people, including a large number of students, teachers, technicians, cleaners and a principal or head.

Other aspects of the person's general scheme may include the types of relationships or attitudes between the people involved, such as friendship, submission and power, and the activities of these people including, going up or down the stairs, writing, talking, playing musical instruments and teaching.

Thus this relatively simple 'scheme' of the high school contains different elements organised among themselves to form a structure. This structure may be linked to schemes in other structures (for example, teachers, students, education, etc.).

* Here the word 'scheme' does not have the meaning attributed to it by Piaget but rather the meaning derived from studies of memory and information processing.

In scientific theory there are some very elaborate 'schemes' representing knowledge in a particular domain such as mechanics, light, or chemical reactions. Such scientific 'schemes', integrated as they are into structures, are composed similarly of elements and relationships between them. However, they differ from the example just used of a high school in that some elements in the structure of a scientific theory do not correspond to direct perceptions.

This model of the organisation of schemes integrated into structures can be used to describe learning or the acquisition of a new piece of knowledge. First we will consider an analogy with the grouping of students in a class. Students relate with one another and form groups for different activities such as sports, drama and science lessons. These groups are not static but change as friendships and interests change; some students may not relate to others at all but remain isolates. Consider what may happen when a new boy arrives in the class. When he arrives, there are various possibilities for what might happen: he might not relate with the other students at all and remain isolated; he might join a group that already exists; or his presence might provoke a reorganisation of friendship groups of the class as a whole. The same student could also be integrated differently depending on the class that receives him.

The analogy with learning is clear; the way a new piece of information is assimilated depends both on the nature of the information and the structure of the learner's 'schemes'. Thus the same experience provided for students in their science lessons may be assimilated differently by each individual.

These images of the organisation of schemes and the acquisition of new schemes may account for the existence of these personal, contradictory and stable ideas. Each one of us has a characteristic organisation of schemes. Acquired information is linked to other information and even if this new information is the same for several people, the link established between this acquired information and already stored information has little chance of being the same from one person to the next.

When a student states several contradictory ideas, different schemes are brought into play; these ideas may all be stable in so far as the schemes leading to them are integrated into structures, and to change any one of them may require the modification of a structure, not merely of an element of that structure.

In learning science, a pupil may note an event that is contrary to his or her expectations, that does not fit in with his or her schemes. Simply noting such a discrepant event however is not necessarily followed by a restructuring of that student's ideas – such restructuring takes time and favourable circumstances. To help students to accomplish such reorganisation in their thinking about natural phenomena, science teaching can play an important role in giving children a wide range of experiences relating to certain key ideas. [. . .]

WHAT PURPOSES ARE SERVED BY UNDERSTANDING STUDENTS' IDEAS?

Taking account of students' prior ideas is one of the strategies, though certainly not the only one, which enables teaching to be better adapted to students. This can occur in a number of ways:

1 *The choice of concepts to teach.* In some teaching schemes used with secondary school pupils, some concepts have been considered to be obvious and have been taken for granted in planning a course. Yet, [...] studies of children's ideas suggest that even some apparently simple notions such as the conservation of matter or the intensive nature of temperature may not be appreciated by many secondary school students. Failure to appreciate such basic ideas then leads to further and more serious learning problems.

2 *The choice of learning experiences.* If students' prior ideas are known then these can be challenged directly by experiences which conflict with expectations, so provoking students to reconsider their ideas. However, challenging students' current ideas is not by itself enough to promote change; alternative ideas have to be offered and these need to be seen by students not only as necessary but also reasonable and plausible. Knowledge of students' ideas enables us to choose teaching activities which are more likely to be interpreted by students in the way intended. The case of the reflection of light by objects [...] is an example of this. Most children aged 13–14 recognise that a mirror has the property of reflecting light, even though they think that the light remains on other objects. To support this idea, they refer to the fact that with a mirror one can light up an object or flash a light at someone. One can introduce similar experiences to convince them that light is reflected by ordinary objects. At noon in midsummer, a piece of white paper will glare when struck by the light from the sun. In a dark room, one can easily perceive a light-coloured object being lit by light reflected by a sheet of white paper. We also see that, on the other hand, knowledge of children's conceptions allows us to reject certain classical teaching experiments, which are not interpreted by the child in the way we expect them to be.

3 *The presentation of the purposes of proposed activities.* In formulating the purposes of learning tasks it is important to bear in mind that pupils may reinterpret the intentions of the teacher in terms of their own understandings. This is illustrated in the following example where secondary pupils were programmed through a series of activities on work-cards. One group of girls carried out an experiment in which an immersion heater was placed in blocks of equal weight but made of different metals (figure 3). The function of the experiment was to demonstrate variation in heat capacity. The pupils had been instructed to draw a temperature-time graph as each block was heated. Towards the end of the lesson the girls were instructed to look at the graphs they had produced and

compare them, suggesting an explanation. The teacher (T) enters their discussion:

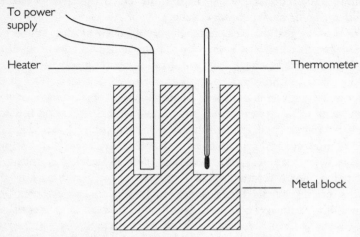

Figure 3 *Experiment to demonstrate variation in heat capacity*

T: What has your experiment shown you?

P2: That different ... um ... that different materials and that ... see how heat could travel through them.

T: What did you find out?

P1: Well ... er ... that heat went through the ... the ... iron more easier than it did through the er ...

P2: Aluminium.

The pupils had had first-hand experience – they had collected their data, but these had been assimilated into a scheme concerned with conductivity, rather than in the way intended.

While it is necessary to bear students' ideas in mind while teaching, it certainly is not easy to put this into practice. The teacher has responsibility for the class as a whole and may consider it quite unrealistic to take the varied ideas of each student into account. [...] Although there is variety in the ideas children use to interpret phenomena, there are clearly some general patterns in the types of ideas that children of different ages tend to use. Studies of children's conceptions relating to a number of scientific topics have been undertaken in different parts of the world with children whose experience of formal science teaching has varied considerably. Despite this, quite independent research studies have reported similar patterns of ideas held by young people. For example, studies in the area of students' conceptions of dynamics, [...] their views of the Earth, [...] and their ideas about heat, [...] have been undertaken in a number of countries and the findings paint a consistent picture with students' early experiences of phenomena dominating their thinking. Studies reported on the particulate theory of matter [...] indicate how difficult it is for many students to assimilate aspects of that model despite carefully designed teaching sequences. The report on children's ideas about electricity [. . .] gives a rather disturbing finding; the proportion of students using an incorrect 'sequence' model for electric current remains dominant as students go through secondary school.

Studies of this kind suggest that despite the apparent variety of ideas suggested in science classrooms, there may be some value in attempting to take account of general trends in children's thinking, both in planning learning activities and in order to improve communication in the classroom itself.

In this chapter we have given an outline of a particular view of learning; a view in which learning is seen to take place through the interaction between, on the one hand, a learner's experiences and, on the other, the 'mental entities', the 'ideas' or 'schemes', used to interpret and give meaning to those experiences. [. . .] Various terms [can be] used to describe these 'mental entities' and each has a slightly different connotation. Some terms, such as 'intuitive notion' or 'intuition' are suggestive of the origins of the ideas; some, such as 'conception', 'rule' or 'prototypic view', hint at the generality of use of the ideas. In some cases the organisation of ideas and the relationship between them is emphasised in the use of such terms as 'cognitive structure', 'frameworks' or 'children's models'. In other cases the term used is qualified with the word 'alternative' (e.g. 'alternative conception', 'alternative framework'), thus emphasising the difference between children's ideas and accepted scientific theory.

In our view, this plurality of terms reflects both the multifaceted nature and the variability which characterises children's ideas; a variability which exists from one type of phenomenon to another, between contexts and between children themselves.

We [do] not, therefore, attempt to impose a common terminology. [. . .] As in the story of the blind men describing an elephant, each of the various terms used reflects some aspects of the central concern: [. . .] the description of children's thinking about phenomena in the natural world.

NOTES

1 Driver, R. (1983) *The Pupil as Scientist?* Open University Press: Milton Keynes.
2 Tiberghien, A. (1980) 'Quel rapport y a-t-il entre ce que les éleves "ont dans la tête" et ce qu'ils font ou disent?', in *Sciences Physiques*, pp. 197–202. Livre du Professeur 3ème coll Libres Parcours, Hachette, Paris.

THE JOINT SOCIALISATION OF DEVELOPMENT BY YOUNG CHILDREN AND ADULTS

1.5

BARBARA ROGOFF

The young child is often thought of as a little scientist exploring the world and discovering the principles of its operation. We often forget that while the scientist is working on the border of human knowledge and is finding out things that nobody yet knows, the child is finding out precisely what everybody already knows (Newman, 1982, p. 26).

This chapter focuses on how young children and adults together manage children's socialisation through children's participation in cultural activities with the guidance of adults. Interactions and arrangements between caregivers and infants or toddlers are the basis for the discussion.

INTRODUCTION

First to be considered is how such joint involvement can be conceptualised. Then the main part of the chapter describes features of adult–child interactions as well as non-interactive arrangements made between adults and children, in order to examine differing aspects of the joint socialisation of children's development. [. . .]

The chapter builds on Vygotsky's concept of the *zone of proximal development*, in which child development is viewed as a social activity with children participating in activities beyond their competence through the assistance of adults or more experienced peers. In social interaction in the zone of proximal development, children are able to participate in activities that are beyond their capabilities when working independently. Through such social guidance, children are presumed to gradually internalise the skills that were practised with adult support so that they can be performed independently (Vygotsky, 1978; Wertsch, 1979). Thus the zone

Source: Gellatly, Rogers and Sloboda (eds), *Cognition and Social Worlds* (Oxford University Press, 1989), pp. 57–82. Originally published in M. Lewis and S. Feinman (eds), *Social Influences and Behaviour* (Plenum, New York).

* The thoughtful comments of Saul Feinman are acknowledged with thanks.

of proximal development is a dynamic region of sensitivity to learning experiences in which children develop, guided by social interaction.

In Vygotskian theory, children's interaction within the zone of proximal development is part of a larger sociocultural theory that places human skills and achievements in the context of the technologies, practices, and values available through cultural history. These sociocultural technologies and skills include inventions such as literacy, mathematics, mnemonic skills, and approaches to problem-solving and reasoning. In effect, cultural inventions channel the skills of each generation, with individual development mediated by the guidance of people who are more skilled in their use. Children are introduced to the culture through the guidance of its more experienced members (Laboratory of Comparative Human Cognition, 1983; Rogoff, 1982; Rogoff, Gauvain and Ellis, 1984; Vygotsky, 1978).

Cole (1981) suggests that the zone of proximal development is where culture and cognition meet. It is in this sensitive zone that variations in social interaction may be expected to yield adaptations of individuals to their specific cultural surroundings. Their adaptations will simultaneously show features that are similar across many cultural contexts, based on cross-cultural commonalities in the processes of communication and of child development, and variations according to the specific goals and means available for appropriate development in each culture.

This chapter extends the concept of zone of proximal development by stressing the *inter-relatedness* of children's and adults' roles, in a process of *guided participation*. The thesis is that the rapid development of young children into socialised participants in society is accomplished through a finely tuned combination of children's skills and the guidance of adults (or older children). The elaboration presented in this chapter, while consistent with the Vygotskian approach, differs in its emphasis on the role of children as active participants in their own socialisation. They do not simply receive the guidance of adults, they seek, structure, and even demand the assistance of those around them in learning how to solve problems of all kinds. The aim of this chapter is to stress the complementary roles of children and adults in fostering children's development.

Young children appear to come equipped with ways of ensuring proximity and involvement with more experienced members of society, and of becoming involved with their physical and cultural surroundings. The infants' strategies (if one ignores connotations of intentionality) appear similar to those appropriate for anyone learning in an unfamiliar culture: stay near a trusted guide, watch the guide's activities and get involved when possible, and attend to any instruction the guide provides.

Infants' strategies are complemented by features of adult–child interaction that are well adapted to the gradual immersion of children in the skills and beliefs of the society. Adults arrange the occurrence of children's activities and facilitate learning by regulating the difficulty of the tasks and by modelling mature performance during joint participation in activities. While adults may rarely regard themselves as explicitly teaching infants or young children, they routinely adjust their interaction and structure children's environments and activities in ways consistent with providing support for their learning.

In elaborating the concept of the zone of proximal development, Rogoff and Gardner (1984) emphasised that while more experienced people play an important role in socialisation, this role is meshed with the efforts of children to learn and develop. Rogoff (1986) proposed that guided participation with school-children involves adults leading children through the process of solving a problem, and the child participating at a comfortable but slightly challenging level:

Adults provide guidance in cognitive development through the arrangement of appropriate materials and tasks for children, as well as through tacit and explicit instruction occurring as adults and children participate together in activities. Adults' greater knowledge and skill allow them to assist children in translating familiar information to apply to a new problem, and to structure the problem so that the child can work on manageable subgoals. The effectiveness of adults in structuring situations for children's learning is matched by children's eagerness and involvement in managing their own learning experiences. Children put themselves in a position to observe what is going on; they involve themselves in the ongoing activity; they influence the activities in which they participate; and they demand some involvement with the adults who serve as their guides for socialization into the culture that they are learning. Together, children and adults choose learning situations and calibrate the child's level of participation so that the child is comfortably challenged (Rogoff, 1986, p. 38).

This chapter extends these ideas by focusing on processes of guided participation with younger children. The themes include how adults facilitate the development of infants and toddlers, how children themselves channel their own development and the assistance they receive. [. . .]

First, however, it is necessary to examine the notion of the inter-relatedness of the individual child's role and that of the social context – including the adults and older children that provide guidance.

MUTUALITY OF INDIVIDUAL EFFORT AND SOCIAL FACILITATION

This section examines alternative conceptualisations of how mutual involvement of adults and children may contribute to development. It has been common in developmental psychology to focus attention alternatively on the contribution of either partner, in examining how adults teach children, or how children develop independently. This chapter argues for the necessity of considering the mutual involvement of children and the social world in understanding child development. But such mutual involvement could be understood in different ways. In order to explore ways of conceptualising the mutual roles of adults and children in fostering children's development, it is useful to draw a relationship with the parallel question of nature and nurture, which has long interested psychologists. By analogy, we may regard the role of the child as 'nature' and the role of social partners as 'nurture'.

The history of psychology has long pitted nature against nurture, with questions of how much of development should be credited to one and how much to the other. This traditional view places nature and nurture in opposition. Most developmentalists, as one reads in early chapters of introductory texts, are no longer trying to figure out if development is 'more nature' or 'more nurture'. Instead, they view nature and nurture as interacting to produce development: development does not occur solely through individual effort or pre-programming, nor does it occur entirely under the direction of the environment.

However, the notion of interaction often involves an assumption that the interacting entities are separable (see Rogoff, 1982). In other words, nature and nurture in such a view can be regarded as independent influences – definable in terms not involving each other – that happen to co-occur.

In contrast to the idea that nature and nurture are separate but interacting influences on development, the present chapter is built on the premise that nature and nurture (i.e. the child and the social world) are not separable. They are mutually involved to an extent that precludes regarding them as independently definable. In this view, development is made up of both individual efforts or tendencies and the larger sociocultural context in which the individual is embedded and has been since before conception. Thus biology and culture are not viewed as alternative influences but aspects of a system in which individuals develop.

This stance is reflected in Vygotsky's efforts (Wertsch, 1985) to study development in terms of four interrelated levels. The level with which developmental psychologists traditionally deal is termed ontogenetic development – changes in thinking and behaviour associated with age. But this is merely a grain of analysis differing from the other three: phylogenetic development is the slowly changing species history that leaves a legacy for the individual in the form of genes. Sociocultural development is the changing cultural history that leaves a legacy for the individual in the form of technologies such as literacy, number systems, and computers, as well as value systems, scripts, and norms for the handling of situations met by the individual. Microgenetic development is the moment-to-moment learning by individuals in particular problem contexts, built upon the individual's genetic and sociocultural background. In this system, the roles of the individual and the social world are seen as interrelated in the levels of analysis reflecting learning, ontogenetic development, phylogenetic development, and sociohistorical development.

[...]

SOCIAL FACILITATION OF INDIVIDUAL DEVELOPMENT

Working from observations of adults instructing children aged 6 to 9 years, Rogoff and Gardner (1984) proposed that guided participation involves the following activities:

1 providing a bridge between familiar skills or information and those needed to solve a new problem,
2 arranging and structuring problem-solving, and
3 gradually transferring the responsibility for managing problem-solving to the child.

These activities seem relevant for the guidance of younger children as well. This section elaborates on these three features of adults' and young children's arrangements for socialisation and development. It stresses the entwinement of adults' and children's activities, the active role of both participants, and the possibility that teaching and learning can occur tacitly (as well as explicitly) in the arrangements and interaction between adults and young children.
   [. . .]

PROVIDING BRIDGES BETWEEN FAMILIAR SKILLS OR INFORMATION AND THOSE NEEDED IN NOVEL SITUATIONS

Adults help young children find the connections between what they already know and what is necessary to handle a new situation (D'Andrade, 1981; Erickson, 1982). For older children this may involve specifying exactly how the new situation resembles the old. For example, in a classification task (Rogoff and Gardner, 1984), some mothers made comments such as 'You need to put the things together that go together, just like on Sesame Street when they say "three of these things belong together"'.

For very young children, the bridging role of adults involves assisting children in understanding how to act in new situations by provision of emotional cues regarding the nature of the situation, nonverbal models of how to behave, verbal and nonverbal interpretations of behaviour and events, and verbal labels to classify objects and events. All of these adult activities are coupled with young children's efforts (intentional or not) to pick up information about the nature of situations and their caregivers' interpretations.

EMOTIONAL AND NONVERBAL COMMUNICATION

From the first year of life, children look to adults to interpret situations that are ambiguous from the child's point of view, in a process termed *social referencing* (Feinman, 1982; Gunnar and Stone, 1984). Interpretations offered by adults inform infants about the appropriate approach to take to a new situation. For example, if a child is crawling toward its mother and reaches what appears to be a dropoff, the child searches the mother's face for cues regarding the safety of the situation. If the mother's emotional expression indicates fear, the child does not proceed, but if the mother has an encouraging expression, the child carefully crawls across clear glass suspended a foot above what appears to be the floor (Sorce *et al.*, 1985).

Young children are so skilled in obtaining information from glances, winces, and mood that one of the greatest challenges of testing preschoolers is to avoid nonverbal actions that may be construed as cues. Children press for and use such cues even when given standardised intelligence tests (Mehan, 1976).

Such referencing is facilitated by the ability that appears by 8–12 months of age to obtain information from the direction in which caregivers point and gaze (Bruner, 1983; Butterworth and Cochran, 1980). The development of such skill is supported by the efforts of mothers to regulate joint attention during the first year. If an infant appears not to understand a pointing gesture, mothers facilitate the baby's comprehension by touching the indicated object (Lempers, 1979). As early as three months of infants' age, mothers attempt to achieve joint reference by introducing an object between themselves and the baby as a target for joint attention, using a characteristic intonation and shaking the object (Bruner, 1983). From ages 6 to 18 months, infants are more than four times as likely to engage in joint attention when interacting with their mothers as when interacting with a peer (Bakeman and Adamson, 1984). Bakeman and Adamson attribute this pattern to the mother's socialisation of reference, 'embedding it within the interpersonal sphere well before infants can structure this integration by themselves' (p. 1288). Thus the infant's use of social referencing builds on earlier skills and social guidance, providing more advanced means to gather information regarding their mothers' (and others') interpretations of new situations.

Mothers and other adults may at times intentionally attempt to communicate a particular understanding of a new situation through managing their emotional and nonverbal communication. For example, at a doctor's office a mother may try to mask her apprehension when her baby is receiving an injection, in order to minimise the baby's reaction to the situation. Or parental management of cues may enter into instruction in potentially frightening situations, as suggested in the following advice to parents on teaching three-week-old babies to swim in the bathtub:

> Your attitude toward water is important. An infant who sees her mother wince in terror every time she floats in deep water is not going to have a very confident picture of the strange situation. Since panic is the single most deadly factor in water, parents should be acutely aware of their responsibility in teaching their child a healthy respect for water . . . If you show enjoyment of the water, she will

imitate your excitement and pleasure . . . Lift your baby into the water, and rest her on your bent knees, facing you. Dip your hands into the water, and pat your baby's body to help her adjust to the water temperature. Talk and smile constantly throughout the entire session. Gradually lower your knees until the baby is completely submerged in the water, head resting comfortably on your knees, body on your thighs. Take this part slowly, allowing enough time for your baby to become acquainted with the water (Poe, 1982, pp. 12, 20).

Such intentional communication of how to interpret a situation may be rare. But in a less self-conscious fashion, adults handling babies seem almost inevitably to provide interpretation for the baby's actions, their own actions, and events in the environment (Shotter and Newson, 1982). For example, mothers may respond to the baby's attempt to push an approaching spoon away with a running commentary such as 'You getting full? Try another bite, Mama wants you to grow up big and strong.' For babies learning to eat from a spoon, adults frequently provide supplementary cues regarding the appropriate action for the child – they can be observed to open their own mouths wide at the time the baby is to do the same (Valsiner, 1984). To ensure a happy response to a potentially startling event, adults make an exaggerated face of surprise and enjoyment, for example, commenting 'isn't that funny?' when concerned that a Jack-in-the-box might startle a baby (Rogoff, Malkin, and Gilbride, 1984).

WORDS AS A CULTURAL SYSTEM FOR BRIDGING

In addition to such interpretive comments and actions, the provision of a language system teaches children the meanings and distinctions important in their culture. Labels categorise objects and events in ways specific to the language of the child's culture. Roger Brown pointed out this function of language learning in his comments about the Original Word Game:

The Original Word Game is the operation of linguistic reference in first language learning. At least two people are required: one who knows the language (the tutor) and one who is learning (the player). In outline form the movements of the game are very simple. The tutor names things in accordance with the semantic custom of his community. The player forms hypotheses about the categorical nature of the things named. He tests his hypotheses by trying to name new things correctly. The tutor compares the player's utterances with his own anticipations of such utterances and, in this way, checks the accuracy of fit between his own categories and those of the player. He improves the fit by correction. In concrete terms the tutor says 'dog' whenever a dog appears. The player notes the phonemic equivalence of these utterances, forms a hypothesis about the non-linguistic category that elicits this kind of utterance and then tries naming a few dogs himself . . . In learning referents and names the player of the Original Word Game prepares himself to receive the science, the rules of thumb, the prejudices, the total expectancies of his society (Brown, 1958, pp. 194, 228).

Clearly, the Original Word Game requires two active partners. Language development is facilitated by social involvement as well as deriving from the child's natural propensity to learn language. In this view, Chomsky's Language Acquisition Device cooperates with Bruner's Language Acquisition Support System, which 'frames or structures the input of language and interaction to the child's Language Acquisition Device in a manner to "make the system function"' (Bruner, 1983, p. 19). Consistent with this emphasis on the social supports for language acquisition are Moerk's (1983) careful analyses of maternal language input to Roger Brown's subject Eve. Eve's mother provided sufficiently rich and frequent input, with semantic and linguistic redundancy, and contingent instructional relationships between mother's and child's utterances, for her framing of Eve's language development to be considered an important contribution to the child's efforts to learn language.

The process of communication, itself a social activity, can be regarded as the bridge between one understanding of a situation and another. For an adult and child to communicate successfully, the adult must search for common reference points, translating the adult's understanding of the situation into a form that is within the child's grasp (Rogoff, 1986; Wertsch, 1984). Adults insert their interaction into the ongoing activity of an infant, waiting for the infant to be in the appropriate state and providing verbal and nonverbal commentary on the object or event to which the baby is already attending (Kaye, 1982; Schaffer, 1984).

Adjustment of the adult's perspective in the service of communication is also apparent in the way adults occasionally misclassify an atypical exemplar of a category in order to avoid confusing toddlers about the basic nature of the category. For example, adults may agree that a whale is a fish, or that an electric outlet is 'hot'. Bruner (1983, based on Deutsch and Pechmann) suggests that the fact that a physicist mother is unlikely to share an identical concept of 'electricity' with her four-year-old does not matter as long as their shared meaning is sufficient to allow their conversation about shocks to continue. This effort to communicate draws the child into a more mature understanding that is linked to what the child already knows. In the process of communicating, adults tie new situations to more familiar ones, drawing connections from the familiar to the novel through the adult's verbal and nonverbal interpretation.

STRUCTURING SITUATIONS FOR CHILD INVOLVEMENT

CHOICE AND STRUCTURING OF SITUATIONS

Adults frequently make arrangements for children, selecting activities and materials they consider appropriate for children at that age or interest level (Laboratory of Comparative Human Cognition, 1983; Valsiner, 1984). Such choices may frequently be made without the intention of providing a specific learning experience, but may also be designed explicitly for the socialisation or education of the child. Whiting (1980) cogently states the responsibility of parents and other adults for arranging children's learning environments:

> The power of parents and other agents of socialization is in their assignment of children to specific settings. Whether it is caring for an infant sibling, working around the house in the company of adult females, working on the farm with adults and siblings, playing outside with neighborhood children, hunting with adult males, or attending school with age mates, the daily assignment of a child to one or another of these settings has important consequences on the development of habits of interpersonal behavior, consequences that may not be recognized by the socializers who make the assignments (p. 111).

By making such choices and adjusting tasks and materials to children's competence and needs, adults tacitly guide children's development. Parents designate some objects as appropriate for children, following the recommendations of toy manufacturers and cultural lore. For example, children of different ages are presented with books adjusted to their interests and skills: cardboard or plastic picture books, paper picture books with a few words, books with pictures and text, books with pure text. Adults determine the activities in which children's participation is allowed or discouraged, such as chores, parental work and recreational activities, television shows, the birth of a sibling, or the death of a grandparent. Adults arrange the social environment to promote or avoid certain relationships, by assigning child care to a sibling, grandparent, or babysitter, and encouraging or discouraging particular playmates.

It would be misleading to consider the choice of activities to be the sole responsibility of adults. Children are very active in directing adults towards desirable or away from undesirable activities. Children's preferences are clear in their refusal to enter some activities, and their insistence on others. Their attempts to communicate desire for involvement in specific activities begins during the last half of the first year of life. Rogoff, Malkin, and Gilbride (1984) cite an example of a nine-month-old attempting to get an adult to work a Jack-in-the-box: the baby began by pushing the box across the floor toward the adult, and patted the top of the box when the adult asked 'What?' The adult responded to the baby's actions as a request, and asked 'Should we make Jack come out?' The adult tried to get the baby to turn the handle (an action too difficult for this nine-month-old); and the baby responded with a series of frustrated yet determined moves – whining and fumbling with the box – that expressed his desire to have the box opened. Finally the adult began to turn the handle and the baby immediately relaxed. The adult asked sympathetically, 'Is that what you wanted?' and the baby stared at the handle and let out a big sigh of relief.

STRUCTURING SITUATIONS THROUGH DIVISION OF RESPONSIBILITY

In addition to arranging the structuring learning activities by providing access and regulating the difficulty of tasks, adults structure children's involvement in learning situations by handling more difficult aspects of the task themselves and organising the child's involvement with the more manageable aspects of the activity. In engaging the child in an appropriate handling of the situation, the adult creates a 'scaffolded' or supported situation in which the child can extend current skills and knowledge to a higher level of competence (Wertsch, 1979; Wood, Bruner and Ross, 1976). Note that while the term scaffold could imply a rigid structure or one that does not involve the child, most users of the term include notions of continual revisions of scaffolding to respond to children's advancements. Bruner (1983) characterises scaffolding in language development as the adult acting on a motto of 'where before there was a spectator, let there now be a participant' (p. 60).

An example of adult support is provided by the way adults structure children's developing narration skills by asking appropriate questions to organise children's stories or accounts (McNamee, 1980). If the child stops short or leaves out crucial information, the adult prompts, 'What happened next?' or 'Who else was there?' Such questions implicitly provide children with the cues they need to internalise as they develop narration skills. Adults' questions fill in the outline of what narratives involve. Building on Bruner's perspective, McNamee (1980) suggests that 'if story schemas exist for young children, they hover in the air between adults and children as they converse' (p. 6).

Adults interacting with children may structure tasks by determining the problem to be solved, the goal, and how the goal can be segmented into manageable subgoals. For example, the joint clean-up of a toddler's room may require the adult (even with a co-operative toddler) to define the goal of cleaning up the room, to segment the task into subgoals such as picking up dirty clothes and putting toys in their proper places, and to determine the specifics of each subgoal (e.g. can you find all the blocks and put them in the box?). The adult's structuring of the problem may be tailored to the child's level of skill. With a novice, the adult may take responsibility for managing the subgoals as well as making sure the overall goal is met. A more experienced child may take responsibility for the subgoals, and eventually for the whole task. Such changes in the division of responsibility are an important feature of guided participation, in which the child becomes increasingly responsible for managing the situation as skills increase.

TRANSFER OF RESPONSIBILITY FOR MANAGING SITUATIONS

Children take on increasing responsibility for managing situations over the course of years as well as through the process of becoming familiar with a particular task. Effective transfer of responsibility for managing a situation requires adults to be sensitive to children's competence in particular tasks so that responsibility is given when the child is able to handle it. Similarly, such decisions require knowledge (again, it may be tacit) of what skills and knowledge are needed in order to be able to independently handle that situation, and facilitated by knowledge of the course of development of skill in handling that particular situation. In addition to adults' adjustments of support according to children's skills, children are active in arranging for participation at an appropriate level.

ADULTS' ADJUSTMENT OF SUPPORT

Scaffolding requires revision as the child gains in understanding. One form of scaffolding involves providing sufficient redundancy in messages so that if a child does not understand one aspect of the communication, other forms are available to make the meaning clear. As children develop greater understanding, adults and older children adjust the level of scaffolding necessary to support the young child's learning and performance by reducing the level of redundancy.

For example, mothers assisting preschoolers in a counting task adjusted the level of their assistance to children's correctness (Saxe, Gearhart, and Guberman, 1984). When children made accurate counts, mothers shifted their directives to a more superordinate level in the task structure so that children had more responsibility for determining the subgoals regarding how to obtain one-to-one correspondence, and when children counted inaccurately, mothers shifted to a subordinate level in the task structure, taking over management of the subgoals themselves.

In early parent–child communication, adults facilitate infants' language acquisition by supporting verbal messages with enough redundant nonverbal information to ensure understanding (Greenfield, 1984). As infants become able to comprehend verbal messages, adults decrease the nonverbal information. Messer (1980) observed that maternal discourse was organised in episodes referring to specific objects, and within the episodes the mothers provided great redundancy regarding which thing was the object of reference. This organisation of maternal speech was greatest for younger children, again suggesting that the structure of maternal communication provides a continually modified scaffold for learning.

Researchers in pre-linguistic development have noted that adults carry on conversations with infants in which the adult's role as conversational partner is adjusted to the baby's repertoire:

> The mothers work to maintain a conversation despite the inadequacies of their conversational partners. At first they accept burps, yawns, and coughs as well as laughs and coos – but not arm-waving or head movements – as the baby's turn. They fill in for the babies by asking and answering their own questions, and by phrasing questions so that a minimal response can be treated as a reply. Then by seven months the babies become considerably more active partners, and the mothers no longer accept all the baby's vocalizations, only vocalic or consonantal babbles. As the mother raises the ante, the child's development proceeds (Cazden, 1979, p. 11).

Caregivers simplify their own language, they repeat and expand upon infants' contributions, and they provide visual supports and redundant information to assist an infant's understanding (Bruner, 1981, 1983; Hoff-Ginsberg and Shatz, 1982; Messer, 1980; Moerk, 1983; Snow, 1977; Zukow, Reilly, and Greenfield, 1982). Mothers report that their conversations with two-year-olds help the children learn to talk (Miller, 1979).

The modification of discourse by adults speaking to infants and young children may provide support for children's conversation and language learning. In the earliest months, the restriction of parental baby talk to a small number of melodic contours may enable infants to abstract vocal prototypes (Papousek, Papousek, and Bornstein, 1985).

Caregivers make the context of statements explicit by clarifying their own and the child's intentions and specifying the referents of a statement (Ochs, 1979). Such provision of background knowledge is reduced as children gain language facility. The structure of mother–child discourse allows children to participate in conversations that are beyond their competence in discourse and may help children advance their skills (Bernstein, 1981). Some evidence regarding the impact of adult language input on children's language development is discussed in a later section on the influence of guided participation.

CHILDREN'S ROLE IN ARRANGING PARTICIPATION

While it is certainly true that adults carry great responsibility in socialisation – they are more knowledgeable and have authority – children are also very active in gaining skill through social interaction. Children participate by indicating their readiness for greater responsibility or even by managing the transfer of information. Adults do not simply solve problems and report their solutions, nor do children passively observe adults and extract the relevant information spontaneously. An adult assesses a child's current understanding of the material and adjusts the scaffolding to support the child's developing skill, while the child simultaneously adjusts the pace of instruction and guides the adult in constructing the scaffold.

An example of an infant seeking a more active role is found in Rogoff, Malkin and Gilbride's (1984) description of an adult and a twelve-month-old working a Jack-in-a-box together. Initially, the adult performed all aspects of manipulating the toy (turning the handle to get the bunny out of the box, and pushing the bunny back into the box), while the baby concentrated solemnly on the actions. In the second episode of play with the Jack-in-the-box, the baby attempted to push the bunny back in the box, and the adult encouraged, 'close it up', while helping the baby push the lid down. In the third episode, the baby began to participate in cranking the handle, and in the fourth episode the baby seemed to demand some independence in managing the handle while the adult encouraged this involvement:

> The baby grabbed the box on its sides and shoved it back and forth on the tray, and the adult paused in cranking. The baby looked at the crank and slowly reached for it, confirming the adult's interpretation that he had been demand-

ing a turn. Putting the baby's hand on the crank and turning the crank, the adult said, 'Okay now, you do it' (pp. 40–1).

Over the course of this interaction, the baby eventually participated in winding the handle, pushing the bunny back in the box, and closing the box, while the adult supported the baby's involvement by winding the handle to near the end of the cycle and assisting the baby in holding the lid down on the springy bunny.

Negotiations regarding level of participation and the nature of the activity can be managed by babies through eye contact, joint attention, smiles or cries, and posture changes. Babies can indicate interest by looking eagerly toward an object or event, leaning forward and gesturing toward the object or event with arms, and making enthused grunts. In a negative situation, or if the adult seems not to understand the baby's cues, the baby's activity may change from joint attention to listlessness, then gaze aversion, and finally to turning entirely away. Kaye (1977) found that six-month-old infants' actions, especially gaze aversion, controlled their mothers' efforts to teach them to reach around a barrier.

In addition to their contribution to managing joint interaction, young children influence their participation in adults' ongoing activities that may not have interaction with the child as a focus. Children's attempts to learn from adult activities may go unnoticed by parents, who are likely to view children's attempts to 'help' or be involved in adult activities as just an inevitable aspect of childhood. During the first year, babies seem to be automatically interested in whatever object an adult is handling, and try to grasp it themselves. An adult's manipulation of a toy facilitates contact by 11–13-month-olds with the same toy, with markedly similar actions performed on the toy (Eckerman, Whatley, and McGhee, 1979). Toddlers follow their parents around the house, trying to be involved in ongoing activities. Rheingold (1982) found that children aged 18 to 30 months spontaneously and energetically helped their parents or a stranger in the majority of the household chores that the adults performed in a laboratory or home setting. Many of the parents reported that they commonly circumvented their child's efforts to participate at home by trying to do chores while the child was napping, to avoid the child's 'interference'.

The propensity to seek proximity to and involvement with adults assists infants and toddlers in acquiring information about the environment and about the activities of the person who is followed (Hay, 1980). Their eagerness to be involved may force a busy parent to give them some role in activities, allowing them to stir the batter, put tape on the present, carry the napkins to the table, help turn the screwdriver, and so on.

In such activities, the adult's and child's roles are likely to fit the characteristics of guided participation. For pragmatic reasons, the adult may try to keep the child from getting involved in an aspect of the activity that is too far beyond the child's skill, e.g. to avoid broken eggs, torn wrapping paper, or damage to the child or to objects. Nevertheless, the child is likely not to be satisfied with an aspect of the job that is too simple, and will insist on greater involvement if given an obvious make-work role. Thus even in interaction with a reluctant adult, the adult and child together may contribute to the child's learning through guided participation.

An example of how a child's insistence on involvement may be instrumental is provided by my daughter, who at age 3½ years was interested in sewing. I was getting ready to leave the house, and noticed that a run had started in the foot of my stocking. My daughter volunteered to help sew the run, but I was in a hurry and tried to avoid her involvement by explaining that I did not want the needle to jab my foot. I began to sew, but could hardly see where I was sewing because my daughter's head was in the way, peering at the sewing. Soon she suggested that I could put the needle into the stocking and she would pull it through, thus avoiding sticking my foot. I agreed and we followed this division of labour for a number of stitches. When I absent-mindedly handed my daughter the needle rather than starting a stitch, she gently pressed my hand back toward my foot, and grinned when I glanced at her, realising the error. The same child at four years of age asked me, as we worked in the kitchen, 'Can I help you with the can opener by holding on to your hand while you do it? ... That's how I learn'. These incidents illustrate the eagerness with which children approach the possibility of learning through involvement with adult activities, as well as their active role in the 'instruction'. The child arranges for participation in the activity, and the adult tacitly (sometimes unwillingly) provides access and information.

DOES GUIDED PARTICIPATION INFLUENCE LEARNING AND DEVELOPMENT?

Thus far, I have suggested that the integrated role of children seeking involvement and structuring their participation, and of adults providing information and arranging for children's activities, may in part be responsible on a day-to-day basis for the rapid progress of children in becoming socialised participants in the intellectual and social aspects of their society. But the existence of such interaction and arrangements between adults and children does not prove that they are influential in children's learning and development.

I would argue, however, that guided participation does play a role in children's learning and development. So much of what children are able to do requires being embedded in their culture. They would certainly not learn English without exposure to that language, nor would they develop scripts for restaurants, peek-a-boo, or book reading without involvement in those activities, as observers or participants. Many of the skills that developmental psychologists study are tied closely to the technology (e.g. books, number system, language, logic, television) of the culture in which children develop and which children learn to master, with the assistance of people who already participate skilfully in culturally important activities.

A variety of studies find an association between children's experiences and their independent skills. In Rogoff, Malkin and Gilbride's (1984) observations of adults and infants playing with a Jack-in-the-box, the infants' understanding of the game script and skill in manipulating the toy improved over the course of repeated episodes in single sessions. Babies who participated in monthly games of roll-the-ball with their mothers were able to return the ball almost two months earlier than they returned any items in a standard test of infant development (Hodapp, Goldfield, and Boyatzis, 1984). The extent to which mothers expand on infants' pointing gestures by labelling objects is associated with the number of object names in the child's vocabulary (Masur, 1982), and the pattern of joint adult–child construction of propositions from one-word utterances appears to form the foundation of children's combinations of words (Scallon, 1976).

Several studies provide evidence that an important function of social interaction with adults may be the direction of young children's attention. Attention may be an important individual activity that can be channelled by the highlighting of events by social partners. Mothers who more frequently encourage their four-month-olds' attention to objects, events, and environmental properties have babies with greater speaking vocabularies and Bayley scores at age twelve months, even when the effect of four-month infant vocalisation and the effect of twelve-month maternal stimulation are partialled out (Papousek, Papousek, and Bornstein, 1984). In an experiment in which the level of maternal focusing of attention was increased (by having an encouraging observer comment on the effectiveness of the mother's naturally occurring efforts to stimulate her infant), infants showed greater exploratory competence as much as two months after the intervention (Belsky, Goode, and Most, 1980). Active involvement of a supportive parent or experimenter in children's exploration of novel objects, compared with these adults' more passive presence, led to more active object exploration by 3–7-year-olds (Henderson, 1984*a,b*).

It is hardly surprising that children learn what they are taught; it is but a short extension to argue that on a day-to-day basis what children learn and are taught contributes to the development of what they know. In this perspective, development is built upon learning and, at the same time, learning is based on development. Children contribute to their own development through their eagerness and management of learning experiences as well as through their employment of the knowledge they already have at hand. At the earliest ages this 'knowledge' includes their reflexes and aspects of behaviour necessary for eating and protection, as well as primordial schemas for social interaction and learning systems such as language (Slobin, 1983). Soon, however, their inborn behavioural repertoire is modified with experience to reflect their history of learning experiences in the knowledge they bring to each new situation.

[. . .]

REFERENCES

Bakeman, R. and Adamson, L. B. (1984) 'Coordinating attention to people and objects in mother–infant and peer–infant interaction', *Child Development*, 55, 1278–89.
Belsky, J., Goode, M. K., and Most, R. K. (1980) 'Maternal stimulation and infant

exploratory competence: Cross-sectional, correlational, and experimental analyses', *Child Development*, 51, 1163–78.

Bernstein, L. E. (1981) 'Language as a product of dialogue', *Discourse Processes*, 4, 117–47.

Brown, R. (1958) *Words and Things*. New York: Free Press.

Bruner, J. S. (1981) 'Intention in the structure of action and interaction', in L. P. Lipsitt (ed.), *Advances in Infancy Research Vol. 1*, pp. 41–56. Norwood, NJ: Ablex.

Bruner, J. S. (1983) *Child's Talk: Learning to Use Language*. New York: Norton.

Butterworth, G. and Cochran, G. (1980) 'Towards a mechanism of joint visual attention in human infancy', *International Journal of Behavioural Development*, 3, 253–72.

Cazden, C. (1979) 'Peekaboo as an instructional model: Discourse development at home and at school', in *Papers and Reports on Child Language Development*, No. 17. Stanford University, Department of Linguistics, Stanford, CA.

Cole, M. (1981) 'The zone of proximal development: where culture and cognition create each other', Center for Human Information Processing Report No. 106, University of California, San Diego.

D'Andrade, R. G. (1981) 'The cultural part of cognition', *Cognitive Science*, 5, 179–95.

Eckerman, C. O., Whatley, J. L., and McGhee, L. J. (1979) 'Approaching and contacting the object another manipulates: a social skill of the one-year-old', *Developmental Psychology*, 15, 585–93.

Erickson, F. (1982) 'Taught cognitive learning in its immediate environments: a neglected topic in the anthropology of education', *Anthropology and Education Quarterly*, 13, 149–80.

Feinman, S. (1982) 'Social referencing in infancy', *Merrill-Palmer Quarterly*, 28, 445–70.

Greenfield, P. M. (1984) 'A theory of the teacher in the learning activities of everyday life', in B. Rogoff and J. Lave (eds), *Everyday Cognition: Its Development in Social Context*, pp. 117–38. Cambridge, MA: Harvard University Press.

Gunnar, M. R. and Stone, C. (1984) 'The effects of positive maternal affect on infant responses to pleasant, ambiguous, and fear-provoking toys', *Child Development*, 55, 1231–6.

Hay, D. F. (1980) 'Multiple functions of proximity seeking in infancy', *Child Development*, 51, 636–45.

Henderson, B. B. (1984a) 'Parents and exploration: the effect of context on individual differences in exploratory behaviour', *Child Development*, 55, 1237–45.

Henderson, B. B. (1984b) 'Social support and exploration', *Child Development*, 55, 1246–51.

Hodapp, R. M., Goldfield, E. C., and Boyatzis, C. J. (1984) 'The use and effectiveness of maternal scaffolding in mother–infant games', *Child Development*, 55, 772–81.

Hoff-Ginsberg, E. and Shatz, M. (1982) 'Linguistic input and the child's acquisition of language', *Psychological Bulletin*, 92, 3–26.

Kaye, K. (1977) 'Infants' effects upon their mothers' teaching strategies', in J. D. Glidewell (ed.), *The Social Context of Learning and Development*. New York: Gardner Press.

Kaye, K. (1982) 'Organism, apprentice, and person', in E. Z. Tronick (ed.), *Social Interchange in Infancy*. Baltimore: University Park Press.

Laboratory of Comparative Human Cognition (1983) 'Culture and cognitive development', in W. Kessen (ed.), *History, Theory, and Methods. Handbook of Child Psychology*, ed. P. H. Mussen, Vol. 1, pp. 294–356. New York: Wiley.

Lempers, J. D. (1979) 'Young children's production and comprehension of nonverbal deictic behaviors', *Journal of Genetic Psychology*, 135, 93–102.

Masur, E. F. (1982) 'Mothers' responses to infants' object-related gestures: influences on lexical development', *Journal of Child Language*, 9, 23–30.

McNamee, G. D. (1980) 'The social origins of narrative skills'. Unpublished dissertation, Northwestern University.

Mehan, H. (1976) 'Assessing children's school performance', in J. Beck, C. Jenks, N. Keddie and M. F. D. Young (eds), *Worlds Apart*. London: Collier Macmillan.

Messer, D. J. (1980) 'The episodic structure of maternal speech to young children', *Journal of Child Language*, 7, 29–40.

Miller, P. J. (1979) *Amy, Wendy, and Beth: Learning Language in South Baltimore*. Austin: University of Texas Press.

Moerk, E. L. (1983) *The Mother of Eve: As a First Language Teacher*. Norwood, NJ: Ablex.

Newman, D. (1982) 'Perspective-taking versus content in understanding lies', *Quarterly Newsletter of the Laboratory of Comparative Human Cognition*, 4, 26–9.

Papousek, M., Papousek, H., and Bornstein, M. H. (1985), 'The naturalistic vocal environment of young infants', in T. M. Field and N. Fox (eds), *Social Perception in Infants*. Norwood, NJ: Ablex.

Poe, P. (1982) 'Beginning in the bathtub', *American Baby*, 44(19), 12–20.

Rheingold, H. L. (1982) 'Little children's participation in the work of adults, a nascent prosocial behavior', *Child Development*, 53, 114–25.

Rogoff, B. (1982) 'Mode of instruction and memory test performance', *International Journal of Behavioral Development*, 5, 33–48.

Rogoff, B. (1986) 'Adult assistance of children's learning', in T. E. Raphael (ed.), *The Contexts of School Based Literacy*. New York: Random House.

Rogoff, B. and Gardner, W. P. (1984) 'Guidance in cognitive development: an examination of mother–child instruction', in B. Rogoff and J. Lave (eds), *Everyday Cognition: Its Development in Social Context*, pp. 95–116. Cambridge, MA: Harvard University Press.

Rogoff, B., Gauvain, M., and Ellis, S. (1984) 'Development viewed in its cultural context', in M. H. Bornstein and M. E. Lamb (eds), *Developmental Psychology*. Hillsdale, NJ: Erlbaum.

Rogoff, B., Malkin, C., and Gilbride, K. (1984) 'Interaction with babies as guidance in development', in B. Rogoff and J. V. Wertsch (eds), *Children's Learning in the 'Zone of Proximal Development'*, pp. 31–44. San Francisco: Jossey–Bass.

Saxe, G. B., Gearhart, M., and Guberman, S. B. (1984) 'The social organization of early number development', in B. Rogoff and J. V. Wertsch (eds), *Children's Learning in the 'Zone of Proximal Development'*, pp. 19–30. San Francisco: Jossey-Bass.

Schaffer, H. R. (1984) *The Child's Entry into a Social World*. London: Academic Press.

Scallon, R. (1976) *Conversations with a One-Year-Old*. Honolulu: University Press of Hawaii.

Shotter, J. and Newson, J. (1982) 'An ecological approach to cognitive development: implicate orders, joint action, and intentionality', in G. Butterworth and P. Light (eds), *Social Cognition Studies in the Development of Understanding*, pp. 32–52. Sussex: Harvester.

Slobin, D. I. (1973) 'Cognitive prerequisites for the development of grammar', in C. A. Ferguson and D. I. Slobin (eds), *Studies of Child Language Development*. New York: Holt, Rinehart and Winston.

Snow, C. (1977) 'Mother's speech research: from input to interaction', in C. Snow and C. Ferguson (eds), *Talking to Children*. New York: Cambridge University Press.

Sorce, J. F., Emde, R. N., Campos, J. J., and Klinnert, M. D. (1985) 'Maternal emotional signaling: its effect on the visual cliff behavior of 1-year-olds', *Developmental Psychology*, 21, 195–200.

Valsiner, J. (1984) 'Construction of the zone of proximal development in adult–child joint action: the socialization of meals', in B. Rogoff and J. V. Wertsch (eds), *Children's Learning in the 'Zone of Proximal Development'*, pp. 65–76. San Francisco: Jossey-Bass.

Vygotsky, L. S. (1978) *Mind in Society: The Development of Higher Psychological Processes*. Cambridge, MA: Harvard University Press.

Wertsch, J. V. (1979) 'From social interaction to higher psychological processes', *Human Development*, 22, 1–22.

Wertsch, J. V. (1984) 'The zone of proximal development: some conceptual issues', in B. Rogoff and J. V. Wertsch (eds), *Children's Learning in the 'Zone of Proximal Development'*, pp. 7–18. San Francisco: Jossey-Bass.

Wertsch, J. V. (1985) *Vygotsky and the Social Formation of Mind*. Cambridge, MA: Harvard University Press.

Whiting, B. B. (1980) 'Culture and social behavior: a model for the development of social behavior', *Ethos*, 8, 95–116.

Wood, D., Bruner, J. S., and Ross, G. (1976) 'The role of tutoring in problem solving', *Journal of Child Psychology and Psychiatry*, 17, 89–100.

Zukow, P. G., Reilly, J., and Greenfield, P. M. (1982). 'Making the absent present: facilitating the transition from sensorimotor to linguistic communication', in K. Nelson (ed.), *Children's Language, Vol. 3*. New York: Gardner Press.

part two
LEARNING CONTEXTS

INTRODUCTION

VICTOR LEE

As I mentioned in the General Introduction, the importance of *context* for learning has come to be increasingly emphasised. This importance is reflected here by devoting to it the whole of part 2 of this Reader.

In chapter 2.1 Neville Bennett and Elisabeth Dunne record the initial reporting of a specific investigation regarding 15 primary teachers of 4–11-year-olds. These teachers altered their classroom practices in order to achieve a regime of cooperative groupwork. Neville Bennett and Elisabeth Dunne report the initial analysis of the resulting group talk in mathematics and English, concentrating on task-related language and using a Piagetian system of categorising. They distinguish between abstract tasks and action tasks, and their initial analysis suggests, for example, that when children work as a group more of their language is task-related.

The interest in collaborative learning is further developed in chapter 2.2 by Paul Light and Agnès Blaye. Their context is microcomputers. They point out, for example, that computer work can actually encourage interaction between learners, contrary to popular fears that computer use may lead to pupil isolation. Much of the chapter is concerned with an evaluative overview of computer use by classroom groups. The results generally favour collaborative learning or indicate no difference. The chapter ends with a brief 'Prospects' section where such issues as the use of a computer as a 'working companion' to the child are considered.

Chapter 2.3 takes us into the much more exotic world of the street vendors in the marketplaces of Recife in north-east Brazil. In this case, the street vendors are children selling such items as peanuts, popcorn, coconut milk or corn on the cob. Terezinha and David Carraher and Analúcia Schliemann discuss the results of an experiment where a small group of these street vendors (aged 9–15 years) proved much more successful at mathematical calculations in the context of everyday activities than they did when faced with school-type activities. Why was this? What are the educational implications?

Language occupies centre stage in the last two chapters of part 2. In chapter 2.4, Derek Edwards and Neil Mercer examine classroom discourse, discussing a list of classroom communications that make up much of that discourse. They argue that to a very great extent teachers control classroom dialogue, and, through that, the content of knowledge itself. Even the *spontaneous contributions* of pupils are not entirely free of teacher control, as the teacher sets, for instance, the agenda for such contributions. They pepper their argument with actual illustrations of teacher–pupil dialogue, and end their contribution by drawing together some of the general points about the educational processes involved.

In chapter 2.5, Paul Gee introduces a cross-cultural element into his consideration of orality and literacy. He considers the meaning of the terms, offering a survey of the field. It is not a survey in the conventional sense of a comprehensive review of the literature, but he does discuss what he considers to be 'key works' in the area. One of the major issues he tackles is the relationships between literacy and cognitive skills. Literacy can be seen as cultural practice. He then begins to analyse the position of teachers of English with regard to literacy, seeing them as gatekeepers.

IMPLEMENTING COOPERATIVE GROUPWORK IN CLASSROOMS

2.1

NEVILLE BENNETT AND ELISABETH DUNNE

INTRODUCTION

Our research on groups has, since 1981, passed through three stages – from description, to experimentation, to implementation. We began by describing actual classroom practice from which we discovered that what generally passed for groupwork in English classrooms was in fact collections of children sitting closely together, but engaged on individual tasks (Bennett *et al.* 1984). In such groups the level of cooperation, frequency of explanation and knowledge exchange is low. It was therefore not possible to acquire a clear understanding of the nature or processes of group cooperation from such data.

In order to achieve this understanding, experiments were undertaken in classrooms in which cooperative groups were set up using normal curriculum materials and tasks with the specific aim of seeking relationships between group composition, group processes and pupil understanding (Bennett and Cass 1988). In addition to showing that group composition was an important variable in relation to processes and outcomes, it was apparent that where a demand for cooperation was made by the teacher, cooperative endeavour and on-task behaviour increased to a high level. It was also established that there was a relationship between interaction in the group and pupils' understandings of the task.

These findings generally support the claims made for cooperative group work (cf. Johnson *et al.* 1981; Slavin 1983; Sharan 1980; Webb 1989); however, like most other American and European studies, they provide no information on issues of classroom implementation, nor on the critical role of the teacher.

The need for research on implementation has attained great contemporary relevance in Britain as a consequence of the introduction of a National Curriculum which is demanding assessed skills in cooperative endeavours. For example the language curriculum 'Speaking and Listening' attainment targets demand that by the age of seven children should be able to present real or imaginary events in a connected narrative to a small group of peers, speaking freely and audibly; and by the age of eleven the average child will be able to offer reasoned explanations of

Source: Paper presented at the conference of the European Association for Research in Learning and Instruction, Madrid, 1989.

how a task has been done or a problem solved and to take part effectively in small-group discussion. The particular pedagogical problem in Britain is that the National Curriculum is making demands for cooperative groupwork from a teacher workforce which has little experience or expertise in this kind of teaching.

The major aim of our present study is thus to investigate the impact of changing classroom grouping practices from those requiring individual, to those requiring cooperative, outcomes, on such aspects as group interaction, classroom management, teacher activity and pupil learning. A particular focus is on the choice and design of group tasks in order to ascertain relationships between task demand and types of group talk.

METHOD

A sample of fifteen primary teachers (teaching 4–11 year olds) participated in the study, each of whom had agreed to modify his or her classroom grouping practices in order to implement [a regime of cooperative groupwork. Depending on teacher choice, some tasks were selected which involved children working individually on 'jigsaw' elements for a joint outcome].

In this kind of task, there are as many elements to the task as there are group members. Each child works on one element and the task is divided in such a way that the group outcome cannot be achieved until every group member has successfully completed his or her piece of work. At this point the 'jigsaw' can be fitted together. Cooperation is thus built into the task structure, as indeed is individual accountability. It is difficult in this type of group task for a child to sit back and let others do all the work, especially since group members are likely to ensure that everyone pulls his weight. Examples of such tasks would be the production of a group story or newspaper, or the making of a 'set' of objects in a practical maths activity.

[Other tasks involve children working jointly on one task for a joint outcome or discussion.] For this type of task, children will need to work cooperatively since only one product will be required of the group. Activities will therefore have to be coordinated and it is possible that a group leader will emerge in order to create the necessary organisation. Each individual's work will have an impact on the group product but will be worthless until it becomes part of that product. Examples can be seen in problem-solving in technology, construction activities or in discussion tasks. Although collaborative endeavour is necessary for the group to succeed, it is less easy to ascertain exactly what each group member has contributed and individual accountability is therefore lower.

Six teachers chose to implement change in language work, four in maths, three in science/technology and two in computer tasks. The teachers then worked in small cooperative groups to plan and design the activities to be used.

The study took place over a six-week period during which time the following data were collected:

1 *Group interaction.* Talk was recorded on two occasions, one early, and one towards the end of the period. Each child in the group was fitted with a radio-microphone in order to gain recordings of high quality for later transcription. The length of the recordings varied depending on the nature of the task. None exceeded 45 minutes.

2 *Task and classroom management.* Observations were made at the same time as the group recordings on a pre-specified schedule by a trained observer. These observations focused in particular on the frequency and type of pupil demands on the teacher. These observations were supplemented by accounts from the teachers themselves concerning changes, (a) made to classroom organisation and management; (b) teacher activities as a consequence of implementing cooperative groupwork; (c) their perceptions of difficulties and successes.

3 *Pupil outcomes.* Changes in pupil understanding at the individual level were ascertained by the development and administration of a pre- and post-test designed around the tasks to be completed. Teachers also provided a professional judgement on the quality of any group outcomes.

ANALYSIS

Analysis of group talk required several stages. The recordings were first transcribed, a process which resulted in transcripts of individual members of the group, which had then to be reconstituted in the appropriate time base. The reconstituted transcripts were then analysed using a specially prepared category system.

In our previous studies we have preferred to adopt an inductive approach whereby categories of talk have been generated from the data themselves. This has the advantage of most adequately describing the particular data set, but there is also a major disadvantage in that unique groups of categories are derived from each set of data, thus making comparisons, and therefore the development of explanatory theory, difficult. In order to fulfil the aims of this study, an analytic system was required based on a theory capable of generating conceptual links between types of group talk and types of task demand. The conceptualisation we found most useful in this regard was Piaget's (1959) model of the development of children's conversations. The stages he proposes for children aged 4–7 are shown in figure 4 on page 66.

Briefly, he argues that, after children have progressed through the egocentric stage, various types of interaction or conversation are apparent, based on whether the interaction is in agreement or disagreement, and on differing levels of collaboration in action and abstract thought. It is only within conversation at stage 3 that 'there is any real interchange of thought'.

Our concern is not with developmental aspects of this model; we are simply using it as a heuristic to postulate seven modes of group interaction (*see* table 2) on page 67.

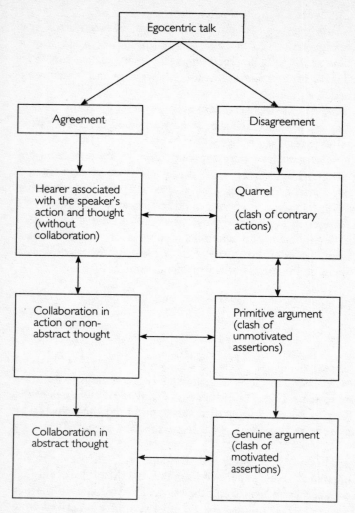

Figure 4   *The development of children's conversations*

The definitions of these modes, and examples, are presented below.

MODE A   COLLECTIVE MONOLOGUE

In the context of a group, but when a child's talk is to the self, without any obvious expectation of a reply; sometimes mumbling or under the breath; egocentric in nature, e.g.

'I need a pencil ... I need thirty-two – that's the end. Thirty-three ... thirty-two ... 1, 2, 3, 4, 5, 6' (etc. to 32).

	Stage	Conversational type	Mode
	1	Collective monologue	A
Action	2	Association with	B
		Sharing in	C
		Collaboration in	D
		Quarrelling	E
		Primitive argument	F
Abstract thought	3	Collaboration	G
		Genuine argument	H

Table 2 *Conversational modes*

Mode B   Association with (action)

Talking about one's own activity or commenting on it; conversational and addressed to the whole group or any group member but not always specifically; not actually collaborative. This is likely to occur when the task demand is the same for all children but there is a request for individual products, e.g.

> 'He's got tears coming down from his eyes – dripping in between his fingers.'
> 'Neil, look at my bog frog. Look at my frog – there – frogs by the score!'
> 'Oh, I like your man – it's good.'

Mode C   Sharing in (action)

Talk centres around a shared activity, often involving demonstration and may be a response to a request for help. As for B, this is likely to occur when there is a request for individual products but the task demand is the same for all children. It also occurs in collaborative tasks with a single product when children interact with individuals rather than the whole group, e.g.

Each child in a group is making a box from a piece of squared paper. To do this, it is necessary to cut out the corners:

James: Do you just go up two by two?
Natalie: One, two. One, two. (She demonstrates how to count and where to cut out the appropriate squares from each other.)

MODE D   COLLABORATION IN (ACTION OR NON-ABSTRACT THOUGHT)

When a group of children are collaborating in their activity and the talk demonstrates this, e.g.

A group of children are making a cart together; most of their talk is similar to that of the discussion below:

Stacey: Come on. Let's begin.
David: Here's our instructions ...
Stacey: Wait a minute, two centimetres on each end, make sure you add on two centimetres.
David: Make sure you add on two centimetres from each end ... Because look ... measure across the box to see how the axle should be, remember to add on two centimetres from each end ... alright?
Stacey: Axle, axle, these are the axles.

MODE E   QUARRELLING

Talk that illustrates a clash of opinion in terms of action; seldom extended in nature.

Primitive   e.g.   'No, you're not drawing the squares.'

With motives e.g.   'That's not the way to do it ... Because that's not what it says.'

MODE F   PRIMITIVE ARGUMENT

Where talk takes the form of simple and opposing statements with no explicit reasoning or justification; it represents a move into abstract thought but is a parallel to quarrelling in action, e.g.

A group are discussing the differences between two pieces of prose – one being in 'story' form, the other being a spoken account written down.

Lucy: The spoken version was boring but no one else seems to think so.
Jo: I don't think it was boring. I don't think *boring*. It was different.
Robyn: I think it was different.

Jo: It was different but it wasn't boring.
Lucy: I think it was boring and not different.

MODE G COLLABORATION

Where children discuss their work in terms of ideas or arguments which are logical and reasoned, sometimes with justification through the use of words such as 'since', 'then' or 'because', e.g.

Children discussing poems make statements such as:

'I think it means he isn't getting any gold at all because he's not selling anything . . . That's what I think it is.'
'I think he's like the King of the Jungle. He sounds like it doesn't he?'

The children discussing the two pieces of prose (see F) make suggestions:

Robyn: I said the written one sounds more like a story.
Lucy: Yeah, same here. The second one sounds more like a story. So I'm going to put, "It had more details".

MODE H GENUINE ARGUMENT

For genuine argument to occur, demonstrations and logical solutions etc. have to be made explicit. Use of 'because' and 'since' as logical connecters. The following example shows mode F moving into mode G.

Sophie: The ending was hopeless.
Holly: Was it? Do you think it was?
Luke: I liked the ending.
Sophie: It was too soppy though.
Luke: Too soppy?
Neil: Well, I like it when they die at endings. It makes it a lot more funnier. It's a lot more good.
Holly: Well that's very nice, isn't it? [sarcastically!]
Neil: It's a lot more good – like – like – if I wrote a story I'd go "As he swings his head with his sword and" – stop the book there and they'd want to buy the next book wouldn't they?
Holly: No, probably wouldn't – because not many people like animals being killed.
Neil: They would.

The categorisation of the conversational modes into Action and Abstract is consistent with Piaget's model, as are the definitions of the two terms:

Action: talk related to the activity of the moment.

Abstract: talk no longer connected with the activity of the moment, but concerned with finding an explanation, reconstructing a story or a memory, discussing the order of events or the truth of a tale.

All talk was first classified as task-related or not. All task-related talk was then allocated to a conversational mode before making decisions concerning the centrality of the talk to task demand, and whether the talk was outcome, or socially, oriented. ('Not central' refers to talk which is clearly related to task completion but not to the cognitive demand – for example, finding paper to write on or collecting together necessary materials. 'Social' is that talk in which children are concerned with the organisation of their group – for example, 'we can't write that . . . it's not a group decision', whereas 'Outcome' relates to the cognitive demand of the task.)

These classifications were carried out by trained observers, all of whom were qualified teachers. Inter-judge reliability has been found to be high.

FINDINGS

The figures to be discussed in this section represent only one-half of the data which are available for analysis, and refer only to language and maths tasks. Thus, at present, we are looking only at general trends which may, or may not, be confirmed by further categorisation.

The high overall level of task-related talk for maths and language in this study can be usefully compared with an earlier study of groupwork in classrooms where children were observed to be seated in groups but to be working individually (Bennett *et al.* 1984). The two sets of figures are shown in table 3.

	Cooperative Groupwork (Bennett and Dunne 1989)	Individualised work (Bennett *et al.* 1984)
Maths	89%	63%
Language	86%	70%
Total	88%	66%

Table 3   *Task-related talk during individual and cooperative groupwork*

The children in an 'individualised' situation did cooperate and talk about their work, yet the 'cooperative' children exhibit a much greater involvement with their tasks, to the extent that talk unrelated to the task in many groups is minimal and sometimes non-existent. Additionally the great majority of this talk is central to the task (85 per cent) and is 'outcome'-oriented rather than 'social' in nature (86 per cent).

Table 4 presents an overall comparison of the language and maths areas.

Mode	Language	Maths
A	6	11
B	10	52
C	43	26
D	14	3
E	2	7
F	2	
G	21	
H	3	

Table 4 *Conversational modes in language and maths* (%)

The table shows marked differences in conversational mode in the two subjects. Talk in maths is heavily concentrated in mode B – 'associating with' – with no abstract talk at all. In contrast one-quarter of the talk in language work is abstract, and the talk relating to action is more sophisticated. Thus, maths tasks can be characterised as demanding action talk whereas language tasks demand both action and abstract talk.

The reason for this dichotomy seems to be fairly clear: in maths and science/technology the tasks set for the children, across the whole age range, could be defined as *action* tasks. Pupils are asked, for example, to make cubes, to make triangular prisms, to make carts that will roll down a slope, to make models for a fairground. These tasks are practical and therefore involve manipulation of materials. The children *have* to be involved in action in order to complete their tasks.

On the other hand, language tasks generally demand a different kind of activity. The children are asked to talk, to discuss, to make decisions unrelated to action. They are given problems to be solved verbally, tasks which ask them to look for meaning, to provide ideas, to compare and contrast. Alongside this, there is a demand to write or draw, sometimes as a group response, sometimes as individuals, in order to show what has been gained from the group discussion. Such tasks are characterised by a predominant demand for *abstract* thought, the action demand being secondary. So, for example, the whole group provides ideas for a single story, so that the emphasis is on creative thought; or the teacher provides a written or drawn stimulus for discussion, sometimes with questions to guide thinking – sometimes without. There is then a demand that this be completed by writing or by drawing.

ACTION TASKS

It will be remembered that action tasks are characterised by talk mostly within modes A to E. Let us now look more closely at the nature of talk occurring within an action task. A group of seven-year-olds is asked to make a set of cubes out of squared paper, each child contributing a cube of a different size, and the range of possibilities being limited by the size of paper. This leads to much interaction similar to:

Tania: Emily's doing the smallest.
James: I'm going to do the biggest.
Tania: I'm doing the smallest.
James: You're doing the biggest because you're the oldest ... I'm doing the smallest even if you say I can't.
Tania: I'm doing the biggest one because I'm doing the best.
(Mode D: Social)

Most of such talk is classified as 'social' since it seems to revolve around vying for status within the group, but there is also a great deal which relates more closely to the cognitive demand:

Emily: I'm doing a five by five.
James: No, I'm doing five by five ...
Tania: How are we going to make it anyway? I don't know anyway?
Lisa: You'll have to do another one like that won't you.
Emily: Uh uh. I did it wrong ...
Lisa: I'm on my second. Is that perfect? That isn't perfect is it?
James: I've made mine and it goes just like a dice.
Lisa: Shall I screw this up and do it again?
Tania: Lisa are you doing the two side one. Hey, I know. You could do three lines.
(Mode D: Outcome)

This kind of interaction is very similar to a collaborative task where a group of seven- and eight-year-olds are asked to make a single cart, following precise instructions. They again discuss who can do what, sometimes arguing, sometimes resolving the problems associated with sharing materials:

Stacey: Can I saw the other part?
Heidi: Stacey can do another bit.
David: Wait a minute. I'm just marking it. I'm just marking it, Stacey.
Heidi: Stacey's doing that part.
David: Stacey, quick! Sorry Paul, Stacey's doing it. Put it on this one for her ... because you're not my best friend ... wait a minute ... there's plenty of sawing, look, these and these. Knocked it off. I'm clumsy. No, don't.

Heidi: See if you can hold it there.
David: And properly.
Heidi: That's it, isn't it.
(Mode D: Social)

Ten minutes later:

Heidi: We don't have to stick that down.
David: No, wait a minute. Scissors . . . scissors, pass me the scissors. Thanks. Cutting that bit of glue off, it's hanging off too much . . . you'll have to go that way . . . sticks to the box . . . it needs to anyway, doesn't it?
Heidi: Yes, but not yet because we are not sticking it . . . Now we need the triangles . . . we have to read the instructions . . . making the axle holders . . . no, because we've already put . . . we need to get the triangles to strengthen the corners, stick the triangles in place, the picture will remind you if you have forgotten how to . . .
David: No, I'll use the scissors it's easier . . .
Heidi: She's cutting out that . . .
David: I know and I need to cut another one off there. They're not the same size . . . could have done with them a bit bigger.
(Mode D: Outcome)

ACTION AND ABSTRACT TASKS

It is clear that decisions about, and therefore talk about, action are important to the task and monopolise all conversation. What is of particular interest is that for tasks which combine action with abstract demands, the talk related to action continues to dominate. It seems as if, given the opportunity to talk about action, the children will take it. Or it may be that, since an end-product is always demanded by the teacher, the action required for this is given the group's greatest attention. Thus, in language lessons where there has been a real attempt verbally to solve a problem as a group, talk relating to the writing up, or to the drawing of ideas and meanings, is always proportionately higher.

An example of this is shown when a group of six- and seven-year-olds are discussing a problem: which choice – of a card, a cup of tea in bed, or a bunch of flowers, would be the best way to surprise Mum on her birthday? The children enter into this hypothetical situation instantly, listening and replying to each other, making decisions, justifying their responses:

Andrew: Yes, but if we choose the flowers one she can put them in a vase.
Louise: Yes, but they'll die so she won't keep them for very long.
Andrew: She will because . . .

Louise: They could be, they could be, those paper flowers couldn't they ...
           because they last a long time.
(Mode H: Outcome)

Then:

Louise: I think the card.
Andrew: Yeah, the card.
Louise: Because Mum can keep it for ages, she could always keep it forever
           ... If we have a cup of tea Mum will drink it all.
Andrew: No, she won't, she'll spill it.
Louise: In bed, she might spill the milk when she's pouring it in for her
           breakfast, so we'll have the card.
Donna: Yes.
Louise: Because, because, when the flowers are in the vase they could knock
           the vase over and the water would go over.
(Mode G: Outcome)

However, as soon as they begin to write and draw, it is this that retains their
attention. They talk about each others' drawings:

Philip: Is that a girl? Is that a girl? Actually this is a boy.
Louise: A boy?
Donna: That's a funny boy ... that's got to be a girl.
(Mode B: Outcome)

They talk under their breath as they write. They ask each other what to do next:

Philip: What else shall I do, Andrew?
Andrew: Don't ask me. Do the writing.
Philip: Oh, now I know.
Alan: Do the writing.
Philip: Right, I've got to do the writing.
(Mode D: Outcome)

Louise takes on a leadership role, expecially helping Donna who finds the writing
difficult:

Louise: Write *for* – for Mum.
Donna: F ... O ... R. No. There. OK?
Louise: F ... O ... a. For Mum. Can you write Mum there?
Andrew: Is that the way? Make a ...
Philip: A ... C ... A ... R ... D.
Andrew: How do you write it? C ... A ... for? How do you write it ...?
Louise: No ... for Mum ... M ... F ... O ... R ...
Alan: C ... A ... R ... D ... F ... O ... R ... M ... U ... M ... for
           Mum.

Andrew: There, done it.
(Mode D: Outcome)

Louise then checks the group's writing and the children decide they have completed their task: high and low attainers have worked together; boys and girls have conversed readily with each other; they have solved all difficulties without bothering the teacher; and, most importantly, they have made a logical and justified choice from their three options, a choice which will then be explained to the rest of the class.

The teacher is slightly disappointed that there is not a lengthier discussion of the problem itself. Yet when one considers the difficulties these children experience with the action – writing simple words, making their drawings look like real people, and even, for Philip, remembering what he has to do next, then it is easy to understand why talk relating to this action is predominant. As soon as the action talk begins, furtherance of the abstract discussion would seem unlikely, at least for children of such young age.

However, nine- and ten-year-olds respond in a slightly different way to a similar task. They are given a long poem which is read both with the teacher and by the group. The children are asked to draw individual posters to illustrate the poem and told also that they may be challenged about its meaning. Throughout their work, the children move across many modes of talk; the action and abstract modes are intermingled. Each drawing needs to reflect the description and sense of the poem, and the children thus search for meaning as this becomes important to their illustration:

Mary Anne: No I'm not. I'm sitting him down with his hands over his face crying. He's an old man, isn't he?
Samantha: I dunno. Yes I think . . . Does it say old? Does it say man?
Mary Anne: An old . . . yeah . . . It says "the old King of the Makers".
Samantha: If it says "King" it must be a man.
(Mode H: Outcome)

They also need to know the meaning of individual words:

Matthew: . . . clayman. What's a clayman?
Mary Anne: How the hell should I know what a clayman is? . . . A clayman is, a clayman is a clayman.
Matthew: No but you wouldn't find a clayman in the jungle.
Samantha: The cayman not a clayman.
Mary Anne: How should I know what a cayman is?
Matthew: Well, go up and ask.
(Mode H: Outcome)

However, it seems that when children are asked to submit a group response, rather than several individual ones, the amount of talk relating to action is significantly diminished. Ironically, this has occasionally led to teachers suggesting that such a lesson has been less worthwhile, since there has been less talk when compared with other sessions, and sometimes more off-task chatter: in fact it may rather be that abstract talk is harder, comes less easily to the children, needs more pause for thought and that their participation is less obvious.

CONCLUSION

These findings of differences between action tasks and abstract tasks do not mean that abstract talk is not available to children who are involved in action tasks. It does occur, but extremely rarely, and is not extended in nature. Nor do the findings mean that children involved in action are not involved in any kind of abstract thought, but simply that they only rarely give evidence of it in their talk. However, it is important to note that post-task interviews and class follow-up periods did give some evidence of teachers promoting talk in terms of abstract ideas, taking up decisions made by children and questioning and challenging. Although the argument was lacking during the children's groupwork, teachers had the opportunity for more organised clashes of opinion in class discussion. For example, those children who had been making carts with wheels and bodies of different shapes and sizes were fully aware of the proportions of their own group's product. The teacher-led discussion as to why some carts rolled further or faster than others now became meaningful to every child as they realised exactly how their own group's cart was different from another's; pupils were prepared to argue the strengths and weaknesses of their own cart.

Further to this, the findings do not show whether it is usual practice for teachers to choose action tasks with no deliberate and explicit demand for abstract discussion; they show only that the teachers in our sample chose this way of working. It may well be widespread, however, for practical activity in maths is often presented as the be-all and end-all of mathematical working for children in British primary schools. To move into the more difficult area of promoting abstract thought as a precursor to, or alongside, action, might be a consideration for future task design.

What stands out from the data is that children are becoming familiar with both materials and ideas without need of the teachers' intervention. The end products whether made, written or drawn are truly the children's own (and if we believe Graves (1983) 'ownership' is all-important). A few of the teachers involved feel concern that discussion might have been improved by their presence in the group; the majority are amazed or delighted at the perseverance of even the youngest, or the lowest achiever. In the action tasks, children are said to produce work of higher quality than usual; they 'nag' each other to 'get on', to 'stop being stupid', to check over writing, to help with spellings. More able children, or sometimes a chosen group leader, virtually take on the role of teacher in dealing with general procedure; the teacher is thus left free to deal with more cognitive affairs, or 'real' teaching. On those rare occasions when an abstract discussion seems slow and lacking in content, and an end-product reflects this, even this struggle without the teacher may be worth while, for, again, what these children can bring to an ensuing discussion with the teacher will be their own, a foundation which may allow them to restructure their thinking later. Thus the end-product of one task becomes the first stage of an ongoing process extended by the teacher after the pupils have familiarised themselves with essential details. It is important to realise that the most faltering discussions are, at least in these data, characterised by talk in mode G accompanied by modes F and H, both rarely seen elsewhere. Since these two categories are those in which real problem-solving is tackled through talk, it is unfair to compare the faltering progression with the often free-flowing spontaneity of talk relating to action.

FURTHER WORK

As already stated, the findings reported here are based on only one-half of the group tasks recorded. Categorisation of the remaining half continues and when completed will be used to refine our analyses of the relationships between task demands and conversation modes.

The data provided by the teachers on pupil and group outcomes, and on their evaluations of the impact of change on their teaching activities and classroom management styles are yet to be analysed. When completed they will allow us to consider such questions as the links between task type, conversation mode and pupil outcomes, changes in classroom practices as a function of implementing cooperative groupwork, and issues relevant to successful implementation on a wider scale.

ACKNOWLEDGMENT

This study is part of a wider research programme on Primary Teacher Education in the School of Education, University of Exeter, funded by the Leverhulme Trust.

REFERENCES

Bennett, N. and Cass, A. (1988) 'The effects of group composition on group interactive processes and pupil understanding', *British Educational Research Journal*, 15, 19–32.
Bennett, N., Desforges, C., Cockburn, A. and Wilkinson, B. (1984) *The Quality of Pupil Learning Experiences*. London: Lawrence Erlbaum.

Graves, D. (1983) *Writing, Teachers and Children at Work*. London: Heinemann.

Johnson, D. W., Manruyama, G., Johnson, R., Nelson, D. and Shaw, L. (1981) 'Effects of cooperative, competitive and individualist goal structures on achievement: a meta-analysis', *Psychological Bulletin*, 89, 47–62.

Piaget, J. (1959) *The Language and Thought of the Child*. London: Routledge and Kegan Paul.

Sharan, S. (1980) 'Cooperative learning in small groups: recent methods and effects on achievement, attitudes and ethnic relations', *Review of Educational Research*, 50, 241–71.

Slavin, R. E. (1983) *Cooperative Learning*. New York: Longman.

Webb, N. M. (1989) 'Peer interaction and learning in small groups', *International Journal of Educational Research*, 13, 21–39.

COMPUTER-BASED LEARNING: THE SOCIAL DIMENSIONS

2.2

PAUL LIGHT AND AGNÈS BLAYE

INTRODUCTION

This chapter concerns the cognitive consequences of peer interaction in the context of educational microcomputer use. The computer has, in the course of its recent appearance on the educational scene, acted as a multi-faceted mirror, reflecting the whole gamut of educational and psychological theories concerning the development of children's thinking. Moreover, the computer has not only lent itself well to assimilation into a wide variety of educational contexts, it also has the potential to transform those contexts.

Without attempting a comprehensive review, we propose to examine some of the broad issues surrounding individualised versus group microcomputer use, to offer an overview of the available experimental literature, and to take a look at some of the possibilities for future development in this field. We will restrict ourselves to situations of 'direct' face-to-face interaction, while acknowledging that the use of networking, of electronic mail and conferencing would all deserve a place in any full discussion of the social dimensions of children's computer use.

THE COMPUTER AS AN EDUCATIONAL TOOL: CONCEPT TO REALITY

There are a number of distinct frameworks within which the computer has been envisaged as contributing to education. One of these is the Piagetian constructivist framework, developed in this context most effectively by Papert (1980). Papert's seminal work with LOGO has done a great deal to shape microcomputer use, especially at younger age levels. He saw in programming a distinctive route toward the development of generalisable problem-solving skills ('powerful ideas'), and emphasised the individual constructive activity of the child him- or herself in

Source: Hugh Foot, Michelle Morgan and Rosalyn Shute (eds), *Children Helping Children*. John Wiley, in press.

acquiring such skills. While Papert's vision was not of the child-computer dyad as *isolated* from other learners, there was little room for any analysis of the social dimensions of the learning process. Programming in a high-level language such as LOGO requires the pupils to have a precise and formal representation of all the necessary steps to a particular goal. The essence of Papert's view was that the writing, testing and 'debugging' of programs offers a uniquely powerful resource for the development of abstract thought and high-level problem-solving abilities. The intellectually constructive aspect of computer use, then, is to be found in the creative engagement of the child with the computer program.

While this perspective has been an influential one, the majority of contemporary school computer use is of a very different ilk. Surveys such as that by Jackson, Fletcher and Messer (1986) confirm that most computer use in primary schools involves 'drill and practice' software. The pedagogical perspective here is that the computer can provide a level of routine individual tutoring which the busy classroom teacher cannot. Any given educational task can be broken down into its elements and the individual child can be taken through a carefully graduated series of subtasks embodying these elements. The child can progress at his or her own pace, being given lots of practice to establish full mastery of each subtask. From this perspective one of the main virtues of the computer is its facility for providing direct and immediate feedback, shaping performance and ensuring a progressive build-up of understanding.

From this standpoint, the computer can be seen as an infinitely patient teaching assistant, a descendent of the Skinnerian 'teaching machine' of an earlier era. Indeed it has been said of this kind of usage that it amounts to employing the technology of the 1980s to embody the curriculum of the 1950s (Baker 1985). While the principles of programmed learning proved difficult to implement in the then-available technology, the computer with its speed and flexibility offers these principles a new lease of life.

The recent development of intelligent tutoring provides a new way to harness the educational potentialities of computers. What characterises 'drill practice' and other 'non-intelligent' computer-assisted learning software is the lack of flexibility which results in all pupils having to undergo essentially the same teaching sequence. By contrast, an intelligent tutoring system offers the possibility of generating the teaching sequence 'online' during the educational interaction (Elsom-Cook 1987). As a result the teaching sequence is tailored to the requirements of each pupil.

An essentially individualistic view of the learning process is fundamental to the tradition which stretches from programmed learning to intelligent tutoring systems, and *progress* in this domain has largely been measured in terms of increasingly flexible and accurate tailoring of the software to the needs of the individual learner. This in turn has provoked concern about the dangers, supposedly inherent in information technology, of losing out on the social and interactional aspects of the learning process. The worrying image of the socially isolated and withdrawn child, hunched over his or her computer for hours at a time, is one which has considerable currency (Baker 1985).

The reality, at least for the early school years in North America and the UK, appears to be very different. For what may prove temporary and pragmatic reasons, the indications are that, far from reducing socially interactive learning, computers in the classroom *increase* the opportunities for such learning. This is especially true in respect of child–child interaction. The most obvious factor here is the scarcity of computer hardware in schools. The survey mentioned earlier by Jackson *et al.* (1986) indicated that in the primary sector the level of provision averaged less than one computer per class. Moreover, whereas over most curricular areas the teacher has vastly more expertise than the pupils, this is often not true in respect of computers. Here, knowledgeable pupils often become valued sources of information for other children in the class (Sheingold, Hawkins and Char 1984).

The net result of these factors is that much educational computer work takes place within relatively autonomous *groups* of pupils. Indeed, Jackson *et al.*'s (1986) survey showed that primary-school teachers saw learning to interact in groups as one of the main *advantages* of computer use in schools. The view of computer-related activities as incentives to social interaction has been supported by many systematic observations of work on the computer in the classroom (e.g. Hawkins 1983; Hawkins, Sheingold, Gearhart and Berger 1982). Sheingold *et al.* (1984) reviewed a number of early studies which point to the conclusion that work with computers promotes both a high level of task-related interaction and a high probability of children calling on one another (rather than the teacher) for help. Far from preventing peer interaction, then, computer work in schools may perhaps offer a peculiarly effective environment for interaction between learners.

EMPIRICAL STUDIES OF COMPUTER USE BY CLASSROOM GROUPS

Classroom-based observational studies have suggested a similar picture for activities specific to computers (e.g. programming and word processing) and for traditional activities transferred to the computer (e.g. most drill and practice and non-intelligent CAL software).

Cummings (1985), on the basis of an Australian study of children using a variety of CAL programs, concluded that the computer can and does provide an effective motivator for groupwork. In particular he saw computer-based work as supplying the context for the kind of genuine discussion between children which the Bullock Report (1975) considered so necessary, but which is so difficult to achieve in teacher-centred classrooms. Broderick and Trushell (1985), observing ten-year-old children using word processors, described a wealth of positive and mutually supportive interactions among the children. Proponents of LOGO in recent years (e.g. Hoyles and Sutherland 1986; Hughes, McLeod and Potts 1985; Hawkins 1983; Hawkins *et al.* 1982) have offered detailed observational support to the view that children working with LOGO in pairs or small groups typically show high levels of spontaneous interaction. Indeed, Hoyles and Sutherland see this as one of the major strengths of this approach to learning mathematics. They suggest that it is the context of social interaction which pushes the children towards adopting an objective attitude to the task in hand. Their ongoing studies are attempting to validate this claim through a fine-grained analysis of the interaction actually going on between pairs of children working together on LOGO over a prolonged period of time.

Hawkins and colleagues (1982) describe the interaction between pupils when they work with LOGO as sometimes taking the form of sustained collaboration on a joint project, sometimes taking the form of children seeking help and advice from one another when they are in difficulties, and sometimes involving children just 'stopping by' at the computer in passing. Not surprisingly, patterns of interaction are affected by the kind of software in use. Crook (1987) for example, observed that a piece of CAL software involving maze-solving tended to produce turn-taking on the part of the children. Another piece of software involving series completion produced more differentiated interaction, with discussion of competing hypotheses. The richest discussion was promoted by an adventure game, though differences in reading ability were limiting. Similarly in wordprocessing, children's very limited keyboard skills imposed severe restrictions on the interaction (Crook 1986).

Though suggestive, these kinds of studies cannot definitively establish the effects of such interaction upon individual children's learning. In the next section we turn to more artificial, experimental studies which have sought to do this.

EXPERIMENTAL STUDIES

One series of experimental studies has stemmed from the mainly American tradition of social-psychological research rooted in the work of Lewin and Deutch on group dynamics and cooperation. These studies put their emphasis on cooperative organisation of groups, tasks and rewards (e.g. Johnson and Johnson 1986; Johnson, Johnson and Stanne 1986) and deal mainly with CAL tasks. For example, Johnson and Johnson describe a study in which 14-year-olds worked in groups of four on a geography simulation task on the computer. In some groups the pupils were given individual goals, independently of one another. In other groups the children within the groups were instructed to work competitively, to see who was best. In the third type of group the children were instructed to work cooperatively, being assigned to specific roles in rotation. The third condition produced significantly higher levels of individual achievement on a number of measures than did either of the other two. Both the cooperative and the competitive conditions produced more positive expressed attitudes towards computers than did the individualised condition.

Johnson and colleagues suggest that such benefits of cooperation may be more evident with more complex and exploratory software of the kind they used. However, rather similar advantages for pupils working in cooperative pairs have been found with relatively simple drill and practice software (Mevarech 1987).

Twelve-year-olds were studied working alone or in pairs of similar ability on arithmetic drill and practice programs. All children were individually post-tested. Those who had worked in pairs achieved significantly better results, and this was especially true among the low-achieving children. However, in another rather similar study involving computer-based instruction in Hebrew, only marginal and non-significant differences favouring homogeneous pairs over individuals were found (Mevarech, Stern and Levita 1987).

Another variable which could potentially play an important role is group size. Trowbridge (1987) observed 13- and 14-year-olds working on CAL software designed to teach them about electrical circuits. The pupils worked either one, two, three or four to a computer. Measures of interactional behaviour taken from videotapes of the sessions indicated that children working in twos or threes engaged in the highest levels of interaction, though those working in threes were more likely to show competitive interaction. The pairs were the most mutually supportive. The children working in pairs made the fewest incorrect entries and formulated higher quality responses than those working in the other conditions, though post-tests failed to show significant superiority in individual learning outcome.

Whereas the work we have discussed thus far has mainly emphasised social motivational and attitudinal concomitants of interaction, treating cognitive attainments simply as an outcome measure, another body of (mainly European) experimental work has attempted a more cognitively oriented analysis of the interaction. For example, Fletcher (1985) has attempted to analyse the role of the verbalisation which typically accompanies collaborative work. In a study with 9–11-year-olds, children worked on a computer simulation game either as individuals or in groups of three. Among the individuals, some were instructed to work silently while others were asked to talk aloud. On most measures, the groups performed substantially better than the silent individuals. The requirement to verbalise reasons for decisions etc. led to some improvement among the children working alone, leading Fletcher to conclude that overt verbalisation may have at least some part to play in group facilitation of performance. However, there was no individual post-test on the task in this study, and a post-test measure of verbal knowledge concerning the task indicated no significant differences between the conditions.

Experimental studies have also been carried out involving rather more 'computer-specific' activities such as programming. Programming the computer can be thought of as a highly technical chore which, mercifully, computer users have to concern themselves with less and less these days. But it can also be thought of as the activity which most fully embodies the educational potentialities of the microcomputer. We saw this earlier with Papert, who envisaged the writing, running, debugging and developing of LOGO programs as an activity which distilled and rendered accessible to the young child a whole range of powerful, abstract ideas. Indeed, as Colbourn and Light (1987) noted, the claims Papert made for the cognitive benefits of programming (especially in terms of the child's metacognitive ability to reflect upon and articulate his or her own problem-solving abilities) bear a distinct resemblance to claims which have been made for the cognitive benefits of peer interaction. So what can we say about the effectiveness of bringing these two phenomena together and employing peer interaction in the service of learning to program?

We saw earlier that classroom observation work involving LOGO indicates its potential for supporting high levels of task-related social interaction, though the evidence that it promotes the generalisable problem-solving skills envisaged by Papert is less than convincing (Clements 1985; DES 1987; Kliman 1985). For present purposes the key question is whether there is any experimental evidence that child–child interaction facilitates the learning of programming concepts and skills. There appear to have been relatively few systematic studies in this area.

One such study involved 11- and 12-year-old children learning to use a programming language called MICROPROLOG (Colbourn and Light 1987; Light, Colbourn and Smith 1987). The children worked in class groups of eight over a number of sessions. Each group of eight pupils was given access to either two, four or eight microcomputers. No differences were found between these conditions in terms of children's individual grasp of MICROPROLOG at post-test. A significant difference between the design of this study and those of most others we have discussed is that, although in one condition the children had a microcomputer each, they were working within a group of eight pupils and could interact freely with one another. Videotapes of selected sessions indicated little difference in level of task-related child–child interaction in the 'individual', 'two to a machine' and 'four to a machine' conditions. This perhaps serves to highlight the artificiality of experimental studies in which the 'control' condition involves children working alone at the computer with no access at all to their fellow students.

Faced with this difficulty, one way forward is to rely on trying to *correlate* the amount or quality of interaction which particular learners engage in and their particular learning outcome. Webb, Ender and Lewis (1986) adopted this approach in a study of 11–14-year-olds learning BASIC programming in pairs over a number of sessions. They looked for evidence that the quality of social interaction and discussion in which children engaged during learning could predict achievement in terms of eventual individual programming skills. Measures were taken of the frequency of such behaviours as giving and receiving explanations, asking questions and getting replies, and verbalising aloud. Correlations with learning outcome were calculated, partialling out variations in initial ability level. The results showed that many of the interaction measures were significantly positively correlated with some (though not all) of the learning outcome measures.

Perhaps the most systematic and theoretically coherent body of experimental work on the cognitive consequences of peer interaction has been that associated with Doise, Mugny and Perret-Clermont in Geneva and Neuchatel [. . .]. While this work has not been concerned with computer based learning, it has exercised considerable influence on work in this field. Doise and colleagues typically used a three-step experimental design involving an individual pre-test, an intervention session in which children work either alone (the control condition) or in groups (usually pairs) and finally an individual post-test. The studies which established this tradition (see for example Doise and Mugny 1984; Perret-Clermont 1980) involved children in the age range 5–7 who, in Piaget's terms, were in the process of mastering concrete operational modes of thought. Where working in pairs facilitated subsequent individual performance the mediating process was characterised as 'socio-cognitive conflict', i.e. conflict between differing wrong answers based on partial centrations, embodied socially in the differing perspectives of the two children. The social dimension of the situation was seen as providing the impetus towards resolving the conflict. Such resolution could be achieved by transcending the different centrations to arrive at a more advanced 'decentred' solution.

This analysis has been adapted by a number of researchers interested in peer-facilitation effects on non-Piagetian tasks, and several of these have involved computer-based work (Blaye 1988; Fraisse 1987; Light, Foot, Colbourn and McClelland 1987). In these cases, the reason for using the computer was principally that it offered advantages in controlling and manipulating task presentation, so as to facilitate detailed study of interactional effects. In some cases these manipulations involve the software, in some the hardware.

As an example of a software manipulation, Fraisse (1985; 1987) followed up a series of studies on recursive reasoning with 11- and 12-year-olds by pitting children, either alone or in pairs, against the computer. When the 'computer-opponent' was programmed to give poor (in fact random) answers the children working in pairs discussed their ideas and showed superior learning to those children who worked alone. But when the 'computer-opponent' was programmed to give perfect answers every time, the children in effect used the computer to check out their hypotheses, did not interact much with their partners, and showed no peer-facilitation of performance.

The effects of different types of hardware and interface devices upon interactive learning has not been extensively studied as yet (Wilton and McClean 1984). However, Scaife (1987) has begun to analyse children's performance with various kinds of input devices. Most such devices have clearly been designed with a single user in mind. However, it is possible to exploit them for cooperative usage, and this has been done in a number of experiments.

Blaye (1988) reports a series of studies in which 5- and 6-year-olds worked on a form/colour matrix filling task either individually or in pairs. Although the task might have been expected to engender conflicts of centration, the children working in pairs showed only a low frequency of verbal disagreement, and there was little to suggest that such disagreements were conducive to learning. Nevertheless, experience in pairs did in some studies lead to greater individual progress than working alone. This was particularly true with a version of the task where the interaction in the pairs was structured so that one child indicated his or her choice with a lightpen and the other had to key in his or her assent via the keyboard before the instruction would be accepted by the computer.

A rather similar procedure for preserving the engagement of both children with the task was used by Light *et al.* (1987). Here pairs and individuals were presented with a problem-solving task on the computer. Superiority of the pairs condition (as judged in terms of individual post-test performance) was only shown when the keyboard was modified so as to require corresponding key entries from both partners to activate a response. Despite rather little verbal interaction of any kind, this 'dual key' condition, resulting in joint participation of both children in every move, was associated with clear peer facilitation of individual performance. As with Blaye (1988), the most likely mechanism underlying progress seems to be the destabilisation of initial inefficient solution strategies, creating novel intermediate stages on the basis of which the children could see their way through to more efficient solutions.

Light and Glachan (1985) and Light and Foot (1987) have reported a number of studies of problem-solving on the computer which suggest that both the likelihood of peer interaction benefits and the underlying mechanisms vary considerably from task to task. For example, whereas benefits in the 'Tower of Hanoi' task seemed to accrue from the essentially nonverbal disequilibration process referred to above, explicit verbal justification of choices seemed to be an important factor in a 'Balance Beam' task. Disagreement and argument about moves proved a good predictor of learning outcome in the code-breaking game 'Mastermind'.

It is clear from these and other studies that pairs or groups of children working at the computer do not always perform better than individuals, and even when they do this advantage is not always reflected in individual learning outcome. On the other hand it is worth remarking that *contrary* results, favouring the individual over the group, do not seem to appear in this literature. The studies we have reviewed either favour learning in groups or indicate no difference in outcome. There are no indications from these studies that, for example, the reduced 'hands-on' experience associated with group use of the computer entails any disadvantages to the learner.

As to the mechanisms of group facilitation, where it occurs, it is apparent that the concept of socio-cognitive conflict which inspired much of the recent work in this field is far from adequate to explain all the effects observed. Much remains to be done in explicating the processes involved. We have seen in some of the studies that we have been considering that manipulations of computer hardware and software can be used as a way of influencing the nature of the socio-cognitive activity and hence the outcome of the interaction. How far can this be taken? To what extent can we envisage the computer actively supporting interaction among learners or participating as a full interactive partner in the learning process? These are some of the issues to which we shall turn in the final section of this chapter.

PROSPECTS: THE SOCIAL INTERFACE

As we noted at the outset of this chapter, the goal of intelligent tutoring systems has often been expressed in terms of *individualising* the learning process (Elsom-Cook 1988), and to this extent it may seem to be very much opposed in spirit to any consideration of social processes in learning. But this is not necessarily the case. Woolf (1988) recently noted the 'most surprising' observation that certain experimental intelligent tutoring systems have been shown to be very effective when used with quite heterogeneous *groups* of students (in this case adults). Hennessy and colleagues are presently developing an arithmetic tutor specially designed to be used by pairs of children (Hennessy, Evertz, Ellis, Black, O'Shea and Floyd 1987).

To pick up the idea touched upon at the end of the previous section, it is possible to envisage an intelligent tutor not only coping with pairs of learners but also as being itself a *member* of such a pair – i.e. a partner in the learning process. If it is the case that children learn certain things in and through peer-group interaction, then can this process itself be modelled? The possibility of the computer's playing the role of a working companion to the child, interacting in such a way as to maximise the child's learning, has recently surfaced in the Intelligent Tutoring literature. For example, Chan and Baskin (1988) propose a system in which the computer plays both the role of teacher and the role of a companion who 'learns' to perform the task at about the same level as the child, and who exchanges ideas with the child as they work together on the same material.

Many problems stand in the way of implementing such a system, not the least of which is our very imperfect understanding of how 'real' learning companions help one another. While there is a long way to go, there are real signs of convergence with some of the work being undertaken by developmental psychologists working in this field. For example, Blaye, Farioli and Gilly (1987), using Blaye's matrix filling task mentioned earlier, experimented with a condition in which the child proposed an entry for a given cell and the computer 'partner' proposed an alternative choice. The alternative selected was based on a diagnosis of the child's proposal – if it reflected a centration on one dimension of the matrix the computer-partner suggested an (equally wrong) alternative based on the other dimension of the matrix. The results were not impressive – in fact as we have seen, Blaye's (1988) other studies seriously question the power of socio-cognitive conflict as a mechanism for progress on this task – but the basic design illustrates well the close convergence of work in cognitive science and developmental psychology at the present time.

Similar issues arise in respect of computer-based 'help' facilities. Researchers in this area seem to be confronted with two basic observations. Firstly, children are typically very ready to use their peers as sources of help when faced with computer tasks. Secondly, when help facilities are available on the computer itself, the children seem to show little interest in them and benefit little from their use (Messer, Jackson and Mohamedali, 1987; Turner 1988). These apparently conflicting results again point to the need to integrate psychological research on peer facilitation with software design work.

We need to be able to specify the ways in which children solicit and gain help from those around them while working at the computer, and then to use this knowledge of socially mediated help to inform the design of machine-based help. In the realm of adults, the need for research on learners' informal support networks when working with computers is increasingly being recognised, as indeed are the potential implications of such research for the design of effective software-based help (e.g. Bannon 1986; O'Malley 1986). Hopefully, similar research with children will generate progress towards more adaptive and 'helpful' software for children (whether working individually or collectively) before too long.

It is striking, given the inherently individualistic assumptions about the learning process which informed so much of the early work in the field of educational computing, that the social dimension of computer-based learning has come so clearly to the fore. It should allay the fears of any who still see the computer as necessarily a threat to social processes in learning. We concur with a recent OECD report that 'there is every prospect for more rather than less interchange among learners thanks to the new information technologies' (1987, p. 105). We hope that we have said enough to indicate why psychologists interested in 'children helping children' should be interested in educational computing. It is an area where more psychological research on the social foundations of learning is sorely needed, and where such research has a real chance of influencing children's educational experience.

ACKNOWLEDGMENTS

The writing of this chapter was facilitated by a joint ESRC/CNRS grant to Professor Paul Light and Professor Michel Gilly (Université de Provence) and by a grant to Dr Agnès Blaye from the Fondation Fyssen, Paris.

REFERENCES

Baker, C. (1985) 'The microcomputer and the curriculum: a critique', *Journal of Curriculum Studies*, 17, 4.

Bannon, L. (1986) 'Helping users help each other', in D. Norman and S. Draper (eds) *User Centred System Design*. Hillsdale, N.J.: Erlbaum.

Blaye, A. (1988) 'Confrontation socio-cognitive et résolution de problème'. Unpublished doctoral thesis, University of Provence.

Blaye, A., Farioli, F. and Gilly, M. (1987) 'Microcomputer as a partner in problem solving', *Rassegna di Psicologia*, 4, 109–18.

Broderick, C. and Trushell, J. (1985) 'Problems and processes: junior school children using wordprocessors to produce an information leaflet', *English in Education*, 19, 2.

Bullock, A. (1975) *A Language for Life*. London: HMSO.

Chan, T.-W. and Baskin, A. (1988) '"Studying with the Prince": the computer as learning companion'. Paper presented to IT-88 Conference, Montreal, June, 1988.

Clements, D. (1987) 'A longitudinal study of the effects of LOGO programming on cognitive abilities and achievement', *Journal of Educational Computing Research*, 3, 1.

Colbourn, C. J. and Light, P. H. (1987) 'Social interaction and learning using microPROLOG', *Journal of Computer Assisted Learning*, 3, 130–40.

Crook, C. (1986) Paper presented at second European Developmental Psychology Conference, Rome, September.

Crook, C. (1987) 'Computers in the classroom: defining a social context', in J. Rutkowska and C. Crook (eds) *Computers, Cognition and Development*. Chichester: Wiley.

Cummings, R. (1985) 'Small group discussions and the microcomputer', *Journal of Computer Assisted Learning*, 1, 149–58.

DES (1987) *Aspects of the work of the Microelectronics Education Programme*. London: Department of Education and Science.

Doise, W. and Mugny, G. (1984) *The Social Development of the Intellect*. Oxford: Pergamon Press.

Elsom-Cook, M. (1987) 'Intelligent computer-aided instruction research at the Open University'. CITE Technical Report No. 10. The Open University.

Elsom-Cook, M. (1988) 'Guided discovery tutoring and bounded user modelling', in J. Self (ed.), *Artificial Intelligence and Human Learning*. London: Chapman and Hall.

Fletcher, B. (1985) 'Group and individual learning of junior children on a microcomputer based task', *Educational Review*, 37, 251–61.

Fraisse, J. (1985) 'Interactions sociales entre pairs et découverte d'une stratégie cognitive chez des enfants de 11 ans'. Unpublished Doctoral Thesis, University of Provence.

Fraisse, J. (1987) 'Étude du rôle pertubateur du partenaire dans la découverte d'une strategie cognitive chez des enfants de 11 ans en situation d'interaction sociale', *Bulletin de Psychologie*, 382, 943–52.

Hawkins, J. (1983) 'Learning LOGO together: the social context'. Tech. Report 13, Bank St. College of Education, New York.

Hawkins, J., Sheingold, K., Gearhart, M. and Berger, C. (1982) 'Microcomputers in schools: impact on the social life of elementary classrooms', *Journal of Applied Developmental Psychology*, 3, 361–73.

Hennessy, S., Evertsz, R., Ellis, D., Black, P., O'Shea, T. and Floyd, A. (1987) 'Design specification for "Shopping on Mars".' CITE report 29, Institute of Educational Technology, The Open University.

Hoyles, C. and Sutherland, R. (1986) 'Using LOGO in the mathematics classroom', *Computers in Education*, 10, 61–72.

Hughes, M., MacLeod, H. and Potts, C. (1985) 'Using LOGO with infant school children', *Educational Psychology*, 5, 3–4.

Jackson, A., Fletcher, B. and Messer, D. (1986) 'A survey of microcomputer use and provision in primary schools'. *Journal of Computer Assisted Learning*, 2, 45–55.

Johnson, D. and Johnson, R. (1986) 'Computer assisted cooperative learning', *Educational Technology*, January 1986.

Johnson, R., Johnson, D. and Stanne, M. (1986) 'Comparison of computer assisted cooperative, competitive and individualistic learning', *American Educational Research Journal*, 12, 382–92.

Kliman, M. (1985) 'A new approach to infant and early primary mathematics'. DAI Research Paper 241, Department of Artificial Intelligence, University of Edinburgh.

Light, P. H., Colbourn, C. J. and Smith, D. (1987) 'Peer interaction and logic programming: a study of the acquisition of micro-PROLOG.' ESRC Information Technology and Education Programme, Occasional Paper ITE/17/87.

Light, P. H. and Foot, T. (1987) 'Peer interaction and microcomputer use', *Rassegna di Psicologia*, 4, 93–104.

Light, P. H., Foot, T., Colbourn, C. and McClelland, I. (1987) 'Collaborative interactions at the microcomputer keyboard', *Educational Psychology*, 7, 13–21.

Light, P. H. and Glachan, M. (1985) 'Facilitation of problem solving through peer interaction', *Educational Psychology*, 5, 217–25.

Messer, D., Jackson, A. and Mohomedali, M. (1987) 'Influences on computer-based problem solving', *Educational Psychology*, 7, 1.

Mevarech, Z. (1987) 'Learning with computers in small groups: cognitive and social processes'. Paper presented at 2nd European Conference for Research on Learning and Instruction, Tubingen, W. Germany, September, 1987.

Mevarech, Z., Stern, D. and Levita, I. (1987) 'To cooperate or not to cooperate in CAI: that is the question', *Journal of Educational Research*, 80, 164–7.

OECD (1987) *Information Technologies and Basic Learning*. Paris: Organisation for Economic Cooperation and Development.

O'Malley, C. (1986) 'Helping users help themselves', in D. Norman and S. Draper (eds), *User Centred System Design*. Hillsdale, N.J.: Erlbaum.

Papert, S. (1980) *Mindstorms: Children, Computers and Powerful Ideas*. Brighton: Harvester Press.

Perret-Clermont, A.-N. (1980) *Social Interaction and Cognitive Development in Children*. London: Academic Press.

Scaife, M. (1987) 'Sensorimotor learning in children's interactions with computerised displays'. Final report to ESRC, No. C08250010.

Sheingold, K., Hawkins, J. and Char, C. (1984) '"I'm the thinkist, you're the typist": the interaction of technology and the social life of classrooms'. Tech. Report 27, Bank St. College of Education, New York.

Trowbridge, D. (1987) 'An investigation of groups working at the computer', in Berger, K. Pezdek and W. Banks (eds) *Applications of Cognitive Psychology: Problem Solving, Education, and Computing*. Hillsdale, N.J.: Erlbaum.

Turner, T. (1988) 'Cognitive development through child-computer interaction using HELP facilities'. Unpublished paper, Department of Psychology, University of Southampton.

Webb, N., Ender, P. and Lewis, S. (1986) 'Problem solving strategies and group processes in small groups learning computer programming', *American Educational Research Journal*, 23, 243–61.

Wilton, J. and McClean, R. (1984) 'Evaluation of a mouse as an educational pointing device', *Computers and Education*, 8, 455–61.

Woolf, B. (1988) 'Representing complex knowledge in an intelligent machine tutor', in J. Self (ed.), *Artificial Intelligence and Human Learning*. London: Chapman and Hall.

2.3 | MATHEMATICS IN THE STREETS AND IN SCHOOLS

TEREZINHA NUNES CARRAHER, DAVID WILLIAM
CARRAHER AND ANALÚCIA DIAS SCHLIEMANN

There are reasons for thinking that there may be a difference between solving mathematical problems using algorithms learned in school and solving them in familiar contexts out of school. Reed and Lave (1981) have shown that people who have not been to school often solve such problems in different ways from people who have. This certainly suggests that there are informal ways of doing mathematical calculations which have little to do with the procedures taught in school.

Reed and Lave's study with Liberian adults showed differences between people who had and who had not been to school. However, it is quite possible that the same differences between informal and school-based routines could exist within people. In other words it might be the case that the same person could solve problems sometimes in formal and at other times in informal ways. This seems particularly likely with children who often have to do mathematical calculations in informal circumstances outside school at the same time as their knowledge of the algorithms which they have to learn at school is imperfect and their use of them ineffective.

We already know that children often obtain absurd results such as finding a remainder which is larger than the minuend when they try to apply routines for computations which they learn at school (Carraher and Schliemann, in press). There is also some evidence that informal procedures learned outside school are often extremely effective. Gay and Cole (1976) for example showed that unschooled Kpelle traders estimated quantities of rice far better than educated Americans managed to. So it seems quite possible that children might have difficulty with routines learned at school and yet at the same time be able to solve the mathematical problems for which these routines were devised in other more effective ways. One way to test this idea is to look at children who have to make frequent and quite complex calculations outside school. The children who sell things in street markets in Brazil form one such group (Carraher et al. 1982).

Source: *British Journal of Developmental Psychology*, Vol. 3, 1985, pp. 21–9.

THE CULTURAL CONTEXT

The study was conducted in Recife, a city of approximately 1·5 million people on the north-eastern coast of Brazil. Like several other large Brazilian cities, Recife receives a very large number of migrant workers from the rural areas who must adapt to a new way of living in a metropolitan region. In an anthropological study of migrant workers in São Paulo, Brazil, Berlinck (1977) identified four pressing needs in this adaptation process: finding a home, acquiring work papers, getting a job, and providing for immediate survival (whereas in rural areas the family often obtains food through its own work). During the initial adaptation phase, survival depends mostly upon resources brought by the migrants or received through begging. A large portion of migrants later become unspecialised manual workers, either maintaining a regular job or working in what is known as the informal sector of the economy (Cavalcanti 1978). The informal sector can be characterised as an unofficial part of the economy which consists of relatively unskilled jobs not regulated by government organs thereby producing income not susceptible to taxation while at the same time not affording job security or workers' rights such as health insurance. The income generated thereby is thus intermittent and variable. The dimensions of a business enterprise in the informal sector are determined by the family's work capability. Low educational and professional qualification levels are characteristic of the rather sizeable population which depends upon the informal sector. In Recife, approximately 30 per cent of the workforce is engaged in the informal sector as its main activity and 18 per cent as a secondary activity (Cavalcanti 1978). The importance of such sources of income for families in Brazil's lower socio-economic strata can be easily understood by noting that the income of an unspecialised labourer's family is increased by 56 per cent through his wife's and children's activities in the informal sector in São Paulo (Berlinck 1977). In Fortaleza it represents fully 60 per cent of the lower class* family's income (Cavalcanti and Duarte 1980a).

Several types of occupations – domestic work, street-vending, shoe-repairing and other types of small repairs which are carried out without a fixed commercial address – are grouped as part of the informal sector of the economy. The occupation considered in the present study – that of street-vendors – represents the principal occupation of 10 per cent of the economically active population of Salvador (Cavalcanti and Duarte 1980b) and Fortaleza (Cavalcanti and Duarte 1980a). Although no specific data regarding street-vendors were obtained for Recife, data from Salvador and Fortaleza serve as close approximations since these cities are, like Recife, state capitals from the same geographical region.

It is fairly common in Brazil for sons and daughters of street-vendors to help out their parents in their businesses. From about the age of 8 or 9 the children will often enact some of the transactions for the parents when they are busy with another customer or away on some errand. Pre-adolescents and teenagers may

---

* In the present report the term 'class' is employed loosely, without a clear distinction from the expression 'socio-economic stratum'.

even develop their own 'business', selling snack foods such as roasted peanuts, popcorn, coconut milk or corn on the cob. In Fortaleza and Salvador, where data are available, 2·2 and 1·4 per cent, respectively, of the population actively engaged in the informal sector as street-vendors were aged 14 or less while 8·2 and 7·5 per cent, respectively, were aged 15–19 years (Cavalcanti and Duarte 1980a,b).

In their work these children and adolescents have to solve a large number of mathematical problems, usually without recourse to paper and pencil. Problems may involve multiplication (one coconut cost x; four coconuts, $4x$), addition (4 coconuts and 12 lemons cost $x+y$), and subtraction (Cr$ 500 – i.e. 500 *cruzeiros* – minus the purchase price will give the change due). Division is much less frequently used but appears in some contexts in which the price is set with respect to a measuring unit (such as 1 kg) and the customer wants a fraction of that unit: for example, when the particular item chosen weighs 1·2 kg. The use of tables listing prices by number of items (one egg – 12 *cruzeiros*; two eggs – 24, etc.) is observed occasionally in natural settings but was not observed among the children who took part in the study. Pencil and paper were also not used by these children, although they may occasionally be used by adult vendors when adding long lists of items.

METHOD

SUBJECTS

The children in this study were four boys and one girl aged 9–15 years with a mean age of 11·2 and ranging in level of schooling from first to eighth grade. One of them had only one year of schooling; two had three years of schooling; one, four years; and one, eight years. All were from very poor backgrounds. Four of the subjects were attending school at the time and one had been out of school for two years. Four of these subjects had received formal instruction on mathematical operations and word problems. The subject who attended first grade and dropped out of school was unlikely to have learned multiplication and division in school since these operations are usually initiated in second or third grade in public schools in Recife.

PROCEDURE

The children were found by the interviewers on street corners or at markets where they worked alone or with their families. Interviewers chose subjects who seemed to be in the desired age range – schoolchildren or young adolescents – obtaining information about their age and level of schooling along with information on the prices of their merchandise. Test items in this situation were presented in the course of a normal sales transaction in which the researcher posed as a customer. Purchases were sometimes carried out. In other cases the 'customer' asked the vendor to perform calculations on possible purchases. At the end of the informal test, the children were asked to take part in a formal test which was given on a separate occasion, no more than a week later, by the same interviewer. Subjects answered a total of 99 questions on the formal test and 63 questions on the informal test. Since the items of the formal test were based upon questions of the informal test, order of testing was fixed for all subjects.

1 *The informal test.* The informal test was carried out in Portuguese in the subject's natural working situation, that is, at street corners or an open market. Testers posed to the subject successive questions about potential or actual purchases and obtained verbal responses. Responses were either tape-recorded or written down, along with comments, by an observer. After obtaining an answer for the item, testers questioned the subject about his or her method for solving the problem.

The method can be described as a hybrid between the Piagetian clinical method and participant observation. The interviewer was not merely an interviewer; he was also a customer – a questioning customer who wanted the vendor to tell him how he or she performed their computations.

An example is presented below taken from the informal test with M., a coconut vendor aged 12, third grader, where the interviewer is referred to as 'customer':

Customer: How much is one coconut?

M: 35.

Customer: I'd like ten. How much is that?

M: (Pause) Three will be 105; with three more, that will be 210. (Pause) I need four more. That is ...* (Pause) 315 ... I think it is 350.

This problem can be mathematically represented in several ways: 35×10 is a good representation of the *question* posed by the interviewer. The subject's answer is better represented by $105 + 105 + 105 + 35$, which implies that 35×10 was solved by the subject as $(3 \times 35) + (3 \times 35) + (3 \times 35) + 35$. The subject can be said to have solved the following subitems in the above situation:

(a) 35×10;
(b) 35×3 (which may have already been known);
(c) $105 + 105$;
(d) $210 + 105$;
(e) $315 + 35$;
(f) $3 + 3 + 3 + 1$.

* (...) is used here to mark ascending intonation suggestive of the interruption, and not completion, of a statement.

When one represents in a formal mathematical fashion the problems which were solved by the subject, one is in fact attempting to represent the subject's mathematical competence. M. proved to be competent in finding out how much 35×10 is, even though he used a routine not taught in third grade, since in Brazil third-graders learn to multiply any number by ten simply by placing a zero to the right of that number. Thus, we considered that the subject solved the test item (35×10) and a whole series of subitems (b to f) successfully in this process. However, in the process of scoring, only *one* test item (35×10) was considered as having been presented and, therefore, correctly solved.

2 *The formal test.*   After subjects were interviewed in the natural situation, they were asked to participate in the formal part of the study and a second interview was scheduled at the same place or at the subject's house.

The items for the formal test were prepared for each subject on the basis of problems solved by him or her during the informal test. Each problem solved in the informal test was mathematically represented according to the subject's problem-solving routine.

From all the mathematical problems *successfully solved* by each subject (regardless of whether they constituted a test item or not), a sample was chosen for inclusion in the subject's formal test. This sample was presented in the formal test either as a mathematical operation dictated to the subject (e.g. $105 + 105$) or as a word problem e.g. Mary bought x bananas; each banana cost y; how much did she pay altogether?). In either case, *each subject solved problems employing the same numbers in his or her own informal test.* Thus quantities used varied from one subject to the other.

Two variations were introduced in the formal test, according to methodological suggestions contained in Reed and Lave (1981). First, some of the items presented in the formal test were the inverse of problems solved in the informal test (e.g. $500 - 385$ may be presented as $385 + 115$ in the formal test). Second, some of the items in the informal test used a decimal value which differed from the one used in the formal test (e.g. 40 *cruzeiros* may have appeared as 40 *centavos* or 35 may have been presented as 3500 in the formal test – the principal Brazilian unit of currency is the *cruzeiro*; each *cruzeiro* is worth one hundred *centavos*).

In order to make the formal test situation more similar to the school setting, subjects were given paper and pencil at the testing and were encouraged to use these. When problems were nonetheless solved without recourse to writing, subjects were asked to write down their answers. Only one subject refused to do so, claiming that he did not know how to write. It will be recalled, however, that the school-type situation was not represented solely by the introduction of pencil and paper but also by the very use of formal mathematical problems without context and by word problems referring to imaginary situations.

In the formal test the children were given a total of 38 mathematical operations and 61 word problems. Word problems were rather concrete and each involved only one mathematical operation.

RESULTS AND DISCUSSION

The analysis of the results from the informal test required an initial definition of what would be considered a test item in that situation. While, in the formal test, items were defined prior to testing, in the informal test problems were generated in the natural setting and items were identified *a posteriori*. In order to avoid a biased increase in the number of items solved in the informal test, the definition of an item was based upon *questions* posed by the customer/tester. This probably constitutes a conservative estimate of the number of problems solved, since subjects often solved a number of intermediary steps in the course of searching for the solution to the question they had been asked. Thus the same defining criterion was applied in both testing situations in the identification of items even though items were defined prior to testing in one case and after testing in the other. In both testing situations, the subject's oral response was the one taken into account even though in the formal test written responses were also available.

Context-embedded problems were much more easily solved than ones without a context. Table 5 shows that 98·2 per cent of the 63 problems presented in the informal test were correctly solved. In the formal test word problems (which provide some descriptive context for the subject), the rate of correct responses was 73·7 per cent, which should be contrasted with a 36·8 per cent rate of correct responses for mathematical operations with no context.

| | Informal test | | Formal test | | | |
| | | | Mathematical operations | | Word problems | |
Subject	Score*	Number of items	Score	Number of items	Score	Number of items
M	10	18	2·5	8	10	11
P	8·9	19	3·7	8	6·9	16
Pi	10	12	5·0	6	10	11
MD	10	7	1·0	10	3·3	12
S	10	7	8·3	6	7·3	11
Totals		63		38		61

Table 5   *Results according to testing conditions*

* Each subject's score is the percentage of correct items divided by 10.

The frequency of correct answers for each subject was converted to scores from 1 to 10 reflecting the percentage of correct responses. A Friedman two-way analysis of variance of score ranks compared the scores of each subject in the three types of testing conditions. The scores differ significantly across conditions ($\chi^2 r = 6.4$, $P = 0.039$). Mann–Whitney Us were also calculated comparing the three types of testing situations. Subjects performed significantly better on the informal test than on the formal test involving context-free operations ($U = 0$, $P < 0.05$). The difference between the informal test and the word problems was not significant ($U = 6$, $P > 0.05$).

It could be argued that errors observed in the formal test were related to the transformations that had been performed upon the informal test problems in order to construct the formal test. An evaluation of this hypothesis was obtained by separating items which had been changed either by inverting the operation or changing the decimal point from items which remained identical to their informal test equivalents. The percentage of correct responses in these two groups of items did not differ significantly; the rate of correct responses in transformed items was slightly higher than that obtained for items identical to informal test items. Thus the transformations performed upon informal test items in designing formal test items cannot explain the discrepancy of performance in these situations.

A second possible interpretation of these results is that the children interviewed in this study were 'concrete' in their thinking and, thus, concrete situations would help them in the discovery of a solution. In the natural situation, they solved problems about the sale of lemons, coconuts, etc., when the actual items in question were physically present. However, the presence of concrete instances can be understood as a facilitating factor if the instance somehow allows the problem-solver to abstract from the concrete example to a more general situation. There is nothing in the nature of coconuts that makes it relatively easier to discover that three coconuts (at Cr\$ 35.00 each) cost Cr\$ 105.00. The presence of the groceries does not simplify the arithmetic of the problem. Moreover, computation in the natural situation of the informal test was in all cases carried out mentally, without recourse to external memory aids for partial results or intermediary steps. One can hardly argue that mental computation would be an ability characteristic of concrete thinkers.

The results seem to be in conflict with the implicit pedagogical assumption of mathematical educators according to which children ought first to learn mathematical operations and only later to apply them to verbal and real-life problems. Real-life and word problems may provide the 'daily human sense' (Donaldson 1978) which will guide children to find a correct solution intuitively without requiring an extra step – namely, the translation of word problems into algebraic expressions. This interpretation is consistent with data obtained by others in the area of logic, such as Wason and Shapiro (1971), Johnson-Laird *et al.* (1972) and Lunzer *et al.* (1972).

How is it possible that children capable of solving a computational problem in the natural situation will fail to solve the same problem when it is taken out of its context? In the present case, a qualitative analysis of the protocols suggested that the problem-solving routines used may have been different in the two situations.

In the natural situations children tended to reason by using what can be termed a 'convenient group' while in the formal test school-taught routines were more frequently, although not exclusively, observed. Five examples are given below, which demonstrate the children's ability to deal with quantities and their lack of expertise in manipulating symbols. The examples were chosen for representing clear explanations of the procedures used in both settings. In each of the five examples below the performance described in the informal test contrasts strongly with the same child's performance in the formal test when solving the same item.

1 First example (M, 12 years)
Informal test

Customer: I'm going to take four coconuts. How much is that?
Child: Three will be 105, plus 30, that's 135 . . . one coconut is 35 . . . that is . . . 140!

Formal test
Child resolves the item 35×4 explaining out loud:
4 times 5 is 20, carry the 2; 2 plus 3 is 5, times 4 is 20.
Answer written: 200

2 Second example (MD, 9 years)
Informal test

Customer: OK, I'll take three coconuts (at the price of Cr$ 40.00 each). How much is that?
Child: (Without gestures, calculates out loud) 40, 80, 120.

Formal test
Child solves the item 40×3 and obtains 70. She then explains the procedure: 'Lower the zero; 4 and 3 is 7.'

3 Third example (MD, 9 years)
Informal test

Customer: I'll take 12 lemons (one lemon is Cr$ 5.00).
Child: 10, 20, 30, 40, 50, 60 (while separating out two lemons at a time).

Formal test
Child has just solved the item 40×3. In solving 12×5 she proceeds by lowering first the 2, then the 5 and the 1, obtaining 152. She explains this procedure to the (surprised) examiner when she is finished.

4 Fourth example (S, 11 years)
Informal test

Customer: What would I have to pay for six kilos (of watermelon at CR$ 50.00 per kg)?
Child: [Without any appreciable pause] 300.
Customer: Let me see. How did you get that so fast?
Child: Counting one by one. Two kilos, 100. 200. 300.

Formal test

Test item: A fisherman caught 50 fish. The second one caught five times the
amount of fish the first fisherman had caught. How many fish did
the lucky fisherman catch?

Child: (Writes down 50 × 6 and 360 as the result; then answers) 36.

Examiner repeats the problems and child does the computation again, writing
down 860 as result. His oral response is 86.

Examiner: How did you calculate that?
Child: I did it like this. Six times six is 36. Then I put it there.
Examiner: Where did you put it? (Child had not written down the number to
be carried.)
Child: (Points to the digit 5 in 50.) That makes 86 [apparently adding 3
and 5 and placing this sum in the result].
Examiner: How many did the first fisherman catch?
Child: 50.

A final example follows, with suggested interpretations enclosed in parentheses.

5 Fifth example

Informal test

Customer: I'll take two coconuts (at CR$ 40.00 each. Pays with a CR$ 500.00
bill). What do I get back?

Child: (Before reaching for customer's change) 80, 90, 100. 420.

Formal test

Test item: 420 + 80.

The child writes 420 plus 80 and claims that 130 is the result. (The procedure
used was not explained but it seems that the child applied a step of a
multiplication routine to an addition problem by successively adding 8 to 2 and
then to 4, carrying the 1; that is, $8 + 2 = 10$, carry the one, $1 + 4 + 8 = 13$. The
zeros in 420 and 80 were not written. Reaction times were obtained from tape
recordings and the whole process took 53 seconds.)

Examiner: How did you do this one, 420 plus 80?
Child: Plus?
Examiner: Plus 80.
Child: 100, 200.
Examiner: (After a 5 second pause, interrupts the child's response treating it
as final.) Hum, OK.
Child: Wait a minute. That was wrong. 500. [The child had apparently
added 80 and 20, obtaining one hundred, and then started adding
the hundreds. The experimenter interpreted 200 as the final
answer after a brief pause but the child completed the computation
and gave the correct answer when solving the addition problem by
a manipulation-with-quantities approach.]

In the informal test, children rely upon mental calculations which are closely linked to the quantities that are being dealt with. The preferred strategy for multiplication problems seems to consist in chaining successive additions. In the first example, as the addition became more difficult, the subject decomposed a quantity into tens and units – to add 35 to 105, M. first added 30 and later included 5 in the result.

In the formal test, where paper and pencil were used in all the above examples, the children try to follow, without success, school-prescribed routines. Mistakes often occur as a result of confusing addition routines with multiplication routines, as is clearly the case in examples (1) and (5). Moreover, in all the cases, there is no evidence, once the numbers are written down, that the children try to relate the obtained results to the problem at hand in order to assess the adequacy of their answers.

Summarising briefly, the combination of the clinical method of questioning with participant observation used in this project seemed particularly helpful when exploring mathematical thinking and thinking in daily life. The results support the thesis proposed by Luria (1976) and by Donaldson (1978) that thinking sustained by daily human sense can be – in the same subject – at a higher level than thinking out of context. They also raise doubts about the pedagogical practice of teaching mathematical operations in a disembedded form before applying them to word problems.

Our results are also in agreement with data reported by Lave *et al.* (1984), who showed that problem-solving in the supermarket was significantly superior to problem-solving with paper and pencil. It appears that daily problem-solving may be accomplished by routines different from those taught in schools. In the present study, daily problem-solving tended to be accomplished by strategies involving the mental manipulation of quantities while in the school-type situation the manipulation of symbols carried the burden of computation, thereby making the operations 'in a very real sense divorced from reality' (see Reed and Lave 1981, p. 442). In many cases attempts to follow school-prescribed routines seemed in fact to interfere with problem-solving (see also Carraher and Schlieman, in press).

Are we to conclude that schools ought to allow children simply to develop their own computational routines without trying to impose the conventional systems developed in the culture? We do not believe that our results lead to this conclusion. Mental computation has limitations which can be overcome through written computation. One is the inherent limitation placed on multiplying through successive chunking, that is, on multiplying through repeated chunked additions – a procedure which becomes grossly inefficient when large numbers are involved.

The sort of mathematics taught in schools has the potential to serve as an 'amplifier of thought processes', in the sense in which Bruner (1972) has referred to both mathematics and logic. As such, we do not dispute whether 'school maths' routines can offer richer and more powerful alternatives to maths routines which emerge in non-school settings. The major question appears to centre on the proper pedagogical point of departure, i.e. where to start. We suggest that educators should question the practice of treating mathematical systems as formal subjects from the outset and should instead seek ways of introducing these systems in contexts which allow them to be sustained by human daily sense.

ACKNOWLEDGMENTS

The research conducted received support from the Conselho Nacional de Desenvolvimento Científico e Tecnológico, Brasilia, and from the British Council. The authors thank Peter Bryant for his helpful comments on the present report.

REFERENCES

Berlinck, M. T. (1977) *Marginalidade Social e Relações de Classe em São Paulo*. Petrópolis, RJ, Brazil: Vozes.

Bruner, J. (1972) *Relevance of Education*. London: Penguin.

Carraher, T., Carraher, D. and Schliemann, A. (1982) 'Na vida dez, na escola zero: Os contextos culturais da aprendizagem da matematica', *Cadernos de Pesquisa*, 42, 79–86. (São Paulo, Brazil, special UNESCO issue for Latin America.)

Carraher, T. and Schliemann, A. (in press) 'Computation routines prescribed by schools: help or hindrance?', *Journal for Research in Mathematics Education*.

Cavalcanti, C. (1978) *Viabilidade do Setor Informal. A Demanda de Pequenos Serviços no Grande Recife*. Recife, PE, Brazil: Instituto Joaquim Nabuco de Pesquisas Sociais.

Cavalcanti, C. and Duarte, R. (1980a) *A Procura de Espaço na Economia Urbana: O Setor Informal de Fortaleza*. Recife, PE, Brazil: SUDENE/FUNDAJ.

Cavalcanti, C. and Duarte, R. (1980b) *O Setor Informal de Salvador: Dimensões, Natureza, Significação*. Recife, PE, Brazil: SUDENE/FUNDAJ.

Donaldson, M. (1978) *Children's Minds*. New York: Norton.

Gay, J. and Cole, M. (1976). *The New Mathematics and an Old Culture: A Study of Learning among the Kpelle of Liberia*. New York: Holt, Rinehart and Winston.

Johnson-Laird, P. N., Legrenzi, P. and Sonino Legrenzi, M. (1972) 'Reasoning and a sense of reality', *British Journal of Psychology*, 63, 395–400.

Lave, J., Murtaugh, M. and de La Rocha, O. (1984) 'The dialectical construction of arithmetic practice', in B. Rogoff and J. Lave (eds), *Everyday Cognition: Its Development in Social Context*, pp. 67–94. Cambridge, MA: Harvard University Press.

Lunzer, E. A., Harrison, C. and Davey, M. (1972) 'The four-card problem and the development of formal reasoning', *Quarterly Journal of Experimental Psychology*, 24, 326–39.

Luria, A. R. (1976) *Cognitive Development: Its Cultural and Social Foundations*. Cambridge, MA: Harvard University Press.

Reed, H. J. and Lave, J. (1981) 'Arithmetic as a tool for investigating relations between culture and cognition', in R. W. Casson (ed.), *Language, Culture and Cognition: Anthropological Perspectives*. New York: Macmillan.

Wason, P. C. and Shapiro, D. (1971) 'Natural and contrived experience in a reasoning problem', *Quarterly Journal of Experimental Psychology*, 23, 63–71.

COMMUNICATION AND
2.4 CONTROL

DEREK EDWARDS AND NEIL MERCER

It is our purpose in this chapter to examine how particular sorts of classroom discourse carry classroom knowledge. Our first impression of the lessons was that they were relatively informal, progressive, child-centred sorts of pedagogy of the type advocated by the Plowden Report. [...] It is an unforeseen consequence of examining the data more closely that we are in fact largely concerned here with control processes, that is, with ways in which the teacher maintained a tight definition of what became joint versions of events, and joint understandings of curriculum content.

The process of creating joint understandings in the classroom is a problematical one. [...] There appear to be a set of properties and constraints under which the educational process works, which are not always harmonious, and which make the process problematical. These include:

1 the assumption on the part of teachers that educational failure in individual pupils can be attributed to individual factors, and principally to innate ability;
2 a philosophy of education which assumes a self-actualising process of inductive and experiental learning through practical activity;
3 the socialising function of education, in which the teacher exercises a large degree of control over what is done, said and understood;
4 the separation of formal education from the contexts of everyday, out-of-school experience and learning;
5 the largely implicit basis of much classroom activity and discourse.

The notions of 'scaffolding' (Bruner) and of the 'zone of proximal development' (Vygotsky) appear to be appropriate to the description of classroom education, but are often compromised by the somewhat inconsistent nature of these listed properties. While teachers engage in a great deal of skilled tuition, prompting and helping children to develop their understanding of curriculum topics, their own conceptions of what they are doing may be at odds with such a process. Success and failure are conceived largely in terms of inherent properties of pupils rather than as outcomes of the communicative process of education itself, and

Source: *Common Knowledge: The Development of Understanding in the Classroom*, Methuen, 1987, pp. 128–59, 183–7.

understandings on the part of pupils are seen as essentially inductive insights that the pupils themselves must achieve on the basis of their own experiences. The fact that a particular syllabus has to be taught, or, at least, that a planned set of concepts and activities has to be covered, leads to [a] sort of 'teacher's dilemma' how to get the pupils to learn for themselves what has been planned for them in advance.

We shall argue that these dilemmas and compromises can have a destructive effect on the effectiveness of education, by spoiling the essential purpose of the Vygotskyan process: that is, the process often remains incomplete, with no final *handover* of knowledge and control to the pupils. The pupils frequently remain embedded in rituals and procedures, having failed to grasp the overall purpose of what they have done, including the general concepts and principles that a particular lesson's activities was designed to inculcate.

In looking for some way of organising our treatment of these communicative processes, we have chosen what appears to be a central theme of classroom talk, the extent of teacher control over both the discourse and, through that, the content of knowledge. The following list of classroom communications is presented as a scale of teacher control of the nature, content and coding of knowledge, with the extent of control increasing as we descend the list. It is not an exhaustive list, and the qualitative nature of its contents precludes any precise notion of hierarchy or order. Nevertheless, it is useful in that it helps us to define the sorts of phenomena that we shall be dealing with, and their role in the establishment of shared understandings. We shall argue that it is essentially through the pervasive phenomena of teacher control over the expression of knowledge that pupils' understandings of things are frequently created as procedural rather than principled – saying and doing what seems to be required, rather than working out a principled understanding of how and why certain actions, expressions and procedures are appropriate or correct.

The following list of features of classroom discourse is cast in terms of the teacher's role in them.

elicitation of pupils' contributions
significance markers, e.g.   special enunciation
                              formulaic phrases
                              ignoring pupils' contributions
joint-knowledge markers, e.g.   simultaneous speech
                                'royal' plurals
                                repeated discourse formats
cued elicitation of pupils' contributions
paraphrastic interpretations of pupils' contributions
reconstructive recaps
implicit and presupposed knowledge

[...]

SPONTANEOUS AND ELICITED CONTRIBUTIONS

The *spontaneous contributions* offered by the pupils were by definition those communications least influenced by teacher control. But they were not devoid of it. It was the teacher who had set the agenda, defined the topic of discussion, and established in advance the criteria of relevance and appropriateness of any contributions that the pupils might offer. And the teacher generally remained in control of the ultimate fate of any such contributions – of whether they were acted on, taken up and incorporated into the development of ideas in further classroom discourse, or whether they were discouraged, disapproved or ignored. [. . .] Most contributions to classroom discourse offered by the pupils were, as other research has abundantly demonstrated (e.g. Galton, Simon and Croll 1980 [. . .]) made by invitation from the teacher. *Elicited contributions* were those that fell into the familiar and pervasive IRF[1] structure, where pupils' contributions were directly constrained by teachers' questions. [. . .]

The importance of IRFs in the establishment of joint understanding lies in the way in which they express the complementarity of teacher's and pupil's knowledge [. . .] Teachers' questions are of a special sort, in that they do not carry the usual presupposition that the speaker does not know the answer to the question asked [. . .] They function as discursive devices through which the teacher is able to keep a continual check on the pupils' understandings, to ensure that various concepts, information or terms of reference are jointly understood, so that subsequent discourse may be predicated on a developing continuity and context of intersubjectivity. IRF structures also function in defining and controlling what that knowledge and understanding will be. They are part of a set of communicative devices whereby the teacher acts as a kind of filter or gateway through which all knowledge must pass in order to be included in the lesson as a valid or useful contribution. This is particularly noticeable in instances of what may be called 'retrospective elicitation', where the teacher invites a pupil's response after it has already been made. [. . .]

A particularly interesting example of retrospective elicitation occurred [. . .] where the teacher was eliciting hypotheses about the effect on period of swing of shortening the pendulum's string:

Sharon:	It would be slower.	
T:	What do you reckon/	Sharon?
Jonathan:	Much faster.	
Sharon:	Slower./	Faster.
	I think it would be faster.	

Sharon first offered the hypothesis 'It would be slower'. The teacher then retrospectively defined Sharon's contribution as welcome and proper, by explicitly inviting it. Sharon then vacillated and changed her mind. Two things may have influenced her. First, Jonathan was simultaneously suggesting that the pendulum bob would swing faster. Second, and at least as important, there may have been another ground-rule at work. Rather than making a retrospective invitation, the teacher may have been interpreted by Sharon as repeating the question, as asking the same question after having received an answer. [. . .] This is generally a signal that the first answer is wrong, and that an alternative answer is expected. What we have here is probably a conflict between two alternative discursive ground-rules. While the teacher sought to make a retrospective elicitation of Sharon's answer, Sharon herself read this as a repeated question and changed her mind.

[In the case] of less welcome responses, the teacher ignored, or simply failed to encourage or develop, several attempts to introduce ideas that were not part of the planned course of the lesson. [. . .]

MARKING KNOWLEDGE AS SIGNIFICANT AND JOINT

Apart from the pervasive phenomenon of inviting pupils' contributions, and of occasionally ignoring them, expressed knowledge was sometimes given special prominence by discursive devices such as special enunciation and the use of formulaic phrases. Shifts of intonation served pedagogic functions by highlighting important information, and marking other comments as 'asides', or as having different functions. Apart from the conventional use of devices such as pauses and rising intonation to mark the asking of questions, or of falling intonation to mark the confirmation of answers, shifts particularly in the rate and loudness of speech generally occurred at the boundaries of shifts of pedagogic significance, rather than merely of conversational function.

SEQUENCE 1   INTONATION AND KNOWLEDGE

(Note: relevant speech segments italicised.)

PENDULUM LESSON 1

T is establishing that the pupils know how to measure pendulum swings, and can calculate an average period of swing.

T: OK? So that makes ten seconds. So how much then is each swing roughly?	*T looks at Antony.*
Antony: Two seconds.	
T: Two seconds. Good. OK. We'll write that down.	*T writes '2 seconds'.*

Everybody understood that bit?	*Spoken quickly.*
Now then. I wonder if this pendulum would also take the same time.	*T reaches for Jonathan's pendulum.*
	T's intonation now slow, deliberate, in marked contrast to preceding speech.

.

.

T: What did you get darling?	*T looks beyond Lucy to Karen.*
Karen: Mine says eight and a half.	
T: Eight point five and a half. What did you get Lucy?	*T writes down '8.5'.*
Lucy: Er I think/I think mine's eight and a half.	*Lucy showing T the watch.*
T: No. Yours is/yes/*yes it is actually I haven't got my glasses on. I can't see. Yes it is. Eight point five the same.*	*T speaking quickly and quietly.* *T writes '8.5'.*
Right. So it looks as if/if we round off the two eight point fives and take into account the ten point twelve/ten point one two/	*Voice louder and slower.*
Jonathan: Five into eight goes one/ and/	*Jonathan pauses, pen over paper, frowning.*

T: Anybody help him?	
Jonathan: I think it's three isn't it?	*In fact the sum is:*
T: Three/yeh/	

$$5 \overline{)8.250} \quad ^{1.65}$$

Jonathan: Fives into three/is that it? Fives into three go	
Pupil: Fives into thirty goes six/	
Jonathan: Fives into thirty goes six. Fives into two goes/ one point six five	*Jonathan mumbles from here.*
T: *One point six five/*	*T's speech slow and loud.*
So it's not very far away from two which was David's	

.

.

.

	T elicits suggestions for the total number of swings from which an average swing will be calculated. [. . .]
T: An even number/ makes it/ you reckon you can divide by six better than you can divide by five.//	*T looking at Antony.*
Will it make any difference to the **accuracy**/ *of what she's doing if she did a* **larger**/ *number of swings?*	*T laughs, then Sharon does.* *T speaking slowly and clearly, with small pauses as indicated.*

[. . .]

The italicised speech in sequence 1 is that to which the contextual comments about intonation apply. It is speech marked by intonation as having a special significance in relation to the rest of what is said. The choice of slow, deliberate enunciation, or of faster and quieter speech, was clearly determined by the content of what was said, and its pedagogic function. The important curriculum-oriented content was given prominence with careful, clear enunciation, while 'asides' about the teacher's vision, and the check on continuity of understanding, were marked by a drop in volume, and a sudden increase in rate of speech.

CUED ELICITATION

The process of cued elicitation was a pervasive one in our data transcripts.
[...]
Cued elicitations are IRF types of discourse in which the teacher asks questions while simultaneously providing heavy clues to the information required. This simultaneous provision of information may be achieved merely by the wording of the question, but is often accomplished via some other communicative channel such as intonation, pausing, gestures or physical demonstrations. It may also be done implicitly, by an unspoken appeal to shared knowledge. Sequence 2 is a clear example.

SEQUENCE 2   CUED ELICITATION: GALILEO'S PULSE

T: Now he didn't have a watch/ but he **had** on **him** something that was a very good timekeeper that he could use to hand straight away/

T snaps fingers on 'straight away', and looks invitingly at pupils as if posing a question or inviting a response.

You've got it. **I**'ve got it. What is it?// What could we use to count beats? What have **you** got?//

T points on 'You've' and 'I've'.
T beats hand on table slowly, looks around group of pupils, who smile and shrug.

You can feel it **here**.
PUPILS: Pulse.
T: A pulse. Everybody see if you can find it.

T puts fingers on T's wrist pulse.
(In near unison.)
All copy T, feeling for wrist pulses.

Cued elicitation is an important process for at least two reasons:

1 It demonstrates a general point of method and theory – that, if we are going to make proper sense of the process of classroom education, then we need careful

records of gesture and activity as well as detailed transcripts of classroom discourse, that these need to be closely integrated, and that we do not make the error of trying to account for educational processes solely in terms of classroom talk and discourse structures.

2 It is a communicative process of substantial intrinsic interest. Classroom questions and answers have peculiar characteristics: [...] the teacher, who knows the answers, asks most of the questions, asks questions to which she already knows the answers, and, additionally, it appears, may ask questions while simultaneously doing her best to provide the answers via an alternative channel. We have to seek an understanding of the pedagogic function of this sort of thing.

The best interpretation that we can make of the pedagogic function of cued elicitation is that it embodies an educational process in which the pupils are neither being drawn out of themselves, in the *e-ducare* sense, nor simply being taught directly, in the 'transmission' sense. Rather, they are being inculcated into what becomes for them a shared discourse with the teacher (discourse in the broadest sense, including concepts and terminology as well as dialogue). As such, it falls neatly into the sort of educational process defined by Vygotsky's 'zone of proximal development', in which pupils' knowledge is aided and 'scaffolded' by the teacher's questions, clues and prompts to achieve insights that the pupils by themselves seemed incapable of. It is a device which requires that the pupils actively participate in the creation of shared knowledge, rather than merely sit and listen to the teacher talking. Cued elicitation is also a process which constitutes a solution to what we have called the *teacher's dilemma* – a necessary compromise between two conflicting requirements that the lesson had to achieve. These requirements were that the pupils should (apparently, at least) generate their own understandings of things through their own thought and experience, and that they should come to do and to understand specific activities and concepts planned at the outset – to test three specified hypotheses, to find that only one of the variables was effective, to calculate average times over twenty swings, and to make matrices and draw graphs of the results. [...]

The danger of cued elicitation is that, until it is examined closely, it can give a false impression (presumably to the participants as well as to the observers) of the extent to which pupils understand, and are ultimately responsible for, what they are saying and doing. It can easily mask rather than bridge the gap between teacher and child that is the basis of Vygotsky's developmental process. [...]

RECONSTRUCTIONS, PRESUPPOSITIONS AND PARAPHRASES

Moving down our scaled list of communicative processes, we come next to a set of discursive devices through which the teacher was able to maintain a strict control over the content of common knowledge. Through paraphrasing what the pupils said, and through reconstructing what occurred in the lesson when recapping later, she was able to redefine these things as altogether neater, nicer and closer to the intended lesson plan. Similarly, by presupposing certain things as known or understood, she was able to forestall disagreement, and shape the direction of the discourse and the interpretations put upon experience. Paraphrases were often seemingly small and accidental, as when, in Pendulum lesson 2, Lucy appeared to misremember one of the timed scores obtained in lesson 1 when she and Jonathan had varied the weight of the pendulum bob.

SEQUENCE 3   PARAPHRASING LUCY

> T: Now what about when you had **one** washer? Can you remember what the time was there Lucy?
> Lucy: Erm/ one point one four.
> T: One point nine four?
> Lucy: ⌠ Yes.
> T: ⌡ That's right there it is.

T points to the '1 washer' position on graph.

T pointing to where the number is plotted on the graph.

The teacher also used paraphrasing more directly as a teaching method, as in sequence 4, when she tried to elicit as much as possible of the explanation from the pupils, and then recast the explanation offered by Antony into a preferred (and, indeed, more precise) form:

SEQUENCE 4   PARAPHRASING ANTONY

PENDULUM LESSON 2

The teacher is discussing what makes the pendulum continue its swing past the mid-point, against gravity; see sequence 1.

> T: OK so it's gravity that pulls it down. What causes it to go up again at the other side?
> Antony: The string/ it forces up the string/ going down.
> T: It gets up speed going down.

T swings one of the pendulums.

.
.
.

And it's the/ energy the force that it
builds up that takes it up the other
side.

These reconstructive paraphrases demonstrate another function of the 'feedback' stage of IRF sequences; they provide an opportunity for the teacher not only to confirm what the pupils say, but to recast it in a more acceptable form, more explicit perhaps, or simply couched in a preferred terminology. The most extensive reconstructions occurred during the second of the pendulum lessons, when the teacher was recapping (via the familiar sorts of IRF elicitations) on the material covered in lesson 1. Both teacher and pupils took advantage of the opportunity to reconstruct a more acceptable version of events.

Information can be *introduced* into a conversation through its role as an implicit context for what is explicitly stated. The implicit part of a message can be recovered from the situational context and from what is explicitly said, and this again is a normal feature of everyday discourse. If someone asks us in the street for directions to the nearest post office, we would have reasonable grounds for assuming that they want to go there, do not know the way, and so on. The use of presuppositional implication in educational contexts has a pedagogic function over and above its uses in many other contexts (though much persuasive rhetoric, propaganda, advertising, and so on, clearly works in a similar fashion); it serves to introduce certain items of knowledge and assumption as things to be accepted without question, as understood but not on the agenda for discussion or disagreement, and, in a more general sense, is therefore available to the teacher as an instrument of control over what is known and understood.

A particular instance of implicit teaching occurred when the teacher introduced preferred terminology, scientific jargon such as 'mass' and 'momentum'. Sometimes these terms would be introduced through what we may call 'direct teaching', where the teacher explicitly introduced the words, defined them and encouraged the pupils to use them. At other times new terms of reference were introduced by elicitation, or cued elicitation, as was the case with the terms 'momentum' and 'acceleration' in lesson 2 ('Does anyone know the word for it when you get up speed/ as in a car when you press the pedal?'). Sequence 5 shows how various terms were introduced simply by the teacher's using them in an understood context, as an alternative, implicitly preferred vocabulary.

SEQUENCE 5   ACQUIRING A SHARED VOCABULARY: TEACHER'S USAGE

(Video camera concentrating on T's actions; pupils sometimes unidentified.)

T: Yes. Let's have a closer look at this one.
Right. Now then. What does the

T takes off the pendant she is wearing and puts it on the table.

pendulum have to have to be a
pendulum?

BOY: String.

T: A string/ yes. In this case it's a/   *T holds pendant chain up.*

PUPILS: Chain.

T: Chain/
So it has to be suspended doesn't it?   *T raises and suspends pendant by its*
                                                         chain.

Boy: A weight.

T: It has to have a weight doesn't it/ a
mass at the end which this one has.
OK?/ Right/ let's have a closer look at
mine. Is it a pendulum// now?   *T lays pendant flat on table, looks at*
                                                         Lucy.

Lucy: No.   *Rising intonation (signalling 'is this*
                                                         the answer you want?').

T: You agreed Jon?   *Jonathan nods.*

Lucy: Mm.

T: Not./ What does it have to do then
to be a pendulum?

Boy: Be straight.

T: It has to be straight.   *T straightens the pendant's chain, still*
                                                         flat on table.

Is it a pendulum now?   *Pupils shake heads.*

Pupils: No.

Girl: Hanging.

T: It's got to hang.   *T lifts pendant and holds chain*
                                                         stretched out between her two hands.

Girl: Hang straight.

Boy: Hang straight down ⎧ from one
finger.   ⎨

T: ⎩ Why isn't it
a pendulum now?

Same boy: ⎧ 'Cause it won't swing.   *Boy quiet, almost mumbles.*

T: ⎩ You've said it's got to have a
weight on the end/ You've said that it
has to have a string to be suspended
and it **has**.// Why isn't it a pendulum
then?

Karen: It has to hang straight down.

T: It has to hang straight down Karen/   *T holds pendant string in the finger*
there it is/ so that's right isn't it? So it   *and thumb of one hand, suspended*
has to/   *now in a straight vertical line with the*
                                                         pendant at the bottom.

hang from a fixed point./   *T points to fingers holding chain with*
                                                         free hand.

It has to be suspended/ from a string   *Runs hand down chain.*
or a chain or whatever/ and it has to
have a mass at the end. Right/

While the pupils have used everyday terms such as 'weight' and 'hang straight down from one finger', the teacher herself not only has used these terms, but has also introduced the more technical jargon 'mass', 'suspended' and 'from a fixed point'. [...] Having established the various component attributes of a pendulum, the teacher then recaps these with the pupils.

SEQUENCE 6   ACQUIRING A SHARED VOCABULARY: PUPILS' USAGE

T: Now what did we say that they had   *Jonathan is next to his pendulum.*
     to have Jonathan? A pendulum?
Jonathan: A weight at the bottom.
T: Yes and yours **has**/ OK? And yours
     is a washer.
Jonathan: Mm.
T: Right. David what else does a
     pendulum have to have?
David: A mass.
T: Jonathan's mentioned that.
David: A string.
T: A string or a chain or some means of
     suspending the mass/ of hanging it
     down.
     Whoops/   *Pendulum topples and is caught by
                                               Sharon and Antony; all laugh.*

     Right/ and Antony what was the third
     thing it had to have?
Antony: Suspended.
T: Right./ From?
Antony: A fixed point.

The pupils have quickly grasped the new terminology introduced by the teacher, and have begun to use it themselves. It is not clear that they immediately understood what it all meant. David's suggestion 'a mass' is ambiguous between his not understanding that 'mass' means something equivalent here to 'weight', and his sense that the teacher simply prefers the term 'mass', which makes it worth mentioning. Despite the absence of direct teaching – the teacher has not explicitly taught these terms, nor required or overtly encouraged the pupils to adopt them – they have become common terms of reference to signal common understanding. Simply by using the terms in a context in which they could be understood, in this case as alternatives for everyday words used by the pupils, the teacher has managed to induct the pupils into a shared scientific discourse, a shared frame of reference and conception. Indeed, this is probably the best description we could offer of the nature of [this] sort of teaching and learning: [. . .] it is all about the induction of children into the academic world of knowledge and discourse inhabited by the teacher. It is a process of cognitive socialisation through discourse, a process akin at least as much to general behavioural and ideological socialisation as to the cognitive psychological notions of mental growth or development.

CLASSROOM DISCOURSE AND CLASSROOM KNOWLEDGE

[. . .]

One general finding that surprised us was the extent of control exercised by the teacher, even in lessons that were characterised by the more progressive sorts of teaching. In the pendulum lessons, for example, the pupils worked in small groups, subdivided into pairs of pupils working jointly on each pendulum, discovering through their own activities the principles that govern the motion of pendulums. At first sight, the teacher's role appeared to be essentially facilitative, shaping the general direction of the lesson, but largely relying on the pupils themselves to invent hypotheses, procedures and criteria for testing, performing the experiments themselves and making their own observations and measurements. On closer examination, the extent of teacher control became clearer. As we have demonstrated in this chapter, the freedom of pupils to introduce their own ideas was largely illusory; the teacher retained a strict control over what was said and done, what decisions were reached, and what interpretations were put upon experience.

We are, of course, wary of generalising from a small sample of classroom discourse to an analysis of the general state of British primary education. That is not our purpose, and this is the reason why we have not coded and counted the various types of phenomena we have identified. Such a procedure would lend itself to the sorts of statistical comparisons between different classrooms and schools that our research was not designed to achieve. Rather, we have chosen to subject small samples of classroom discourse and activity to close quantitative analysis, in the hope of discovering in that discourse clues to how knowledge is actually built and shared between teacher and pupils.

Nevertheless, the discovery of an overwhelming sense of control by the teacher, in setting the agenda, determining in advance of the lesson what the knowledge outcomes should be, and, in general, expressing the authoritative social role of teacher in terms of epistemic as well as behavioural control, is a discovery that others too have made. Some, such as Edwards and Furlong (1978), base their analysis on classroom discourse as we have done. Others use more specific and quantified linguistic indices. Feldman and Wertsch (1976), for example, measured the frequency with which American teachers used a set of auxiliary verbs that express degrees of uncertainty (may, might, could, etc.). They found a greater use of them in the staffroom than in the classroom; classroom talk was judged to be authoritative, certain of its facts, and 'closed' in comparison to the more open, hypothetical and uncertain talk between teachers.

Our findings suggest these main conclusions about the educational processes we have observed:

1 *Experiential learning and teacher control.* Despite the fact that the lessons were organised in terms of practical actions and small-group joint activity between the pupils, the sort of learning that took place was not essentially a matter of experiential learning and communication between pupils. The role of the teacher was crucial throughout, both in shaping the general pattern and content of the lesson, and in producing the fine-grained definition of what was done, said and understood. The pupils were in no sense left to create their own understandings and interpretations.

2 *Ritual and principle.* While maintaining a tight control over activity and discourse, the teacher nevertheless overtly espoused and attempted to act upon the educational principle of pupil-centred experiential learning, and the importance of pupils' engagement in practical activity and discovery. This led to the pupils' grasp of certain important concepts being essentially 'ritual', a matter of what to do or say, rather than 'principled', i.e. based on conceptual understanding. Particular sorts of classroom discourse that appeared to underlie the creation of such procedural knowledge included a heavy reliance on 'cued elicitation', together with an overriding concern to conduct the lessons in terms of getting through the set of planned activities, rather than, say, making sure that a planned set of concepts were understood by everyone. The sheer extent of teacher control over activity, discourse and interpretation was also likely to have contributed to the fact that the pupils' understanding of the lessons often became a matter of knowing what was done (or, at least, the official reconstructed version of this), and what one was required to say.

3 *Language and the socialisation of cognition.* We have concentrated on the 'content' of knowledge and discourse, on what was said and done, the words used, the concepts at issue, the actions performed. Others have looked largely at the 'form' of classroom discourse, either its sociolinguistic structures (e.g. Sinclair and Coulthard 1975; Mehan 1979), or its relations to formal properties of thought, such as logical reasoning abilities (Walkerdine 1984). The overriding impression from our studies is that classroom discourse functions to establish joint understandings between teacher and pupils, shared frames of reference and conception, in which the basic process (including the problematical features of that process) is one of introducing pupils into the conceptual world of the teacher and, through him or her, of the educational community. To the extent that the process of education can be observed taking place in the situated discourse of classrooms, it is on our evidence essentially a process of cognitive socialisation through language.

The relation of power and control to the creation of joint understandings is both problematical and of great importance. According to Habermas (1970, p. 143), 'pure intersubjectivity' is achieved only under conditions of 'complete symmetry in the distribution of assertion and disputation, revelation and hiding, prescription and following, among the partners of communication'. But education is inherently concerned with introducing children and adults into a pre-existing culture of thought and language. However active a part pupils are allowed to play in their learning, we cannot assume that they can simply reinvent that culture through their own activity and experience. It is necessarily a social and communicative process, and one which has as an inherent part of it an asymmetry of roles between teacher and learner. Pre-school cultural learning, and especially the learning of a first language, has been described by Lock (1979) as a process of 'guided reinvention'. In schools the power asymmetry is more marked; schooling is compulsory, separated from life at home, more formal, and with a more arbitrary syllabus. Many children go unwillingly to school. Teachers are often perceived primarily as sources of punishment (Hood, McDermott and Cole 1980). If the educational process is not to be completely compromised by the asymmetry of teacher and learner, then we need to develop an understanding of the process which recognises and encourages that asymmetry in a manner that fosters rather than hinders learning.

Part of the problem for pupils is that much of the process remains mysterious to them. In however friendly and informal a manner, they are frequently asked to do things, learn things, understand things, for no apparent reason other than that it is what the teacher wants them to do. The goals and purposes of the lesson are not revealed. Indeed, neither often are the concepts that the lesson may have been designed to 'cover'. In the ethos of pupil-centred inductive learning, it is not acceptable to tell the pupils what they were supposed to discover for themselves, even after they have completed the various activities involved. [. . .]

The major components of the teacher–pupil learning process as we have presented it are present in Vygotsky's conception of it. The asymmetry of teacher and learner is essential to the 'zone of proximal development', and so also is the notion of control. Children do not simply acquire knowledge and vocabulary. They acquire at the same time the capacity for self-regulation. Just as verbal thought originates as social discourse, so self-regulated behaviour begins with the regulation of one's behaviour by other people. The successful process involves a gradual handover of control from teacher to learner, as the learner becomes able to do alone what could previously be done only with help. In formal education, this part of the process is seldom realised. For most pupils, education remains a mystery beyond their control, rather than a resource of knowledge and skill with which they can freely operate. The contrast between formal schooling and first-language learning is stark, as Bruner (1985) and others have pointed out. Here, for example, formal education is contrasted with learning to play peekaboo:

> the mother initially enacts the entire script herself and then the child takes an increasingly active role, eventually speaking all the parts initially spoken by the mother. The contrast between such learning environments and the classroom is

striking. In school lessons, teachers give directions and children nonverbally carry them out; teachers ask questions and children answer them, frequently with only a word or a phrase. Most importantly, these roles are not reversed ... Children never give directions to teachers, and questions addressed to teachers are rare except for asking permission. (Forman and Cazden 1985, p. 344)

A successful educational process is one which transfers competence to the learner. It is almost as if formal education, for most pupils, is designed to prevent that from happening.

NOTE

1 'The basic "I-R-F" exchange structure [. . .] – an *initiation* by a teacher, which elicits a *response* from a pupil, followed by an evaluative comment or *feedback* from the teacher – is, once seen, impossible to ignore in any observed classroom talk' (Edwards and Mercer 1987, p. 9). See also Sinclair and Coulthard (1975).

REFERENCES

Bruner, J. S. (1985) 'Vygotsky: a historical and conceptual perspective', in J. V. Wertsch (ed.), *Culture, Communication and Cognition: Vygotskian Perspectives*. Cambridge: Cambridge University Press.

Edwards, A. D., and Furlong, V. J. (1978) *The Language of Teaching*. London: Heinemann.

Feldman, C., and Wertsch, J. V. (1976) 'Context dependent properties of teachers' speech', *Youth and Society*, 8, 227–58.

Forman, E. A., and Cazden, C. B. (1985) 'Exploring Vygotskian perspectives in education: the cognitive value of peer interaction', in J. V. Wertsch (ed.), *Culture, Communication and Cognition: Vygotskian Perspectives*. Cambridge: Cambridge University Press.

Galton, M., Simon, B., and Croll, P. (1980) *Inside the Primary Classroom* (the ORACLE project). London: Routledge and Kegan Paul.

Habermas, J. (1970) 'Toward a theory of communicative competence', in H. P. Dreitzel (ed.), *Recent Sociology*. New York: Macmillan.

Hood, L., McDermott, R., and Cole, M. (1980) '"Let's try to make it a good day" – some not so simple ways', *Discourse Processes*, 3, 155–68.

Lock, A. J. (1979) *The Guided Reinvention of Language*. London: Academic Press.

Mehan, H. (1979) *Learning Lessons: Social Organization in the Classroom*. Cambridge, Mass.: Harvard University Press.

Plowden Report (1967) *Children and their Primary Schools*. London: Central Advisory Council for Education.

Sinclair, J. McH., and Coulthard, R. M. (1975) *Towards an Analysis of Discourse: The English used by Teachers and Pupils*. London: Oxford University Press.

Vygotsky, L. S. (1978) *Mind in Society: The Development of Higher Psychological Processes*. London: Harvard University Press.

Walkerdine, V. (1984) 'Developmental psychology and the child-centred pedagogy: the insertion of Piaget into early education', in J. Henriques, W. Hollway, C. Urwin, C. Venn and V. Walkerdine, *Changing the Subject*. London: Methuen.

Orality and Literacy: From *The Savage Mind* to *Ways with Words*

2.5

James Paul Gee

It is now a common claim that there is a 'literacy crisis' in the United States (Gee 1986; Gumperz 1986; Kozol 1985). This claim is based on two social facts: (1) an unacceptably large number of children, a disproportionate number of whom are from low-income and minority homes, fail to gain functional literacy in school; and (2) partly as a result, an unacceptably large number of adults are functionally illiterate or only marginally literate (about one-third of the nation). At first sight, it seems obvious what this has to do with the English teacher; after all, literacy is what English teachers teach. But what is literacy? Once we answer this question, the English teacher's role becomes even more crucial and yet at the same time much more problematic.

This [chapter] demonstrates how in anthropological studies the term *literate* in the dichotomy *literate/nonliterate* came to replace the term *civilised* in the older dichotomy *civilised/primitive* and then how a distinction between different cultures (nonliterate versus literate ones) came to be applied to different social groups within modern, technological societies like ours, characterising some as having 'restricted literacy' and others as having 'full literacy'. The importance of these developments is the link often assumed to exist between literacy and higher order mental skills, such as analytic, logical, or abstract thinking.

But a contrary current has developed, a current which sees literacy as necessarily plural: different societies and social subgroups have different types of literacy, and literacy has different social and mental effects in different social and cultural contexts. Literacy is seen as a set of discourse practices, that is, as ways of using and making sense both in speech and writing. These discourse practices are tied to the particular world views (beliefs and values) of particular social or cultural groups. Such discourse practices are integrally connected with the identity or sense of self of the people who practise them; a change of discourse practices is a change of identity. [...]

This [chapter] surveys recent work on orality (nonliteracy) and literacy, not by dealing in depth with this now massive literature, but rather by discussing a few key works. These are treated as forming a particular progression, leading to a point of view I advocate. [...]

Source: *TESOL Quarterly*, Vol. 20, 1986, pp. 719–46.

THE ORAL/LITERATE DISTINCTION WITHIN MODERN 'LITERATE' SOCIETIES

Chafe (1982), in contrasting writing (essays) and speech (spontaneous conversation), suggests that differences in the processes of speaking and writing have led to specific differences in the products. The fact that writing is much slower than speech, while reading is much faster, allows written language to be less fragmented, more syntactically integrated, than speech. The writer has the time to mould ideas into a more complex, coherent, integrated whole, making use of complicated lexical and syntactic devices seldom used in speech (such as heavy use of nominalisations, participles, attributive adjectives, and various subordinating devices). In addition to its integrated quality, Chafe calls attention to the fact that written language fosters more detachment than speech, which is face-to-face and usually more highly socially involved than writing. Thus, writing is integrated and detached, while speech is fragmented and involved.

Chafe is aware that these are in reality poles of a continuum and that there are uses of spoken and written language that do not fit these characterisations (e.g. lectures as a form of integrated and detached speech; letters as a form of fragmented and involved writing; literature, in which involvement features are used for aesthetic effects). However, integration and detachment are part of the potential that writing offers, thanks to the processes by which it is produced. [. . .]

The distinction between writing and speech that Chafe draws bears some similarity to Michaels's (1981) distinction between different ways that black and white children tell 'sharing time' stories in the early years of school. Many black children of lower socioeconomic status told what Michaels calls 'topic-associating' stories, while white and black middle-class children tended to tell 'topic-centred' stories. Topic-centred stories are tightly structured around a single topic and lexically explicit, have a high degree of thematic coherence and a clear thematic progression, and feature intonational cues used by the child to mark out syntactically complete, independent clauses. The stories tend to be short and concise. Topic-associating stories associate a series of segments through an implicit link to a particular topical event or theme, rely heavily on inferences to be drawn by the listener on the basis of shared knowledge, and use intonational cues to mark out episodic shifts in the story rather than to make syntactic structure clear.

Gee (1986) has shown that the black children in Michaels's study also used a number of devices reminiscent of Havelock's and Ong's characterisations of orality, for example, the creation of a rhythmical structure through formulaic devices, repetition, and syntactic parallelism. These differences, which are ultimately founded on practices in the home, lead eventually to the middle-class children having control over forms of speech that in their integration and detachment resemble essay-text writing, while the black children retain speech that in its fragmentation and social involvement contrasts with the canons of essay-text literacy.

There has, however, been confusion in much of the linguistics and educational literature about what *orality* actually means. Chafe's work (and much of that of Hymes, e.g. 1981) can set us on the right track here. Chafe points out that in many oral cultures the formal ritual-traditional language or forms of language often referred to as 'high rhetoric' are analogous to the integration and detachment of essayist writing. These forms of language, used on sacred, ritual, or otherwise socially important occasions, involve some degree (often a great deal) of memorisation or sorts of special learning. They very often involve the formulaic, rhythmical, patterned use of language Havelock and Ong call attention to in Homer, but they may also involve a good deal of lexical and syntactic complexity and explicit reference that relies little on hearer inference.

Thus, the formulaic and rhythmic features of orality are by no means in opposition to the linguistic formality, explicitness, and complexity we associate with writing. Looked at in this way, the speech/writing, or orality/literacy, distinction begins to become problematic: what seems to be involved are different cultural practices that in certain contexts call for certain uses of language, language patterned in certain ways and trading on features like fragmentation and involvement to various degrees.

LITERACY AND HIGHER ORDER COGNITIVE SKILLS

The previous section suggests the need for a new approach to the oral/literate divide, one that would study different uses of language, spoken and written, in their cultural contexts. But one major factor keeps literacy, apart from any cultural context, in focus: the claim that literacy leads to higher order cognitive skills. This claim is founded on a large number of empirical studies that go back to the famous work of Vygotsky (see Wertsch 1985) and Luria (1976) in Soviet Central Asia in the 1930s, when this area was in the midst of collectivisation. Many previously nonliterate populations were rapidly introduced to literacy and other practices of modern technological society. Vygotsky and Luria compared nonliterate and recently literate subjects on a series of reasoning tasks.

The tasks consisted of categorising familiar objects or deducing the conclusion that follows from the premises of a syllogism. For example, in one task subjects were given pictures of a hammer, a saw, a log, and a hatchet and asked to say which three went together. Literate subjects were generally willing to say that the hammer, hatchet, and saw went together because they were all tools, thus grouping the objects on the basis of abstract word meanings. In contrast, the answers of nonliterate subjects indicated a strong tendency to group items on the basis of concrete settings with which they were familiar. Thus, they said things like 'the log has to be here too' and resisted the experimenter's suggestions, based on decontextualised word meanings, that the hammer, hatchet, and saw could be grouped together. Performance on syllogistic reasoning tasks yielded analogous results.

It was concluded that major differences exist between literate and nonliterate subjects in their use of abstract reasoning processes. The responses of nonliterates were dominated by their immediate practical experience, and they resisted using language in a decontextualised manner. [...]

However, there is a major empirical problem in the Vygotsky-Luria work. It is unclear whether the results were caused by literacy, by schooling, or even by the new social institutions that the Russian Revolution exposed these subjects to. It is extremely difficult to separate the influence of literacy from that of formal schooling, since in most parts of the world the two go together. But school involves much more than becoming literate: 'A student is involved in learning a set of complex role relationships, general cognitive techniques, ways of approaching problems, different genres of talk and interaction, and an intricate set of values concerned with communication, interaction, and society as a whole' (Wertsch 1985, pp. 35–6).

Scribner and Cole and *The Psychology of Literacy*

The whole question of the cognitive effects of literacy was redefined by the groundbreaking work on the Vai in Liberia by Scribner and Cole in *The Psychology of Literacy* (1981). (All citations below are from this work.) They examine two crucial questions: is it literacy or formal schooling that affects mental functioning and can one distinguish among the effects of different forms of literacy used for different functions in the life of an individual or a society?

Among the Vai, literacy and schooling are not always coterminous. In addition to literacy in English acquired in formal school settings, the Vai have an indigenous (syllabic, not alphabetic) script transmitted outside an institutional setting and with no connection with Western-style schooling, as well as a form of literacy in Arabic. Each of these literacies is tied to a particular set of uses: English literacy is associated with government and education; Vai literacy is used primarily for keeping records and for letters, many of them involving commercial matters; Arabic literacy is used for reading, writing, and memorising the Koran (many Arabic literates do not know Arabic but have memorised and can recite large sections of the Koran). Since some Vai are versed in only one of these forms of literacy, others in two or more, and still others are nonliterate altogether, Scribner and Cole could disentangle various effects of literacy from effects of formal schooling (which affected only the English literates).

Scribner and Cole examined subjects' performance on categorisation and syllogistic reasoning tasks similar to those used by Vygotsky (see Wertsch, 1985) and Luria (1976). Their results call into question much work on the cognitive consequences of literacy. Neither syllabic Vai script nor Arabic alphabetic literacy was associated with what have been considered higher order intellectual skills.

Neither form of literacy enhanced the use of taxonomic skills, nor did either contribute to a shift toward syllogistic reasoning. In contrast, literacy in English, the only form associated with formal schooling, was associated with some types of decontextualisation and abstract reasoning. However, all the tasks on which schooling was the highest ranking determinant of performance were 'talking about' tasks. Schooled subjects showed no such superiority on tasks which did not involve verbal exposition, leading Scribner and Cole to conclude that 'school fosters abilities in expository talk in contrived situations' (pp. 242–3; see also Scribner and Cole 1973).

Furthermore, Scribner and Cole did not find that schooled, English-literate subjects, many of whom had been out of school a number of years, differed from other groups in their actual performance on categorisation and abstract reasoning tasks. They simply talked about them better, providing informative verbal descriptions and justifications of their task activity. However, those who had recently been in school actually did do better on the tasks, suggesting that both task performance and verbal description of task performance improved as a result of schooled literacy but that the former was transient, unless practised in the years following school.

Another very important finding in the Scribner and Cole work is that each form of literacy was associated with some quite specific skills. For example, Vai script literacy was associated with specific skills in synthesising spoken Vai in an auditory integration task (repeating back Vai sentences decomposed, by pauses between syllables, into their constituent syllables), in using graphic symbols to represent language, in using language as a means of instruction, and in talking about correct Vai speech.

All of these skills are closely related to everyday practices involved in Vai script literacy. For instance, the ability to synthesise spoken Vai appears to follow from the large amount of practice in synthesising language that one gets in trying to decode a syllabic script that does not mark word divisions. (To construct meaning out of a chain of syllables, the Vai script reader must often hold a sequence of syllables in working memory until the unit of meaning, what words they belong to, is determined.) Or, to take another example, the Vai, in writing letters, often discuss the quality of the letters and whether they are written in 'good Vai'. This practice appears to enhance their ability to talk about correct speech on a grammar task.

Scribner and Cole, on the basis of such evidence, opt for what they call 'a practice account of literacy'. A type of literacy enhances quite specific skills that are practised in carrying out that literacy. Grandiose claims for large and global cognitive skills resulting from literacy are not, in fact, indicated. One can also point out that the effect of formal schooling – being able to engage in expository talk in contrived situations – is itself a fairly specific skill practised a good deal in school. Thus, we might extend Scribner and Cole's practice account to schooling as well as literacy.

STREET AND *LITERACY IN THEORY AND PRACTICE*

The work of Scribner and Cole (1981) calls into question what Street, in his book *Literacy in Theory and Practice* (1984), calls 'the autonomous model' of literacy: the claim that literacy (or schooling for that matter) has cognitive effects apart from the context in which it exists and the uses to which it is put in a given culture. Street criticises this model through a discussion of Olson's (1977) work, some recent work by Hildyard and Olson (1978), as well as Greenfield's (1972) study of the Wolof of Senegal.

Olson's (1977) claims for the cognitive effects of literacy – that, for example, it 'unambiguously represents meanings' (p. 264) – refer only to one type of literacy, the essay-text form of writing prevalent in Western culture and supported by our schools. In fact, his claims rest on descriptions of the 'British essayists' of the seventeenth and eighteenth centuries, who were

> among the first to exploit writing for the purpose of formulating original theoretical knowledge ... Knowledge was taken to be the product of an extended logical essay – the output of the repeated application in a single coherent text of the technique of examining an assertion to determine all of its implications (pp. 268–9).

This form of literacy is the basis, ideologically, if not always in practice, of our schools and universities. Claims for literacy *per se* are often in fact tacit claims for essay-text literacy, a form of literacy that is neither natural nor universal, but one cultural way of making sense among many others. Of course, this way of making sense is associated with mainstream middle-class and upper middle-class groups and is, in fact, best represented by the ideology and sometimes the practice of academics, the people who most often make claims for it.

One can go further in showing how claims for literacy are often tacit ways to privilege one social group's ways of doing things as if they were natural and universal. Many of the tasks used to measure such things as cognitive flexibility, logical reasoning, or abstractness, tasks like those used by Vygotsky (see Wertsch 1985) and Luria (1976), Greenfield (1972), Scribner and Cole (1981), and many others, are, in fact, tests of the ability to use language in a certain way. In particular, they are tests of what we might call explicitness.

[. . .]

For example, in our culture there is a convention that in certain contrived situations, one does not take it for granted that the listener or audience can see or is aware, through shared knowledge, of what is being referred to (even when they indeed are); thus, one is explicit in referring to it (as children are encouraged to do, for instance, at sharing time). Certain other cultures, as well as unschooled people in our culture, simply do not have, and thus do not use, this convention. In fact, such explicitness may be seen as rude because it is either distancing, blunt, or condescending to the hearer's intelligence or relation to the speaker.

Claims for literacy, in particular for essay-text literacy values, whether in speech or writing, are thus 'ideological'. They are part of 'an armoury of concepts, conventions and practices' (Street 1984, p. 38) that privilege one social formation as if it were natural, universal, or, at least, the end point of a normal developmental progression of cognitive skills (achieved only by some cultures, thanks either to their intelligence or their technology).

Street proposes, in opposition to the autonomous model of literacy, an 'ideological model', in which literacy is viewed in terms of concrete social practices and the various ideologies in which different cultural expressions of literacies are embedded. Literacy – of whatever type – only has consequences as it acts together with a large number of other social factors, including a culture's or a social group's political and economic conditions, social structure, and local ideologies. Any technology, including writing, is a cultural form, a social product whose shape and influence depend upon prior political and ideological factors.

Despite Havelock's (1963; 1982) brilliant characterisation of the transition from orality to literacy in ancient Greece, it now appears that the Greek situation has rarely if ever been replicated. The particular social, political, economic, and ideological circumstances in which literacy (of a particular sort) was embedded in Greece explain what happened there – the flowering of Greek classical civilisation. Abstracting literacy from its social setting in order to make claims for literacy as an autonomous force in shaping the mind or a culture simply leads to a dead end.

There is, however, a last refuge for someone who wants to see literacy as an autonomous force. One could claim that essay-text literacy and the uses of language connected with it, such as explicitness and the syntactic mode, lead, if not to general cognitive consequences, then to social mobility and success in the society. While this argument may be true, there is precious little evidence that literacy in history or across cultures has had this effect either. Street discusses, in some detail, Graff's (1979) study of the role of literacy in nineteenth-century Canada.

While some individuals did gain through the acquisition of literacy, Graff demonstrates that this effect was not statistically significant and that deprived classes and ethnic groups as a whole were, if anything, further oppressed through literacy. Greater literacy did not correlate with increased equality and democracy nor with better conditions for the working class, but in fact with continuing social stratification. The teaching of literacy involved a contradiction: illiterates were considered dangerous to the social order; thus, they must be made literate; yet the potentialities of reading and writing for an underclass could well be radical and inflammatory. So the framework for the teaching of literacy had to be severely controlled, and this involved specific forms of control of the pedagogic process and specific ideological associations of the literacy being purveyed.

Although the workers were led to believe that acquiring literacy was to their benefit, Graff produces statistics that show that in reality this literacy was not advantageous to the poorer groups in terms of either income or power. The extent to which literacy was an advantage or not in relation to job opportunities depended on ethnicity. It was not because you were 'illiterate' that you finished up in the worst jobs but because of your background (e.g. being black or an Irish Catholic rendered literacy much less efficacious than it was for English Protestants).

The story Graff tells can be repeated for many other societies, including Britain and the United States (see Street 1984, as well as Cook-Gumperz 1986; Donald 1983; Gilmore 1985). In all these societies literacy served as a socialising tool for the poor, was seen as a possible threat if misused by the poor (for an analysis of their oppression and to make demands for power), and served as a means for maintaining the continued selection of members of one class for the best positions in the society.

[. . .]

HEATH AND *WAYS WITH WORDS*

Heath's already classic *Ways With Words* (1983) is an ethnographic study of how literacy is embedded in the cultural context of three communities in the Piedmont Carolinas in the United States: Roadville, a white working-class community that has been part of mill life for four generations; Trackton, a working-class black community whose older generation was brought up on the land but which now is also connected to mill life and other light industry; and mainstream, middle-class, urban-oriented blacks and whites.

Heath analyses the ways these different social groups 'take' knowledge from the environment, with particular concern for how 'types of literacy events' are involved in this taking. *Literacy events* are any event involving print, such as group negotiation of meaning in written texts (e.g. an ad), individuals 'looking things up' in reference books or writing family records in the Bible, and the dozens of other types of occasions when books or other written materials are integral to interpretation in an interaction. Heath interprets these literacy events in relation to the *larger sociocultural patterns* which they may exemplify or reflect, such as patterns of care-giving roles, uses of space and time, age and sex segregation, and so forth.

The oral/literate contrast makes little sense because in fact many social groups, even in high-technology societies, fall into such mixed categories as residual orality (Ong 1982) or restricted literacy (Goody 1977). The members of many US communities, though they may write and read at basic levels, have little occasion to use these skills as taught in school. Much of their daily lives is filled with literacy events in which they must know how to respond orally to written materials. Different social groups do this in different ways. How the members of a community use print to take meaning from the environment and how they use knowledge gained from print are interdependent with the ways children learn language and are socialised in interaction with peers and care givers. Language learning and socialisation are two sides of the same coin (Ochs and Schieffelin 1984). Thus, Heath concentrates on how children in each community acquire language and literacy in the process of becoming socialised into the norms and values of their communities.

As school-oriented, middle-class parents and their children interact in the preschool years, adults give their children, through modelling and specific instruction, ways of using language and of taking knowledge from books which seem natural in school and in numerous other institutional settings such as banks, post offices, businesses, or government offices.

To illustrate this point, Heath (1982) analyses the bedtime story as an example of a major literacy event in mainstream homes. (All citations below are to this article, which contains much of the same material as *Ways With Words*.) The bedtime story sets patterns of behaviour that recur repeatedly through the life of mainstream children and adults at school and in other institutions. In the bedtime-story routine, the parent sets up a 'scaffolding' dialogue (see Cazden 1979) with the child by asking questions like *What is X?* and then supplying verbal feedback and a label after the child has vocalised or given a nonverbal response. Before the age of two, the child is thus socialised into the 'initiation–reply–evaluation' sequences so typical of classroom lessons (e.g. Mehan 1979; Sinclair and Coulthard 1975).

In addition, reading with comprehension involves an internal replaying of the same types of questions adults ask children about bedtime stories, and *what-*explanations are replayed in the school setting in learning to pick out topic sentences, write outlines, and answer standardised tests. Through the bedtime-story routine and many similar practices in which children learn not only how to take meaning from books but also how to talk about it, they repeatedly practise routines which parallel those of classroom interaction: 'Thus, there is a deep continuity between patterns of socialisation and language learning in the home culture and what goes on at school' (p. 56).

Children in both Roadville and Trackton were unsuccessful in school, despite the fact that both communities placed a high value on success in school. Roadville adults did read books to their children, but they did not extend the habits of literacy events beyond book reading. For instance, they did not, upon seeing an event in the real world, remind children of similar events in a book or comment on such similarities and differences between a book and real events.

The strong Fundamentalist bent of Roadville tended to make the members of this community view any fictionalised account of a real event as a *lie*. Since they regarded reality as being better than fiction, they did not encourage the shifting of the context of items and events characteristic of fictionalisation and abstraction. They tended to choose books which emphasised nursery rhymes, alphabet learning, and simplified Bible stories. Even the oral stories that Roadville adults told, and that children modelled, were grounded in the actual. These stories, which were drawn from personal experience, were tales of transgression which made the point of reiterating the expected norms of behaviour.

Thus, Roadville children were not practised in decontextualising their knowledge or in fictionalising events known to them and shifting them about into other frames. In school, they were rarely able to take knowledge learned in one context and shift it to another; they did not compare two items or events and point out similarities and differences.

Trackton presents a quite different language and social environment. Babies in Trackton, who were almost always held during their waking hours, were constantly in the midst of a rich stream of verbal and nonverbal communication. Aside from Sunday school materials, there were no reading materials in the home just for children; adults did not sit and read to children. Children did, however, constantly interact verbally with peers and adults.

Adults did not ask children *What is X?* questions, but rather analogical questions calling for nonspecific comparisons of one item, event, or person with another (e.g. *What's that like?*). Though children could answer such questions, they could rarely name the specific feature or features which made two items or events alike. Parents did not believe they had a tutoring role and did not simplify their language for children, as mainstream parents do, nor did they label items or features of objects in either books or the environment at large. They believed children learned when they were provided with experiences from which they could draw global, rather than analytically specific, knowledge.

Children seemed to develop connections between situations or items by gestalt patterns, analogues, or general configuration links, not by specification of labels and discrete features in the situation. They did not decontextualise; rather, they heavily contextualised nonverbal and verbal language. Trackton children learned to tell stories by rendering a context and calling on the audience's participation to join in the imaginative creation of the story. In an environment rich with imaginative talk and verbal play, they had to be aggressive in inserting their stories into an ongoing stream of discourse. Fictionalisation, imagination, and verbal dexterity were encouraged.

Indeed, group negotiation and participation were prevalent features of the social group as a whole. Adults read not alone but in a group. For example, someone might read from a brochure on a new car while listeners related the text's meaning to their experiences, asking questions and expressing opinions. The group as a whole would synthesise the written text and the associated oral discourse to construct a meaning for the brochure.

At school, most Trackton children failed not only to learn the content of lessons but also to adopt the social interactional rules for school literacy events. Print in isolation carried little authority in their world, and the kinds of questions asked about reading books were unfamiliar (for example, *what*-explanations). The children's abilities to link two events or situations metaphorically and to recreate scenes were not tapped in school. In fact, these abilities often caused difficulties because they enabled children to see parallels teachers did not intend and, indeed, might not have recognised until the children pointed them out. By the time in their education when their imaginative skills and verbal dexterity could really pay off (usually after the elementary years), they had failed to gain the necessary written composition skills they would need to translate their analogical skills into a channel teachers could accept.

Heath's characterisation of Trackton, Roadville, and mainstreamers leads us to see not a binary (oral/literate) contrast, but a set of features that cross-classifies the three groups in various ways. Each group shares various features with the other groups but differs from them in other ways: the mainstream group and Trackton both valued imagination and fictionalisation, while Roadville did not; Roadville and Trackton both shared a disregard for decontextualisation not shared by mainstreamers. Both mainstreamers and Roadville, but not Trackton, believed parents have a tutoring role in language and literacy acquisition (they read to their children and asked questions that required labels). However, Roadville shared with Trackton, not the mainstream, an experiential, nonanalytic view of learning (children learn by doing and watching, not by having the process broken down into its smallest parts). [. . .]

In *Ways With Words*, Heath has suggested that in order for a non-mainstream social group to acquire mainstream, school-based literacy practices, with all the oral and written language skills this implies, individuals, whether children or adults, must 'recapitulate', at an appropriate level for their age of course, the sorts of literacy experiences the mainstream child has had at home. Unfortunately, schools as currently constituted tend to be good places to practise mainstream literacy once you have its foundations, but they are not good places to acquire those foundations.

Heath suggests that this foundation, when it has not been set at home, can be acquired by apprenticing the individual to a school-based literate person (the teacher in a new and expanded role), who must break down essay-text literacy into its myriad component skills and allow the student to practise them repeatedly. Such skills involve the ability to give *what*-explanations; to break down verbal information into small bits of information; to notice the analytic features of items and events and to be able to recombine them in new contexts, eventually to offer *reason*-explanations; and finally to take meaning from books and be able to talk about it.

Heath has actually had students, at a variety of ages, engage in ethnographic research with the teacher (e.g. studying the use of language or languages or of writing and reading in their communities) as a way of learning and practising the various subskills of essay-text literacy (e.g. asking questions; taking notes; discussing various points of view, often with people with whom the student does not share a lot of mutual knowledge; writing discursive prose and revising it with feedback, often from nonpresent readers).

CONCLUSION: LITERACY AND THE ENGLISH TEACHER

The literature on orality and literacy is rife with implications for teachers of English, most of which I hope are readily apparent from the preceding discussion. Let me conclude, however, by touching on some major themes. Teachers of English are not, in fact, teaching English, and certainly not English grammar, or even 'language'. Rather, they are teaching a set of discourse practices, oral and written, connected with the standard dialect of English.

Language and literacy acquisition are forms of socialisation, in this case socialisation into mainstream ways of using language in speech and print, mainstream ways of taking meaning, of making sense of experience. Discourse practices are always embedded in the particular world view of a particular social group; they are tied to a set of values and norms. In learning new discourse practices, a student partakes of this set of values and norms, this world view. Furthermore, in acquiring a new set of discourse practices, a student may be acquiring a new identity, one that at various points may conflict with the student's initial acculturation and socialisation.

Different literacy practices allow the student to practise different, quite specific skills, and the student indeed gets better at these. Literacy in and of itself leads to no higher order, global cognitive skills; all humans who are acculturated and socialised are already in possession of higher order cognitive skills, though their expression and the practices they are embedded in will differ across cultures.

Essay-text literacy, with its attendant emphasis on the syntactic mode and explicitness, while only one cultural expression of literacy among many, is connected with the form of consciousness and the interests of the powerful in our society. As Western technology and literacy spread across the globe, this form of consciousness is influencing, interacting with, and often replacing indigenous forms all over the world [. . .]

We should not fool ourselves into thinking that access to essay-text literacy automatically ensures equality and social success or erases racism or minority disenfranchisement. But, nonetheless, English teachers are gatekeepers: short of radical social change, there is no access to power in the society without control over the discourse practices in thought, speech, and writing of essay-text literacy and its attendant world view.

English teachers can cooperate in their own marginalisation by seeing themselves as 'language teachers' with no connection to such social and political issues. Or they can accept the paradox of literacy as a form of interethnic communication which often involves conflicts of values and identities, and accept their role as persons who socialise students into a world view that, given its power here and abroad, must be looked at critically, comparatively, and with a constant sense of the possibilities for change. Like it or not, English teachers stand at the very heart of the most crucial educational, cultural, and political issues of our time.

ACKNOWLEDGMENTS

My thinking about orality, literacy, and related issues has been greatly influenced, over the last few years, by conversations with Courtney Cazden (Harvard University), David Dickinson (Tufts University), Ruth Nickse (Boston University), and Sarah Michaels (Harvard and the University of Massachusetts, Boston), to all of whom I am deeply indebted. I am also indebted to Shirley Brice Heath, Michael Cole, Dell Hymes, and Karen Watson-Gegeo for the lucidity and importance of their written work, which, apparent or not, has influenced me a great deal.

REFERENCES

Cazden, C. (1979) 'Peekaboo as an instructional model: discourse development at home and at school', *Papers and Reports in Child Language Development*, 17, 1–29.

Chafe, W. (1982) 'Integration and involvement in speaking, writing, and oral literature', in D. Tannen (ed.), *Spoken and Written Language: Exploring Orality and Literacy*, pp. 35–53. Norwood, NJ: Ablex.

Cook-Gumperz, J. (1986) 'Literacy and schooling: an unchanging equation?', in J. Cook-Gumperz (ed.), *The Social Construction of Literacy*, pp. 16–44. Cambridge: Cambridge University Press.

Donald, J. (1983) 'How illiteracy became a problem (and literacy stopped being one)', *Journal of Education*, 165, 35–52.

Gee, J. P. (1986) 'Literate America on illiterate America: a review of Jonathan Kozol's *Illiterate America*', *Journal of Education*, 168, 126–40.

Gee, J. P. (in press) 'Units in the production of narrative discourse', *Discourse Processes*.

Gilmore, P. (1985) '"Gimme room": school resistance, attitude, and access to literacy', *Journal of Education*, 167, 111–28.

Goody, J. (1977) *The Domestication of the Savage Mind*. Cambridge: Cambridge University Press.

Greenfield, P. (1972) 'Oral or written language: the consequences for cognitive development in Africa, U.S. and England', *Language and Speech*, 15, 169–78.

Gumperz, J. J. (1986) 'Interactional social linguistics in the study of schooling', in J. Cook-Gumperz (ed.), *The Social Construction of Literacy*, pp. 45–68. Cambridge: Cambridge University Press.

Havelock, E. A. (1963) *Preface to Plato*. Cambridge, MA: Harvard University Press.

Havelock, E. A. (1982) *The Literature Revolution in Greece and its Cultural Consequences*. Princeton, NJ: Princeton University Press.

Heath, S. B. (1982) 'What no bedtime story means: narrative skills at home and at school', *Language in Society*, 11, 49–76.

Heath, S. B. (1983) *Ways With Words*. Cambridge: Cambridge University Press.

Hildyard, A. and Olson, D. (1978) *Literacy and the Specialization of Language*. Unpublished manuscript, Ontario Institute for Studies in Education.

Hymes, D. (1981) 'In vain I tried to tell you': essays in native American ethnopoetics.' Philadelphia: The University of Pennsylvania Press.

Kozol, J. (1985) *Illiterate America*. Garden City, NY: Anchor Press/ Doubleday.

Luria, A. R. (1976) *Cognitive Development: Its Cultural and Social Foundations*, ed. M. Cole, trans. M. Lopez-Morillas and L. Solotaroff. Cambridge, MA: Harvard University Press.

Mehan, H. (1979) *Learning Lessons*. Cambridge, MA: Harvard University Press.

Michaels, S. (1981) '"Sharing time": children's narrative styles nd differential access to literacy', *Language in Society*, 10, 423–42.

Ochs, E. and Schieffelin, B. B. (1984) 'Language acquisition and socialization: three developmental stories and their implications', in R. Shweder and R. LeVine (eds), *Culture Theory: Essays on Mind, Self and Emotion*, pp. 276–320. Cambridge: Cambridge University Press.

Olson, D. R. (1977) 'From utterance to text: the bias of language in speech and writing', *Harvard Education Review*, 47, 257–81.

Ong, W. J. (1982) *Orality and Literacy: the Technologizing of the Word*. London: Methuen.

Richardson, R. C., Jr., Risk, E. C. and Okun, M. A. (1983) *Literacy in the Open Access College*. San Francisco: Jossey Bass.

Sapir, E. (1921) *Language*. New York: Harcourt Brace and World.

Scollon, R. and Scollon, S. B. K. (1981) *Narrative, Literacy and Face in Interethnic Communication*. Norwood, NJ: Ablex.

Scribner, S. and Cole, M. (1973) 'Cognitive consequences of formal and informal education', *Science*, 182, 553–9.

Scribner, S. and Cole, M. (1981). *The Psychology of Literacy*. Cambridge, MA: Harvard University Press.

Sinclair, J. M. and Coulthard, R. M. (1975) *Toward an Analysis of Discourse*. New York: Oxford University Press.

Street, B. V. (1984) *Literacy in Theory and Practice*. Cambridge: Cambridge University Press.

Wertsch, J. V. (1985). *Vygotsky and the Social Formation of Mind*. Cambridge, MA: Harvard University Press.

part three
LEARNING IN ACTION

Introduction

Victor Lee

As we move into the last chapters of the Reader, into part 3, the emphasis on curriculum concerns deepens, and mathematics, science, thinking skills and English take centre stage.

Chapter 3.1 by Paul Cobb is concerned with mathematics. He sees the very close following of the transmission view as leading to teaching by *imposition*, while a constructivist view leads to teaching by *negotiation*. This poses a problem for teachers and for teacher education, as these two models, it is argued, are the two broad options for improving the teaching of mathematics. The first option he sees as expert-driven with the teachers channelling information along specific paths. The second option frees the teacher to develop his or her own practices, but there are dangers. For Paul Cobb, this second option presents huge difficulties, as it requires so much more of the teacher. The very fact that we are aware of these dangers, he argues, is the first step in solving them.

With chapter 3.2 the focus changes to science. There, the debate of recent years regarding the importance of concept and process has been given a tighter focus, Richard Gott and Judith Mashiter argue, with the arrival of the National Curriculum. Central to the debate lies the role of practical work. They review a number of models such as the knowledge transmission and the knowledge refinement model. Their solution is a task-based approach to the curriculum where appropriateness of task and motivation are high on the agenda. The chapter closes with a brief consideration of aspects of the National Curriculum in science.

'Thinking skills' is a relative newcomer, striving for a place in the mainstream curriculum. In chapter 3.3 Bob Burden and Anton Florek offer an introductory guide to one particular thinking skills programme, *Instrumental Enrichment*, developed by the Israeli psychologist, Reuven Feuerstein. It has largely been used with children with learning difficulties, but it has also been developed with mainstream children. The teaching programme itself is grounded firmly in theory, a fact considered particularly important by its originator. Significant issues include teaching children how to learn to learn and the mediating role of teacher, parent or significant other in developing the child's learning. Feuerstein's is essentially an optimistic viewpoint of human ability and of what can be done to improve children's learning.

The concluding chapter, 3.4, by Michael Armstrong, centres around a lively analysis of stories written by five members of a class of 9–11-year-olds. They were responding to a short story by Tolstoy used as a stimulus to get them writing. Michael Armstrong is concerned with product rather than with process, and he analyses aspects of the children's narrative styles. He is particularly interested in the idea of 'appropriation', or the ways in which children take knowledge and use it for their own purposes. Unlike some, he does not see their work as prerational, but finds in the five stories a sophisticated awareness of form and content.

The Tension between Theories of Learning and Instruction in Mathematics

3.1 Education

Paul Cobb

As Berieter (1985) observed, 'A core belief in contemporary approaches to learning is that knowledge and cognitive strategies are actively constructed by the learner' (p. 201). This widely held assumption has a solid epistemological foundation and is generally consistent with literature that documents students' cognitive development in specific areas of mathematics, particularly their misconceptions. Although constructivist theory is attractive when the issue of learning is considered, deep-rooted problems arise when attempts are made to apply it to instruction. In particular, the seemingly obvious assumption that the goal of instruction is to transmit knowledge to students stands in flat contradiction to the contention that students construct knowledge for themselves by restructuring their internal cognitive structures.

In this [chapter] I reflect on the tension between applications of constructivism in psychological and instructional settings. I first argue that the general nature of instructional interactions must be reconceptualised if constructivism is to be taken seriously. The implications of this analysis for instruction are then considered.

TWO PARADIGMS FOR COMMUNICATION

The transmission view of teaching attributes two general functions to the teacher's words and actions. They can carry meanings in and of themselves that are waiting to be apprehended by students, or they can serve to draw students' attention to mathematical structures in the environment. These structures might, for example, be embodied in manipulative materials, pictures, diagrams, or problem statements. The central assumption of the transmission view of teaching and learning is that meaning is inherent in the words and actions of the teacher or in objects in the environment. This assumption works well in many everyday situations, particularly those involving successful communication between adults about topics of mutual interest.

Constructivism challenges the assumption that meanings reside in words, actions, and objects independently of an interpreter. Teachers and students are

Source: *Educational Psychologist*, Vol. 23, 1988, pp. 87–103.

viewed as active meaning-makers who continually give contextually based meanings to each others' words and actions as they interact. The mathematical structures that the teacher 'sees out there' are considered to be the product of his or her own conceptual activity. From this perspective, mathematical structures are not perceived, intuited, or taken in but are constructed by reflectively abstracting from and reorganising sensorimotor and conceptual activity. They are inventions of the mind. Consequently, the teacher who points to mathematical structures is consciously reflecting on mathematical objects that he or she has previously constructed. Because teachers and students each construct their own meanings for words and events in the context of the ongoing interaction, it is readily apparent why communication often breaks down, why teachers and students frequently talk past each other. The constructivist's problem is to account for successful communication.

For the transmission view of teaching, breakdowns in communication are explained by means of an at least implicit reference to the successful case, because failure is the anomaly. Perhaps the student failed to encode all the relevant information in the teachers' words because of limitations in working memory, or perhaps he or she failed to encode a structure because of its complexity or lack of salience. The constructivist, in contrast, has to explain situations in which students do understand what the teacher is saying or do 'see' the mathematical structure. The key move in accounting for these situations is to view the teacher's and students' successful communication as cases in which they are continually not miscommunicating. If this seems outlandish, think for a moment of a simple physical act that we perform almost without thinking, such as standing upright. We may feel as steady as a rock, but physiological evidence indicates that we are, in fact, continually preventing ourselves from falling over. The tightrope walker who continually moves his balancing pole is an extreme example of this phenomenon. Similarly, teachers and students who might be said to share mathematical meanings are each making imperceptible accommodations in their ways of knowing. From this perspective, the process of successfully sharing or exchanging mathematical thoughts and ideas is not viewed as one of transmission. Instead, it is characterised as a dynamic, continually changing fit between the meaning-making of active interpreters of language and action.

From the transmission perspective, instructional issues tend to be addressed by developing ingenious and often creative curriculum materials and pedagogical strategies designed to help students acquire the mathematical knowledge. Constructivists clearly agree that the teacher's actions and instructional activities are of crucial importance in that they are potential sources of problematic situations for students. However, they are typically analysed as elements embedded within the network of social interactions that characterise classroom life. Attention then focuses on what happens in situations where the teacher and students do communicate successfully and what goes wrong when they fail to do so. Therefore, it is possible to expand the analyses to include the teacher's and students' beliefs about the nature of mathematics, their beliefs about their own and each others' roles (i.e. the 'social contract' they have negotiated), and their forms of motivation while doing and talking about mathematics.

There are two primary reasons why a constructivist analysis should be seriously considered as an alternative to the transmission view of instruction. First, there is an important difference between instructional and typical everyday interactions. A fundamental goal of mathematics instruction is or should be to help students build structures that are more complex, powerful, and abstract than those that they possess when instruction commences. The teacher's role is not merely to convey to students information about mathematics. One of the teacher's primary responsibilities is to facilitate profound cognitive restructuring and conceptual reorganisations. By analogy, we do not say that Newton provided information about the physical universe but instead credit him with formalising a radical new way to account for physical phenomena. Not surprisingly, Newton's ideas were initially unintelligible to many of his contemporaries. Similarly, the classroom situation is ripe for miscommunication when the teacher possesses structures and can 'see' mathematical objects that the learners are yet to construct. They will talk past each other unless the teacher makes accommodations to students' current understandings that are far more radical than those usually required in most everyday situations. Investigations of students' understandings of a variety of mathematical concepts indicate that miscommunication is, in fact, as much the norm as the exception. For example, students' understandings of number and addition and subtraction (Carpenter, Hiebert and Moser 1983; Ginsburg 1977; Steffe, von Glasersfeld, Richards and Cobb 1983), place value (Ross 1986; Steffe and von Glasersfeld 1983), multiplication and division (Greer, in press), decimal fractions (Hiebert 1986), variable (Wagner 1981), and geometric proof (Schoenfeld 1985) are very different from the specified goals of the instruction they have received.

The second reason for considering a constructivist perspective concerns the formulation of goals for mathematics instruction and the criteria for assessing instruction. An abundance of research indicates that students routinely use prescribed methods to solve particular sets of tasks on which they have received instruction without having developed the desired conceptual knowledge. Such instruction is judged to be successful when goals are stated in terms of the acquisition of specific skills. Constructivist analyses of learning in particular content domains can allow the question of what mathematics is worth knowing to be addressed in terms of conceptual developments rather than skills to be acquired. Recent research also indicates that non-cognitive goals that pertain to beliefs, affects, and metacognitions must also be considered.

Within this framework, the criteria for assessing instruction must be broader than demonstrating that the performance of students who have been taught to solve a narrow set of tasks is superior to that of students who have not received training on those tasks. Indications that students have constructed powerful conceptual structures include their ability to solve problems in a wide variety of situations a considerable length of time after instruction is completed and their ability to build on the structures when learning in other domains. In other words, the structures are a permanent part of the students' problem-solving repertoire.

Generalising from the second reason, I argue that it is desirable to have theories of instruction that are compatible with analyses of learning. At times, there seems to be inconsistencies when the conceptual development of individual children is considered in isolation and when learning in instructional settings is analysed. I have, for example, read clear, concise constructivist analyses of development coupled with the recommendation that the teacher should devise transparent instructional representations that inevitably lead students to make the correct constructions (e.g. Resnick 1983). In this context, *transparent* means that abstract relationships are presented in an easily apprehended form so that the teacher can draw students' attention to them. The view that abstract relationships are apprehended appears to clash with the claim that 'cognitive acquisition is a process of knowledge restructuring' (Resnick 1983, p. 27). A second instructional recommendation that has been tied to constructivism but does not, for me, follow from the theory is that of teaching students to use methods or strategies that indicate increasingly sophisticated conceptual levels. The assumption that there is a one-to-one correspondence between students' observable behaviours and the underlying conceptual structures does not follow from constructivism. It is quite possible for students to use the prescribed methods to solve a particular set of tasks on which they have received instruction without having developed the desired conceptual structures.

The clash of paradigms illustrated by these two examples is problematic in that constructivism is used to support conventional instructional recommendations that do not follow from the theory. This is not to say that the instructional recommendations will necessarily be ineffective. Rather, the recommendations need an alternative rationale.

Now that we have clarified what does not follow from constructivism, we can begin to consider the theory's instructional implications by first discussing instructional interactions in more detail.

INSTRUCTIONAL INTERACTIONS

The contention that teachers and students actively give meaning to each others' actions implies that students who complete tasks successfully in the context of direction instruction cannot be said to have taken in the knowledge the teacher believes he or she has transmitted. Rather, the students have found a way of acting that is compatible with the teacher's expectations about the outcome of instruction. For example, Ross (1986, pp. 34–5) reported that

> children are able to succeed on a variety of tasks typically found in their textbooks and standardized tests, such as the following:
>
>> In 27, which digit is in the ones' place?
>> How many tens are in 84?
>> $35 = \underline{\hspace{1cm}}$ tens and $\underline{\hspace{1cm}}$ ones.
>> 7 tens + 5 ones = $\underline{\hspace{1cm}}$.

According to Ross, 'the child's knowledge of place value is limited, however, to the position of the digits and does not encompass the quantities indicated by each' (p. 34). The children produce correct answers by relying on purely syntactic cues. At a more advanced level, Hiebert and Wearne (1985) developed a model that accounts for students' solutions to tasks involving decimal computation (e.g. $5.1 + .46$, $.86 - .3$, $8 \times .06$, $.56 - 7$).

> Conceptual bases for computation rules were not built into the system and were not missed. Predictions of performance were made without considering conceptual knowledge, and most of the predictions were verified ... It appears that students' improved performance with age results from an increased facility with syntax rather than from a better conceptual understanding of the procedures (p. 200).

In general, the most that can ever be said is that the constructions children make *fit* those that the teacher assumes they have made (von Glasersfeld 1983). The teacher can never know with absolute certainty what is going on inside each student's head. This does not imply that attempts to infer students' understandings should be abandoned, but it does mean that the teacher should continually be aware of the fallibility of his or her inferences.

Because problems arise for students when they give meaning to instructional situations and because there are wide variations in the cognitive resources that they have available, the teacher's actions do not directly determine students' cognitive constructions. However, teachers' actions do influence the problems that students attempt to solve and thus the knowledge they construct. The crucial relationship is one of constraints. This can be illustrated by considering an analogy between students' construction of mathematical knowledge and the scientist's construction of theoretical knowledge.

> As is the case for a scientific theory, a schema [conceptual structure] is compared with observations, and if it fails to account for certain aspects of these observations, it can be accepted temporarily, rejected, modified, or replaced (Glaser 1984, p. 100).

Just as a scientific theory remains unchallenged until conceptual or empirical anomalies become apparent (Laudan 1977), students operating on the frontiers of their conceptual knowledge have no reason to build new conceptual structures unless their current knowledge results in obstacles, contradictions, or surprises (von Glasersfeld 1983). The difference between the scientist and the student is that the student interacts with a teacher, who can guide his or her construction of knowledge as the student attempts to complete instructional activities. Consequently, the meanings students give to the teacher's actions serve as an additional set of observations that can indicate that their current conceptions are inadequate. Just as empirical data constrains but does not determine the construction of scientific theories, teachers' actions constrain students' construction of new knowledge structures. As an example, consider a case in which a teacher Socratically questions a student and is successful in helping the student complete a mathematics task. Typically, the teacher's questions are intended to pose successive subgoals of the entire task. The student contributes to the success of the instruction by responding appropriately to each of the questions and by reflecting on these separate responses and integrating them into a single, coherent solution. By doing so, the student, in effect, figures out what the teacher might have had in mind all along. Thus, the student has actively constructed mathematical knowledge. However, the opportunity to do so was made possible by the teacher's interventions. In particular, the student would not have produced a sequence of responses that he or she realises constitutes a solution to the task.

The preceding discussion suggests a way of reconciling the assumption that students construct their own knowledge with the fact that they do sometimes learn what was intended from instruction. The task is not to explain how students take in knowledge transmitted by the teacher and integrate it with their individual cognitive structures. Instead, it is to explain how they actively construct knowledge in a way that satisfies the constraints inherent in instruction. The following example illustrates how a teacher's actions constrain a student's construction of knowledge and how a constructivist analysis of the teaching-learning process can influence a teacher's actions.

A SAMPLE ANALYSIS

Melissa, the first-grade student of the following episode, routinely was able to solve missing addend sentences such as $8 + \underline{\hspace{1cm}} = 12$. She consistently solved these tasks and addition and subtraction sentences by using finger patterns associated with number words up to 15. These patterns could include both visible and imaginary fingers. Consider, for example, her solution to a subtraction task in which she was asked to find how many marbles remained in a cup given that there were initially 14 marbles and 11 had been removed. Melissa put up all 10 fingers simultaneously as she said, 'Fourteen'. She then pointed to four locations to the right of her right hand as she whispered '1, 2, 3, 4' and continued '5, 6, ..., 11' as she sequentially closed seven fingers. Finally, she looked at her remaining three fingers and answered, 'Three.' For this task and in solutions to addition and missing addend tasks, Melissa seemed to visualise a third hand. This inference is consistent with limitations in her methods that became apparent when she was asked to solve tasks that involved a total of 16 or more items. In each case, she was unsuccessful and explained that she did not have enough fingers.

Melissa's reliance on direct modelling solutions led to the inference that she could only express her relatively sophisticated concept of number by creating a collection of visible and imagined items. Previous investigations indicate that children inferred to be at about the same conceptual level as Melissa can also express their number concepts by imagining themselves counting (Cobb 1985; Steffe *et al.* 1983). To give meaning to the first addend of $8 + 5 = \underline{\hspace{1cm}}$, for example, the child might take the activity of counting '1, 2, ..., 8' as having been completed without ever imagining a collection of items and solve the sentence by counting-on '8, 9, 10, 11, 12, 13'. Therefore, the teacher speculated that Melissa would only have to express her number concept in terms of imagined counting activity rather than collections of items in order to overcome the limitations of her direct modelling methods. On the basis of this hypothesis, the teacher made several highly directive interventions to investigate whether Melissa could learn to solve subtraction sentences by counting backwards (e.g. solve $17 - 4 =$ by counting '17, 16, 15, 14, 13'). This method was chosen because it is children's first natural method to subtraction sentences beyond direct modelling and because children inferred to be at the same conceptual level as Melissa frequently construct this method without direct instruction (Steffe *et al.* 1983).

The teacher first checked that Melissa had developed the prerequisite ability of reciting the standard backward number word sequence starting at 20. He then asked her to say how many marbles remained in a cup when he removed them one at a time. She answered appropriately on each occasion, and the activity was then repeated with the variation that she was also required to put up a finger each time a marble was removed. Melissa again responded appropriately. The teacher then presented the sentence $15 - 3 =$ _____, but Melissa solved it by using her finger pattern method. Finally, he asked her to solve it by counting backwards and she started to do so before saying, 'Okay, I know it – I just can't get it in my mind'.

The instruction provided up to this point was a form of direct training in which the teacher assessed the child's methods, chose the next method in the developmental sequence as the goal of instruction, assessed prerequisite skills, and attempted to simplify the target method as much as possible. Unfortunately, something seemed to be going wrong. Melissa's final comment and her general demeanour indicated to the teacher that she saw no point in trying to solve the task by counting backwards. He therefore inferred that if he persisted he might merely train her to behave as he desired rather than encourage her to express her number concept in a novel way. In other words, Melissa's primary goal might become to do exactly what she was told and thus get out of an unpleasant situation as quickly as possible. On the basis of these inferences, the teacher engaged her in an alternative activity for 10 minutes before presenting further subtraction sentences. No hints or prompts to count backwards were given in the remainder of the session.

Melissa solved the first subtraction sentence presented, $13 - 4 =$ _____, by using her finger pattern method. The teacher then presented the sentence $21 - 4 =$ _____. Because 21 was beyond the range of her finger patterns the teacher hypothesised that she might count backwards. She muttered quietly to herself for 50 seconds before whispering '20, 19, 18, 17'. Finally, the teacher asked her to solve $32 - 5 =$ _____ and she struggled with the problem for 2½ minutes before counting backwards '31, 30, 29, 28, 27' as she sequentially closed five fingers.

The teacher's prior direct instruction clearly influenced Melissa's production of these two backward-counting solutions, but three observations suggest that she did not merely recall what she had been told to do. Instead, she constructed a backward counting method that expressed her concepts. First, she did not use a new method until she was in a situation where her finger-pattern methods did not work. The tasks $21 - 4 =$ ___ and $32 - 5 =$ ___ were genuine problems for her. As she had previously explained, 'I'm really used to having something to help me and stuff like little numbers with my hands and big numbers with the little cubes that we have [in class]'. This contrasts with the situation in which the teacher attempted to train her to count backwards. Second, the time it took her to solve the two sentences, particularly $2\frac{1}{2}$ minutes to solve $32 - 5 =$ ___ after she had just counted backwards to solve $21 - 4 =$ ___, suggests that her difficulty was not merely one of recall. Third, the methods she used differed from the one that she had been taught. She did not put up fingers or use any other observable keeping-track procedure to solve $21 - 4 =$ ___, and she closed fingers as she counted to solve $32 - 5 =$ ___. In fact, her problem with $32 - 5 =$ ___ appeared to be to find a way to keep track of her backward-counting activity.

This analysis characterises Melissa as an active constructor of knowledge who strove to overcome problems that arose as she interacted with the teacher. More generally, learning that involves conceptual reorganisation is, from the constructivist perspective, an active problem-solving process. This implies that one of the teacher's primary responsibilities should be to engage students in activities that give rise to genuine mathematical problems for them. The practice of discussing the limitations of students' current methods and suggesting alternatives is compatible with constructivism. Even more direct forms of instruction such as lecture and directed discussion can be effective with older students who can conduct an internal, reflective dialogue (Siegel 1981). However, difficulties arise when the teacher is oblivious to students' possible meanings and persists in making interventions that can be interpreted as demands rather than suggestions. When the teacher attempts to impose a method on students, the constraints on students' constructive activities are such that they are likely to try and find ways to give the impression they are producing behaviours that the teacher expects (Voigt 1985). In other words, the teacher's persistent directions to solve tasks in prescribed ways may constrain students' attempts to express their concepts by using alternative methods. This drastically reduces the opportunities for reflective problem solving that are crucial to the construction of increasingly powerful conceptual structures. In the episode with Melissa, for example, the teacher changed his instructional strategy as soon as he became aware that she might not have a reason to construct a new method. He placed the goal of nurturing her apparent intellectual autonomy above that of teaching her a specific method. To this end, he tried to ensure that her activity was subject to the constraint that it should express her numerical concepts.

To conclude this discussion of the sample episode, we note that it also illustrates the value of models of cognitive development in specific areas of mathematics. The teacher was able to infer Melissa's conceptual level, speculate about a possible zone of proximal development, and devise initial instructional activities. However, knowledge of development is not, by itself, sufficient for good instruction. The teacher needs to be aware that he or she cannot inevitably lead the child to make the correct construction. Initial inferences and speculations might be wrong or, for a variety of reasons, the child might give unanticipated meanings to the teachers' actions.

IMPOSITION AND NEGOTIATION IN TEACHING

Teaching can be characterised as involving varying degrees of imposition and negotiation. When teaching by imposition, the teacher attempts to constrain students' activities by insisting that they use prescribed methods. This can be contrasted with teaching by negotiation:

> The teacher has certain goals and intentions for pupils and these will be different from the pupils' goals and intentions in the classroom. Negotiation is a goal-directed interaction, in which the participants seek to [modify and] attain their respective goals (Bishop 1985, p. 27).

The episode with Melissa was characterised more by negotiation than by imposition.

Negotiation and imposition are best thought of as endpoints of a continuum rather than as two all-embracing categories. Observations made by Goodlad (1983) and Stake and Easley (1978) indicated that most mathematics teaching lies far closer to the imposition pole. Indicators of teaching by imposition at the elementary school level include:

1 believing that elementary school mathematics is basically arithmetic and that arithmetic consists of learning basic facts and standard computational procedures;
2 regarding specific facts and skills as isolated instructional goals;
3 inflexibly relying on the textbook;
4 teaching by direct explanation or demonstration and then assigning individual seatwork on paper-and-pencil exercises;
5 dealing with instructional failures by repeating the demonstration–seatwork cycle one or more times;
6 regarding students' alternative methods as undesirable behaviours to be eliminated.

I attempted to investigate the consequences of teaching mathematics by imposition in two recent studies at the first- and second-grade levels (Cobb 1985; 1987; Cobb and Wheatley, in press). The general conclusion of both studies was that the children increasingly did arithmetic in two separate contexts. They had constructed self-generated methods that expressed their concepts and used these to solve mathematical problems in nonschool settings. These contrasted with their versions of academic, school arithmetic procedures that were not connected to their self-generated methods and, at best, expressed alternative, highly figurative concepts. The dichotomy between school arithmetic and self-generated arithmetic can be illustrated by considering the behaviour of one second-grade child, Auburn. She was inferred to be at a relatively advanced conceptual level on the basis of an interview, and her classroom teacher considered her to be one of the best three students in mathematics. Near the beginning of the interview, Auburn was asked to solve the horizontal sentences $16 + 9 =$ _____, $28 + 13 =$ _____, $37 + 24 =$ _____, and $39 + 53 =$ _____. On each occasion, she counted-on by ones as she sequentially put up fingers. She gave the correct answer to the first three sentences and 82 rather than 92 as her answer to $39 + 53 =$ _____. When she was asked about her last solution, she explained, 'I counted five 10s and then I did three 1s.' Her method seemed to involve organising counting-on by ones into units of 10 as she went along by keeping track of the number of times she put up all 10 fingers. She probably lost track and counted around her hands four rather than five times.

At the end of the second part of the interview conducted two days later, Auburn was asked to complete a worksheet that included, in sequence, the following tasks:

$$
\begin{array}{cccc}
16 & 28 & 37 & 39 \\
+\ 9 & +13 & +24 & +53 \\
\hline
\end{array}
$$

(Note that these are the same number combinations as the horizontal sentences.) For each of these tasks, Auburn first added the 1s' column and then the 10s' column. However, she failed to carry the 1 and produced answers of 15, 31, 51, and 82. As soon as she completed the worksheet, the interviewer presented the horizontal sentence $16 + 9 =$ _____ and she counted-on and gave 25 as her answer. The exchange continued as follows:

I: So when we count we get 25 and when we do it this way (points to the worksheet) we get 15. Is that okay to get two answers or do you think there should be only one?

A: (Shrugs her shoulders.)

I: Which one do you think is the best answer?

A: 25.

I: Why?

A: I don't know.

I: If we had 16 cookies and 9 more, would we have 15 altogether?

A: No.

I: Why not?

A: Because if you counted them up together, you would get 25.

I: But is this (points to the answer of 15 on the worksheet) right sometimes or is it always wrong?

A: It's always right.

Given her previous comments, her last statement is interpreted to mean that the answer of 15 is always correct when the task is presented in standard worksheet format.

The contrast between Auburn's behaviour in the two parts of the interview and her final comment indicate that the arithmetic she was currently studying in school had nothing to do with the world of physical objects and real-life problems or her self-generated methods. For her, school arithmetic seemed to be an isolated, self-contained context in which the possibility of doing anything other than attempting to recall prescribed methods did not arise. Her activity in this context did not seem to be directed to understanding and developing increasingly powerful conceptual structures. Instead it was constrained by her interpretation of the classroom teacher's instructions to use explicitly taught methods.

One consequence of children's construction of two separate contexts is that unreasonable responses become increasingly common, a phenomenon documented by Cobb and Wheatley (in press), Hiebert (1984), DeCorte and Verschaffel (1981), and others. For example, the study by Cobb and Wheatley (in press) investigated 16 second-grade children's knowledge of place value concepts. By October of second grade only the three most conceptually advanced children interviewed seemed to be aware of an alternative to attempting to use methods prescribed by the teacher when they completed worksheets. These three children produced the right answer to:

$$\begin{array}{r} 16 \\ + \ 9 \\ \hline \end{array}$$

Only one of the three used the school-taught method. Seven children gave 15 as their answer and six responded 115. The latter group of children were questioned about the reasonableness of their answer, and all appeared to be untroubled. In this setting, there were no indications that they could estimate whether an answer was acceptable. Instead, they seemed to rely on an authority such as the teacher or an answer key. Their loss of intellectual autonomy seemed to be almost complete in the worksheet setting. This indicates some of the limitations of teaching by imposition to replace or repress methods that expressed conceptual knowledge. Schoenfeld (1982) made the same point more generally.

> All too often we focus on a narrow collection of well-defined tasks and train students to execute these tasks in a routine, if not algorithmic fashion. Then we test students on tasks that are very close to the ones they have been taught. If they succeed on those problems, we and they congratulate each other ... To allow them, and ourselves, to believe that they 'understand' the mathematics is deceptive and fraudulent (p. 29).

CONSTRUCTIVISM AND INSTRUCTION

The practice of teaching by imposition follows from a *rigid* adherence to the transmission view of instruction. I have argued that teaching by imposition is incompatible with two general goals of mathematics instruction that follow from constructivism, the construction of increasingly powerful conceptual structures and the development of intellectual autonomy. Constructivism does, however, provide a rationale for teaching by negotiation. It should be said at the outset that this form of teaching requires far more of the teacher. Ideally, the teacher should have a deep, relational understanding of the subject matter and be knowledgeable about possible courses of conceptual development in specific areas of mathematics. In addition, the teacher should continually look for indications that students might have constructed unanticipated, alternative meanings. But this requires that the teacher transcend the common sense transmission view of communication derived from everyday experience. In other words, the teacher must have undergone a conceptual revolution of his or her own. This, to put it mildly, is a serious problem for teacher education.

Further difficulties must be acknowledged before a serious attempt is made to implement constructivist mathematics instruction. As Resnick (1983) observed when referring to the work of Thorndike and Skinner,

> the theories that are strong on prescribing interventions are theories that do not have much to say about thought processes. Even worse, they are theories that almost entirely ignore structure, organization, and meaning as central aspects of learning (p. 12).

Conversely, it is difficult to derive precise instructional recommendations from theories that emphasise structure and meaning. There is a simple reason for this: currently we cannot explain how students construct concepts that are more advanced and complex than those they have available when instruction commences (Berieter 1985). We can identify developmental levels and develop viable models of students' conceptual operations at each of the levels. Further, Piaget's construct of reflective abstraction can be used to specify possible activities from which children might abstract and the resulting structures. However, we are unable to model precisely how students make the transition from one level to the next other than by appealing to intellectually unsatisfactory accretion and absorption arguments. According to Silver (1985), 'A currently popular view ... is that learning is simply an accretion of productions, but I believe that view will prove inadequate for providing a useful understanding of the acquisition of problem-solving expertise in complex domains' (p. 252). Further,

> [We] must go beyond process-sequence strings and coded protocols ... We need to develop new techniques for describing problem-solving behavior not only in terms of the procedures utilized but also in terms of the conceptual systems that influence performance. [These developments] might provide more suitable models for learning, since they could account for the phenomena of cognitive restructuring and conceptual reorganization that are observed as people learn in complex domains (p. 258).

Recent developments such as Anderson's (1983) Adaptive Control of Thought (ACT) theory notwithstanding, Norman's (1980) observation that 'the study and understanding of the learning process remains at a minuscule level' (p. 21) still holds true. The problem of learning seems to be bound up with such intractable issues as the phenomenology of consciousness and the growth of self-awareness (Kilpatrick, 1985).

As a consequence of our inability to explain satisfactorily the type of learning prized by constructivists, we cannot tell teachers that engaging students at a particular conceptual level in certain activities will inevitably lead them to make the correct constructions. The best that can be done is to propose general instructional heuristics compatible with teaching by negotiation and to suggest a variety of specific activities and interventions that might work with some children. In addition to the knowledge requirements discussed at the beginning of this section, it is clear that the constructivist view of instruction implies that the teacher must be a reflective pedagogical problem solver who, in effect, conducts an informal research programme.

It appears that we have two broad options for improving mathematics instruction. We can ignore the goals of developing powerful structures and nurturing intellectual autonomy and attempt to improve traditional instruction based on the transmission view, or we can attempt to effect radical change that is consistent with current cognitive theories. In one option, teachers can be treated as conduits of information who follow specific directions formulated by experts. The second option requires that teachers become mature, autonomous professionals who take responsibility for the development of their own practices. Immense difficulties must be faced if the second option is chosen. However, we are at least becoming aware of the nature of the problem and, as Polya (1957) told us, this is a prerequisite for successful problem-solving.

ACKNOWLEDGMENTS

The research reported in this chapter was supported in part by grants from the Spencer Foundation and the National Science Foundation (Grant No. MDR-8470400). The opinions expressed are, of course, solely those of the author and do not necessarily reflect the positions of the foundations.

My thanks to Tom Carpenter, Phil Winne, and two anonymous reviewers for numerous helpful comments on a previous draft.

REFERENCES

Anderson, J. R. (1983) *The Architecture of Cognition*. Cambridge: Harvard University Press.
Berieter, C. (1985) 'Towards a solution of the learning paradox', *Review of Educational Research*, 55, 201–26.
Bishop, A. (1985) 'The social construction of meaning – a significant development for mathematics education?' *For the Learning of Mathematics*, 5(1), 24–8.

Carpenter, T. P., Hiebert, J. and Moser, J. M. (1983) 'The effect of instruction on children's solutions of addition and subtraction word problems', *Educational Studies in Mathematics*, 14, 55–72.

Cobb, P. (1985) *An Investigation of the Relationship between First Graders' Beliefs, Motivations, and Conceptual Development in Arithmetic* (Final report). Chicago: Spencer Foundation.

Cobb, P. (1987) 'An investigation of young children's academic arithmetic contexts', *Educational Studies in Mathematics*, 18, 109–24.

Cobb, P. and Wheatley, G. (in press) 'Children's initial understandings of ten', *Focus on Learning Problems in Mathematics*.

DeCorte, E. and Verschaffel, L. (1981) 'Children's solution processes in elementary arithmetic problems: analysis and improvements', *Journal of Educational Psychology*, 73, 765–79.

Ginsburg, H. (1977) *Children's Arithmetic: The Learning Process*. New York: Van Nostrand.

Glaser, R. (1984) 'Educational thinking: the role of knowledge', *American Psychologist*, 39, 93–104.

Goodlad, J. I. (1983) *A Place Called School: Prospects for the Future*. New York: McGraw-Hill.

Greer, B. (in press) 'Non-conservation and multiplication and division involving decimals', *Journal for Research in Mathematics Education*.

Hiebert, J. (1984) 'Children's mathematical learning: the struggle to link form and understanding', *Elementary School Journal*, 84, 497–513.

Hiebert, J. (1986, April) *The Nature of Students' Symbol Rule Systems*. Paper presented at the annual meeting of the American Educational Research Association, San Francisco.

Hiebert, J. and Wearne, D. (1985) 'A model of students' decimal computation procedures', *Cognition and Instruction*, 2, 175–205.

Kilpatrick, J. (1985) 'Reflection and recursion', *Educational Studies in Mathematics*, 16, 1–26.

Laudan, L. (1977) *Progress and its Problems*. Berkeley: University of California Press.

Norman, D. A. (1980) 'Twelve issues for cognitive science', *Cognitive Science*, 4, 1–32.

Polya, G. (1957) *How to Solve It* (2nd edn). New York: Doubleday.

Resnick, L. B. (1983) 'Towards a cognitive theory of instruction', in S. G. Paris, G. M. Olson, and W. H. Stevenson (eds), *Learning and Motivation in the Classroom*, pp. 5–38. Hillsdale, NJ: Lawrence Erlbaum Associates, Inc.

Ross, S. H. (1986, April) *The Development of Children's Place-Value Numeration Concepts in Grades Two through Five*. Paper presented at the annual meeting of the American Educational Research Association, San Francisco.

Schoenfeld, A. H. (1982) 'Some thoughts on problem-solving research mathematics and education', in F. K. Lester and J. Garofalo (eds), *Mathematics Problem Solving: Issues in Research*, pp. 27–37. Philadelphia: Franklin Institute Press.

Schoenfeld, A. H. (1985) *Mathematical Problem Solving*. New York: Academic.

Siegel, I. E. (1981) 'Social experience in the development of representational thought: distancing theory', in I. E. Siegel, D. M. Brodzinsky and R. M. Golinkoff (eds), *New Directions in Piagetian Theory and Practice*, pp. 203–17. Hillsdale, NJ: Lawrence Erlbaum Associates, Inc.

Silver, E. A. (1985) 'Research on teaching mathematical problem solving: some underrepresented themes and needed directions', in E. A. Silver (ed.), *Teaching and Learning Mathematical Problem Solving: Multiple Research Perspectives*, pp. 247–66. Hillsdale, NJ: Lawrence Erlbaum Associates, Inc.

Stake, R. E. and Easley, J. (1978) *Case Studies in Science Education* (Vol. 2). Urbana, IL: University of Illinois Center for Instructional Research and Curriculum Evaluation.

Steffe, L. P. and von Glasersfeld, E. (1983) 'The construction of arithmetical units', in J. C. Bergeron and N. Herscovics (eds), *Proceedings of the Fifth Annual Meeting of the North*

American Chapter of the International Group for the Psychology of Mathematics Education, pp. 292–304. Montreal: Université de Montreal, Faculté de Science de l'Education.

Steffe, L. P., von Glasersfeld, E., Richards, J. and Cobb, P. (1983) *Children's Counting Types: Philosophy, Theory, and Applications*. New York: Praeger Scientific.

Voigt, J. (1985). 'Patterns and routines in classroom interaction', *Recherches en Didactique des Mathematiques*, 6, 69–118.

von Glasersfeld, E. (1983) 'Learning as a constructive activity', in J. C. Bergeron and N. Herscovics (eds), *Proceedings of the Fifth Annual Meeting of the North American Chapter of the International Group for the Psychology of Mathematics Education*, pp. 41–69). Montreal: Université de Montreal, Faculté de Science de l'Education.

Wagner, S. (1981) 'Conservation of equation and function under transformations of variable', *Journal for Research in Mathematics Education*, 12, 107–18.

PRACTICAL WORK IN SCIENCE: A TASK-BASED APPROACH?

3.2

RICHARD GOTT AND JUDITH MASHITER

INTRODUCTION

Science education is in a state of rapid change. Over recent years we have experienced an ongoing debate concerning the importance of concept and process in our science courses. This debate has been brought into a tighter focus in the last year or so in England with the advent of the National Curriculum in science. At its centre is the role of practical work; there is no great disagreement as to its importance, the argument concerns its aims – what pupils are to learn from their experiences in the laboratory.

In the classroom, the immediate and overriding preoccupation is with the implementation of the National Curriculum. Its emergence, together with its associated, but untested national system of assessment, requires English science teachers to reconsider the concept–process argument in the light of the restrictions it imposes and the opportunities it offers for innovation. It is being seen in some quarters as a heaven-sent opportunity to retain a concept-based course, while those who have set off down the 'process-science' route are left in some doubt as to the extent to which they will need to cast aside an approach to which many are philosophically committed. To others it offers the framework for a genuine change. What is certainly true is that the urgency for change is now determined by the timetable for the implementation of the National Curriculum. The time is clearly ripe for a reconsideration of the science courses on offer, and in particular of the emphasis they place on practical work.

This chapter will not deal with specific examples of practical work. Rather it will argue for a curriculum based upon 'tasks' or investigative work which may or may not be practical (in the traditional sense of apparatus and experimentation) but which involve the pupil in active data collection or analysis. The roles of practical work in various science schemes will be examined and will serve as an illustration of the argument being developed.

Source: Brian Woolnough (ed.), *Practical Science* (Open University Press, in press).

THE SOCIAL CONTROL OF THE CURRICULUM

We believe that many of our problems in science teaching stem from our blinkered vision as to what constitutes 'science for all'. We wish to suggest that pupils' lack of success in science and their consequent disillusionment can be attributed, at least in part, to *our* failure to match the curriculum to their needs, preferring to deliver science courses that *we*, not they, feel comfortable with. We will begin by examining the underlying causes for that narrowness of purview.

The heart of most science courses has been the acquisition of scientific concepts. Those knowledge-based concepts are often very difficult, abstracted from any real context, and, in the case of Nuffield schemes for instance, embedded in an unreal world of ticker timers and trolleys that cannot be found outside the pages of school science equipment catalogues. As a consequence, pupils perceive no relevance to their science lessons other than the remote and, not necessarily very appealing, prospect of becoming the stereotypical white-coated scientist beloved of popular television advertisements. As Hodson (1987) notes, these 'high status, academic courses are characterised by their abstractness, emphasis on written presentation, use of individual rather than group work, competitiveness and unrelatedness to everyday life' and that this curriculum 'represents a triumph of a particular interest group'.

The members of that interest group – the curriculum developers and opinion formers – operate from within a view of science which is based upon and attempts to emulate their own educational experiences which, at school and university alike, focused upon concept acquisition and explanation. Notions of investigative work which rely on the *use* of concepts rather than their acquisition or verification, are either considered and discarded (or assigned to the CDT or technology department), or simply not considered at all.

This social control of the curriculum (perhaps subconscious social selection is a better description) does not operate solely on the 'content', that is the knowledge-based concepts, of science. The philosophy of science education and approaches to its implementation in the classroom are also largely governed by the historical inertia of inductivism. Most text-books adopt this perspective of science as, arguably, does the policy statement, *Science 5 to 16* (DES, 1985). The majority of HMI documents, for instance, include a series of criteria which include observation, selection of observations for further study and so on; an ordering which is driven, possibly unconsciously, from an inductivist position. This 'scientific method' derives from a retrospective examination of how scientists made great discoveries; it is by definition, then, tied to concept acquisition since this provides its evidence. It is therefore not surprising that practical work is seen as being concerned with illustration and verification.

Research evidence from the Assessment of Performance Unit (APU), as well as the everyday experience of teachers, suggests that this view of science has failed many of our pupils, particularly those of average and below average ability, in that 'a significant proportion of pupils appear to be unable to *apply* the scientific ideas that are being taught' in any other context than that used for their introduction (Gamble *et al.* 1985).

There is a need to challenge the prevailing culture which, because of its elitist view of science in schools, is condemning so many of our pupils to failure and frustration. We suggest that there are several key aspects to the problem of pupil failure in that the aims of the science curriculum are:

- too abstract in terms both of the ideas themselves and of the contexts in which those ideas are usually taught. The difficulty of the ideas for many pupils means that their experience of secondary school science is one of repeated and demoralising lack of success resulting in a vicious circle of failure, demotivation and more failure;
- not sufficiently motivating, in that they lack perceived relevance to pupils' own lives;
- reliant on practical work as a means of enhancing 'conceptual learning rather than acting as a source for the learning of essential skills' (Fensham 1985); and
- based (wrongly) on the premise that pupils will be able to use ideas, spontaneously, in a wide variety of situations.

(The reader is referred to Fensham's reflective essay (1985) for a detailed and well argued discussion of these issues.)

By examining the nature of the 'traditional' science curriculum and then considering some recent innovations attempting to change the curriculum and its teaching, an argument for a task-based approach will now be developed.

THE KNOWLEDGE TRANSMISSION MODEL

As we have already noted, the preoccupation in the 1960s and 1970s was with conceptual understanding, culminating in the influential Nuffield schemes. The pupil was seen as having a mind empty of preconceptions. The aim of science education was to fill that mind with the 'truths' of science. The scientist was portrayed, often quite explicitly, as a man (and very occasionally as a woman) in a white coat in a 'high-tech lab' engaged in incomprehensible but, by implication, extremely difficult and important work. By studying science pupils could avail themselves of the opportunity to become members of this elite. Indeed, the course frequently suggested that pupils be allowed to become 'scientists for the day', as if being a scientist is something that one casts off before returning to the real world. The underlying philosophy of science was, and often remains, inductivist in origin. That is to say, pupils were introduced to a topic via experiments during which neutral observations were made. Hypotheses could then be generated from that neutral data and pupils would subsequently 'discover', or be helped to discover, the particular concept to be acquired.

With particular reference to the nature of *practical* work within this view, the purpose was to illustrate concepts so that pupils could 'see' them in action. '... The aim does not lie in the discovery process ... (but in) the understanding of certain basic concepts' (Woolnough 1988). In practice, the Nuffield approach became very didactic in the hands of teachers not well versed in its philosophy and faced with the broad range of ability in the emerging comprehensive schools. (For a fuller discussion of the Nuffield schemes see Woolnough 1988, *op. cit.*).

The pertinent point here is that all of this practical work had one aim only – that of introducing, illustrating or refining *concepts*. The consequence, in terms of pupil learning, has been that many pupils acquire fragments of knowledge which they can recall only in the context in which they were taught or reinforced. 'Good' pupils collect more knowledge fragments than their 'weak' peers. Opportunities to put science to use in relevant situations were limited since the practical work was so tightly defined and often used purpose-built and 'pupil-proof' (in theory!) apparatus.

THE KNOWLEDGE REFINEMENT MODEL

Most courses aimed at knowledge transmission have an implicit view of learning centred on the premise that pupils have an empty mind into which a body of knowledge, called science, is to be transferred. An alternative view is based on the constructivist model of learning and teaching which emphasises the alternative frameworks, or naive preconceptions, which research suggests that pupils already hold (Millar and Driver 1987). Essentially, the alternative frameworks' view supposes that pupils have their own perceptions of the environment involving language, beliefs and relationships and that these personal perceptions are frequently in conflict with the 'correct' concepts of the agreed body of scientific knowledge. Indeed these perceptions are often referred to as preconceptions, as the intention is that they will be supplanted by the 'proper' concepts.

The constructivist approach focuses on the bringing about of change through revised teaching strategies but the overall objective is still the acquisition of the concepts that traditionally constitute school science. The challenge of teaching is then seen to be the effecting of change from preconceptions to the 'correct' conceptual understanding by providing experiences which either prevent pupils developing *mis*conceptions or which force them to confront the mismatch which exists between their ideas and the actual behaviour of the environment.

This approach suffers from two major drawbacks. First and foremost, its basic aim is identical to that of the concept approach – the acquisition of more, and more powerful, concepts. We are still primarily concerned with pupils' ability to explain phenomena such as evaporation, say, with the 'powerful tool' of the kinetic theory. Evidence suggests that many, and probably most, pupils are not able to do this. Whether alternative teaching strategies will remedy this remains a matter of doubt. Several years' experience of various programmes for accelerating development have produced little in the way of success. It could be dangerous to rest our hopes on this as a solution. And, secondly, the approach still allows concepts to drive and steer the curriculum. All attention is directed towards concept illustration, the logical conclusion of which is the devising, often contriving, of methods, including experimental work, for doing this. The cleaner and more clinical the experiment can be, by the removal of the messy clutter which is reality, then the greater the chance of pupils understanding the underlying idea. As a consequence, and with the best will in the world, the opportunity for choosing a context which is relevant to the pupils' experiences, rather than our own, is very limited.

Practical work can reveal the mismatch between pupils' preconceptions and the concept which is the desired learning objective. Thus its purpose is more than simple illustration and has more structure and direction than enquiry or discovery. Nevertheless, its role is primarily to facilitate the change in conceptual understanding and it therefore exists for and is driven by that collection of concepts to be acquired. This is not to suggest that such practical work has no value but rather to note its restricted and restricting role in the curriculum.

The point at issue here, as Fensham comments, is that 'the majority of the school population learns that it is unable to learn science as it has been defined for schools'. We think the problem is even deeper in that public perception of science almost *requires* that it be incapable of understanding; it only becomes science when it is not understood.

THE 'PROCESS' MODEL

Over the past few years several courses have emerged which have been given the label 'process science'. Often the 'process approach', as epitomised in such curriculum developments as *Science, A Process Approach* (SAPA) (American Association for the Advancement of Science, 1975), *Science in Process* (Heinemann 1987) and the *Warwick Process Science Project* (Screen 1987), has been understood by teachers in a rather vague, ill-defined way as being somehow 'active', 'practical', skills-based and student-centred. SAPA arose from work in the United States on a study of what eminent scientists do as part of their everyday activity. It is interesting to note, in passing, the reliance on this high-status view of science. Why do we not examine the use that 'ordinary' people have for science; the nurses, plumbers and intelligent laypeople?

Putting this to one side for now, let us examine the nature of a 'process approach' in more detail. The premise of the approach is that science should place more emphasis on its methods rather than focusing exclusively on its products. This is a challenge, at least in principle, to the accepted endpoint of science education as a body of conceptual knowledge. The processes include observing, classifying, describing, communicating, drawing conclusions, making operational definitions, formulating hypotheses, controlling variables, interpreting data and experimenting.

In practice, the 'process approach' has come to have two strands. In the early years of secondary school science, the processes acquire a metacognitive role in which lessons are *about* 'observing', 'classifying' etc. The processes assume the status of goals which mirror the concepts of the traditional or the constructivist approaches in importance. A lesson may focus on 'Observation' and proceed to illustrate what it is to observe. But do pupils need to know that they are 'observing' or 'inferring'? The question as to whether or not metacognition will assist *pupils*, as distinct from teachers, to *use* the processes does not have an obvious answer. That does not mean that making such terms explicit to the teacher, so that they become part of teaching and learning, is not important. But perhaps they are better seen as a checklist to ensure that varieties of cognitive process are included. Simply learning a definition, rather than being made aware of the 'correct' term for an activity with which they are already familiar, is unlikely to advance pupils any further in their understanding of science.

Typically, courses in the later secondary school years then deal with processes as a more efficient means to acquire concepts; they become the means rather than the ends of instruction. This is the viewpoint adopted by the constructivists who claim that processes are 'the vehicles by which children develop more effective conceptual tools ... For science, we would argue, is characterised by its concepts and purposes, not by its methods' (Millar and Driver 1987, *op. cit.*). So we find that the redefinition of science is only partial. While acknowledging that the methods of science are important, the methods are those of induction and operate within a concept acquisition framework. It is not likely, therefore, that the problems of relevance and motivation will be tackled effectively.

PROCEDURAL UNDERSTANDING IN SCIENCE – THE MISSING ELEMENT

Gott and Murphy (1987) have suggested that science is about the solving of problems in everyday and scientific situations. They chose to define a problem as a task for which the pupil cannot immediately see an answer or recall a routine method for finding it. To investigate and solve any problem, be it practical or not, there are a set of *procedures* which must be understood and used appropriately. In brief these procedures include:

- identifying the important variables;
- deciding on their status – independent, dependent or control;
- controlling variables;
- deciding on the scale of quantities used;
- choosing the range and number of measurements, their accuracy and reliability;
- selecting appropriate tabulation and display.

Such activities are sometimes referred to as practical skills and as such are often taught in isolation. How many courses have 'circus'-type experiments involving the use of measuring instruments or the creation of tables, graphs and charts? Procedural understanding is not simply a collective term for such skills. The Non-Statutory Guidance for the National Curriculum in Science describes procedural understanding as an 'understanding of how to put all these specific skills together' via the identification and operationalisation of variables and the display and interpretation of data (DES 1989).

Parallels occur in non-practical problems. The idea of deciding which are the independent and dependent variables and which variables must be controlled applies equally to multi-column tables such as those found in *Which?*-type magazine reports (comparing the relative strengths and weaknesses of different makes of some commercial device) or in complex data on environmental effects, say, as it does to planning and performing practical investigations; interpreting such tables often means 'cutting' the data – holding one or more variables constant, whilst looking at the effect of one variable on another. Data on the effects of pollution, for instance, can be accompanied by details of wind strengths and directions, maps showing the location of factories, farming patterns and so on which require a hypothesis to be formulated which can be tested, not necessarily conclusively, against the data.

We must beware of a temptation to think that such understanding is trivial. APU evidence suggested that, for instance, well over half of 13-year-olds were unable to manipulate two independent variables successfully (Gott and Murphy 1987, *op. cit.*). Pupils must have considerable practice before they can apply procedural understanding with confidence.

As we argued in an earlier section, most of the practical work in which we ask pupils to engage involves the illustration or 'discovery' of concepts. We ask pupils to follow instructions or 'do as I have done', fill in a table and display the data in a certain standard way. This is acceptable, even necessary, in experimental work designed to deliver a concept. But in a broader, task-based view, such a narrow conception of practical work must be rejected. The extra element of procedural understanding comes into play if this recipe of instructions is removed. It follows, as a natural corollary, that the science can be more 'open'.

THE STRATIFICATION OF THE SCIENCE CURRICULUM

To summarise the discussion so far, practical work has been used for a variety of purposes. Most commonly it has been used to illustrate *concepts* on the basis that 'seeing is believing'. More recently it has become fashionable to argue that practical work can be arranged in order to disturb and refine preconceptions – the idea of illustrating concepts has been replaced by the idea of active confrontation of preconceptions. The third approach, of 'process science', takes the elements of a 'scientific method' and elevates them to the same status as that given to concepts in the traditional approach. It may become necessary to add to that list the procedural approach to open ended investigative work, which, through its influence on the National Curriculum, will begin to inform curriculum development in the short and medium term.

We wish to suggest that there is an underlying problem here of stratification which is distorting, even artificially polarising, the curriculum. In each of the above views, the key elements of science are extracted and taught in isolation. One stratum is represented by the powerful concepts of, for example, energy transfer. Another stratum consists of the processes of inferring and so on. (Yet another could, in the future, be the procedures of investigational science.)

Learning experiences, even models of learning itself, are then tailored to deliver these strata, often in deliberate and clinical isolation from each other. So, to take heat transfer as an example, experiments are selected *because* they will, we hope, deliver an understanding of the concept as efficiently as possible; the choice of context is secondary, at best. The process stratum, usually taught before the harder concept stratum, is designed to equip pupils with the tools necessary to deal with these concepts. On leaving school we expect the understanding from each stratum to merge, spontaneously, enabling pupils to solve a problem such as identifying and remedying areas of a house which are not energy efficient. The advantage claimed by this approach is one of economics; the ideas are applicable to any example in any situation, so we do not need to cover all situations, or indeed any, of them. As Tobin points out in the context of a process approach, 'Process skills are not separated from science content when problems are encountered in real life situations. However, in classroom contexts, it is often convenient to isolate the processes so that activities can be planned to provide students with intensive practice on the skills' (Tobin 1984).

The argument seems very logical and quite attractively neat and tidy. We know that it has worked for us, the controllers of the curriculum. But, of course, we have defined science from our inherited viewpoint. And, more importantly, the majority of pupils cannot share this perspective. Far from being powerful ideas for solving a variety of problems, science becomes an attachment of status and power for the few and fragments of disjointed knowledge for the many.

As Layton notes in connection with the historical development of science education and in the context of concept driven curricula:

> Schools and colleges, in so far as they incorporated science in the curriculum, adopted a canonical version marked by abstraction and social disconnection . . . As science had succeeded in establishing a place in education for the people, so it had become insulated within the contexts of knowledge generation and validation and withdrawn from the contexts of use . . . In short, science for specific social purposes was replaced by science for science's sake (Layton *et al.* 1986).

Perhaps even more crucially, such a stratified approach denies the way pupils learn. It assumes that they will take on trust our assurance that all this knowledge will be useful to them, even as we deny them the opportunity to put it to use, there and then, in relevant situations. Such an abstract and deferred gratification is unlikely to motivate and encourage the majority of pupils. Indeed, evidence is accumulating which suggests that, to take one example, 'process skill learning appeared to be more effective when process skill lessons were infused into the regular science curriculum ... rather than teaching the process in a brief topic as is often done' (Tobin *et al.* 1984).

A TASK-BASED APPROACH TO CURRICULUM DESIGN

What sort of science should we be teaching? What role should practical work play? How can concepts, processes and procedures be brought together in a more relevant and effective manner? How is science to be made at once less abstract, more relevant and more motivating?

Our first step must be to re-examine the definition of procedures and processes since there is some overlap. If we take procedures to be concerned with operations on variables (in an heuristic sense), then some of the 'processes' will come under such a definition, most obviously such ideas as 'controlling variables'. Those which remain under the process banner sit happily with Tobin's definition in which 'processes' are concerned with different modes of thought or 'intellectual operations involved when solving problems encountered in science and, more generally, in everyday life situations' (Tobin *et al.* 1984 *op. cit.*).

The view to be advanced here is one which attempts to move away from a stratified and, to the pupils, fragmented, position to an holistic approach in which processes weld together and refine both procedural and conceptual understanding. We believe that the way forward is to construct a curriculum around a series of tasks that have within them the elements of motivation that stem from confidence in and a sense of ownership of the activity by the pupils.

We would then have a model for science which engages all the elements we have discussed (see figure 5 on page 162).

It may be useful to consider an example of such an approach. The first requirement is to identify a context in which the task is to be set. For younger pupils, in primary schools (age 5–11), this may well be an everyday situation such as road safety. A task might involve them initially in investigating how plasticene models are deformed in collisions with toy cars of various masses travelling at different speeds. It may develop these ideas using published data on accident statistics with a view to creating a news sheet about the dangers on our roads.

For pupils in secondary school a series of tasks may involve them in investigating structures for cars which compress on collision, or how one such structure crushes under different forces. (Other non-practical tasks may involve the collection and analysis of secondary data on stopping distances, manufacturers' data on the construction of collapsible box sections or steering columns, or data on the

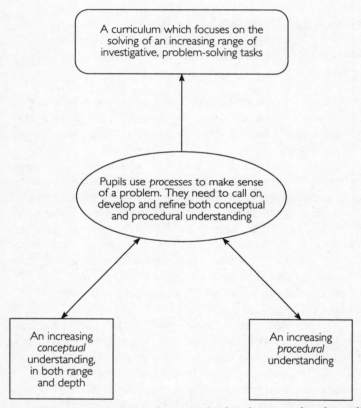

Figure 5   *How processes mediate procedural and conceptual understanding in deriving task solutions*

effectiveness of safety belts at different speeds and restraining different mass bodies.)

The role of 'processes', as defined earlier, now becomes apparent. The *processes* are the various 'ways of thinking' that will be needed to coordinate the pupils' conceptual and procedural understanding into an overall plan for the task. As the task develops, they will *use and develop concepts* such as strength, force and deceleration *while utilising and refining the procedural elements* of the task – the strategies of deciding what to vary, to measure and control and how to do it effectively to give valid and reliable results.

Would such activities be too hard, too abstract? Experience suggests that problems can be selected that are within the reach of the vast majority of pupils. It is true that there are differences in performance. Some pupils will carry out more sophisticated investigations in response to a particular task than others; but all feel they have achieved something. So motivation is enhanced because it depends so crucially on success. Moreover, the setting of the activities within meaningful contexts provides probably the best chance of encouraging transfer of procedures and concepts since the stratified elements of understanding are no longer divorced from purposeful problem-solving activities but are contained within them.

The key to such an approach would lie in the selection of appropriate tasks. They would need to be both practical and written. They would need to be selected for their intrinsic interest and motivation and would have to require pupils to draw on their increasing understanding of concepts and procedures, thus continuously refining them.

PROGRESSION WITHIN A TASK-BASED CURRICULUM

Progression can be defined for a curriculum more easily than it can for assessment purposes. A curriculum, unless we are attempting to create an individualised learning package, can prescribe progression by reference to group behaviour, which is likely to be a little more predictable than that of any individual. Assessment, on the other hand, is by definition personal and subject to all the idiosyncrasies of the individual's interests, experience out of school, home background and so on, which we know to be so influential in pupil attainment. Given the limitations of space here, we will consider only progression in the curriculum.

The evidence to hand suggests that a large number of factors are influential in determining task difficulty. Among the more important are [the following].

CONTEXT

Evidence exists from a variety of sources that the context in which a task is set may be one of the most important determinants of pupil success. Clearly a pupil with a particular interest in gardening, say, will be motivated and knowledgeable in a task involving the investigation of the effectiveness of weedkillers. Pupils' interests and background knowledge will broaden as they grow older, influenced by peer pressures and the immediate environment of home and school. It is against this increasingly complex and diverse contextual background that tasks should be set.

CONCEPTUAL UNDERSTANDING

Concepts interact with tasks in complex ways which require further investigation before we can begin to predict task difficulty with any confidence. Two examples may help to illustrate that complexity.

If the task requires pupils to work with concepts with which they have some acquaintance (heat and temperature say), then they are likely to make progress – to the point where those implicit ideas can become clarified as they evaluate their solution against the demands of the task. If on the other hand, the concepts are not available even in an implicit form (electrical current say), then pupils will have no basis on which to even begin the task, and what is more, little motivation to do so.

Once started on a task, the need to control variables becomes apparent in those circumstances where the pupils have sufficient understanding of the underlying concept to recognise its importance. For instance, in a comparison of the insulation properties of two thermos flasks, the need to control the initial temperature of the liquid relies on an understanding that the rate of cooling will be dependent on the instantaneous temperature. Many pupils who control other more obvious variables, the volume of the liquid, for example, fail to see the necessity for controlling the initial temperature. Add to this picture the fact that concepts themselves present gradients of difficulty which may well be pupil-specific, and the problems of progression through concepts become all too apparent.

PROCEDURAL UNDERSTANDING

Although gradients of difficulty in procedural understanding are largely a matter for conjecture in the face of a dearth of evidence, there is a small amount available from APU work (*op. cit.*) and Foulds and Gott (1988, *op. cit.*). We suggest that one way to begin the structuring of investigative work centres on the procedural aspects of the number and complexity of the variables involved.

Thus a *Which?*-type test involving independent and dependent variables both of which are categoric serves as a starting point (for instance, which of two sorts of jelly dissolves most quickly?, in which younger children may simply watch them and 'see which is fastest'). A second level would be a *Which?*-type test in which the dependent variable is continuous; we would be expecting pupils to quantify the rate of dissolving. Pupils would need to deploy the additional element of procedural understanding represented by the recognition and measurement of such a variable.

The next level would involve the move from categoric to a continuous independent variable. Pupils would now need to decide how many values of that variable to use, over what range and at what intervals: for instance, *how* does the rate of dissolving depend on the temperature of the water? The resulting data is best represented in a line graph, rather than the bar line chart appropriate to the preceding level.

Increasing the number of independent variables to two adds another level of complexity which, through research in the Piagetian tradition we know to present difficulties to a significant minority of pupils at all ages in the secondary-school phase (about a third of 16-year-olds). Pupils would be asked to find out whether the temperature *or* the size of the jelly pieces affects the rate of dissolving. The two independent variables would be categoric (the temperature of the water and the size of the jelly pieces, given two fixed temperatures and sizes, for instance) while the dependent variable, the rate of dissolving, would be continuous.

Once the idea of separation of these independent variables is mastered, the task can be changed by presenting pupils not with two sizes and temperatures, but with a packet of jelly and a source of heat. The task would ask pupils to determine *how* the temperature and the size of the jelly pieces affects the rate of dissolving and becomes a complex one, involving them in decisions as to number and range of measurements for independent variables, both of which are now continuous.

Given this complex picture, how is task progression to be defined? We have argued in this chapter that a key issue in motivating pupils is that of relevance; choice of a context which sustains that motivation while catering for the development of the concepts that constitute a realistic curriculum is clearly therefore a vital element of curriculum design.

As to the more complex issue of procedural and conceptual understanding, we have suggested that to separate out the two would be a mistake; that to progress wholesale along first one strata and then another is ineffective and demotivating. But that does not preclude an emphasis on one or the other in a particular task.

In structuring such a curriculum it may be useful to select an initial series of tasks, set in an appropriate context, in which pupils are asked to advance only along one of the strata (for example, working with a familiar concept, but advancing procedural skills). Once familiar with the procedural skills of *Which?*-type tasks, say, it may then be appropriate to deploy those procedural skills in contexts which involve less well understood concepts – dissolving jelly might become linked to rates of reaction. The concepts can be developed within investigations, providing that pupils have some initial ideas which will allow them some purchase on the task. Other concepts which are very new to them may require an explicit introduction along more traditional lines before the ideas can be refined through use in investigative situations.

The trick will be to sequence the tasks so that the motivation derived from the relevance and completeness of the activity is not subverted by the need to control progression in concept and procedure, whether that need derives from assessment purposes or the structuring of schemes of work. Such a curriculum is, at present, not much more than a gleam on the horizon, but nonetheless a gleam worth striving towards.

THE NATIONAL CURRICULUM – AN OPPORTUNITY AND A CHALLENGE

The English National Curriculum in science revolves around two Profile Components (PC1 and PC2). The first of these has within it just one Attainment Target (AT1 – Exploration of Science) whilst PC2 has 16, all of which are concerned with elements of Knowledge and Understanding. As with the other subjects, the science proposals have met with a mixed and surprisingly muted response. To some it represents a backward step into yet more concept acquisition. Certainly the sheer number of attainment targets in the Knowledge and Understanding Profile Component is somewhat forbidding. But there is more than a glimmer of hope. In Key Stages 1 and 2 (ages 5–11) something close to half of the curriculum in science is to be devoted to AT1 (Exploration of Science), the fraction reducing to about a third in Key Stages 3 and 4 (ages 11–16). AT1 has been construed by many as being simply practical work. This is not the case. Much of what we have called illustrative practical work in fact finds its place in the Knowledge and Understanding attainment targets; which is where it rightly belongs, since its purpose is to help demonstrate concepts.

AT1, by contrast, is concerned with procedural understanding as we have defined it here. In the words of the Non-Statutory Guidance for Science, 'this understanding of the way in which skills are subsumed into the tactics and strategy of an investigation is referred to as procedural understanding and is fundamental to Attainment Target 1' (DES 1989, *op. cit.*).

There is, however, an inherent danger in the separation of the two profile components. By definition, these components are separated for reporting (i.e. assessment) purposes. But they may well influence the curriculum in such a way that it becomes stratified with all the consequences we have identified in this chapter. It will be very tempting for schools to modularise their science curriculum and 'do' AT1 in a concentrated lump before moving on to the 'real' science. The Non-Statutory Guidance for Science advises strongly against this move. It recommends that AT1 should permeate the entire science curriculum, to say nothing of Design and Technology which has adopted a similar philosophy. [...] This permeation is, in our view, best achieved through a task-based curriculum. From this perspective, the progression defined in the Statements of Attainment, with the profile components seen as existing in isolation, represents an incomplete and rather simplistic view of pupil attainment but one which, nonetheless, gives a starting point.

To date, little work has been done to discover either how effective such a task-based curriculum would be, or how pupil attainment can effectively be described. Where tasks have been used in small-scale studies, the evidence, such as it is, suggests that the motivation and success of the pupils has been improved (Foulds and Gott 1988). More research must be carried out into the creation of banks of tasks, structured and indexed upon their procedural and conceptual complexity. Only then will we be in a position to develop and test the ideas presented here.

It is our hope that if this challenge is met, the science curriculum may become available and enjoyable to all pupils, and not just to the most able.

ACKNOWLEDGMENTS

The authors would like to thank Patricia Murphy of the Open University for extensive comment and discussion during the writing of the early drafts of this chapter.

REFERENCES

American Association for the Advancement of Science (1973) *The Science Process Measure for Teachers Form B.*

American Association for the Advancement of Science (1975) *Science – A Process Approach.* Lexington, MA: Ginn.

DES (1985) *Science 5–16: A Statement of Policy.* London: HMSO.

DES (1989) *Science in the National Curriculum.* London: HMSO.

Fensham, P. J. (1985) 'Science for all: a reflective essay', *Journal of Curriculum Studies*, 17, 4, 415–35.

Foulds, K. and Gott, R. (1988) 'Structuring investigations in the science curriculum', *Physics Education*, 23, 6, 347–51.

Gamble, R., Davey, A., Gott, R. and Welford, G. (1985) *Science at Age 15: Assessment of Performance Unit Science Report for Teachers, Number 5.* London: HMSO.

Gott, R. and Murphy, P. (1987) *Assessing Investigations at Ages 13 and 15. Science Report for Teachers: 9.* London: DES.

Heinemann (1987) *Science in Process.* London: Heinemann.

Hodson, D. (1987) 'Social control as a factor in science curriculum change', *International Journal of Science Education*, 9, 5, 529–40.

Layton, D., Davey, A. and Jenkins, E. (1986) 'Science for Specific Social Purposes (SSSP): perspectives on adult scientific literacy', *Studies in Science Education*, 13, 27–52.

Millar, R. and Driver, R. (1987) 'Beyond processes', *Studies in Science Education*, 14, 33–62.

Screen, P. (1987) *Warwick Process Science Project.* Southampton: Ashford Press.

Tobin, K. (1984) 'Student engagement in science learning tasks', *European Journal of Science Education*, 6, 4, 339–47.

Tobin, K., Pike, G. and Lacey, T. (1984) 'Strategy analysis procedures for improving the quality of activity oriented science teaching', *European Journal of Science Education*, 6, 1, 79–89.

Woolnough, B. E. (1988) *Physics Teaching in Schools 1960–1985.* Lewes: The Falmer Press.

3.3 INSTRUMENTAL ENRICHMENT

BOB BURDEN AND ANTON FLOREK

Instrumental Enrichment is a programme, developed by the Israeli psychologist and educator Reuven Feuerstein and his colleagues over many years, to help retarded performers become fully effective learners. It is worth noting the terminology used in this statement because it reflects some important aspects of Feuerstein's work and ideas.

Firstly, the use of the term 'retarded performer' is a useful one as it focuses upon the 'performance', leaving the person potentially intact in the labelling process – a feature which is still often lacking in our teaching culture today. Secondly, Instrumental Enrichment (commonly referred to as IE or FIE) is not primarily concerned with teaching 'thinking skills'. In fact, the term is something of an anathema to Feuerstein since he sees the purpose of his theory and methods as having a profound effect upon the underlying cognitive structures of all thinking and learning. In this sense, the teaching of skills can be seen as a peripheral activity which will only have a lasting and far-reaching effect if it is incorporated within a sound theoretical framework.

This point cannot be emphasised too strongly because it marks the essential difference between Feuerstein and most other producers of cognitive skills programmes. IE is merely the tip of an iceberg. It arises out of a belief system about human potential, a sophisticated theory of human learning, a revolutionary view of assessment and years of clinical and educational practice. In supporting such a position Feuerstein has argued that for him 'the chromosomes do not have the last word', alluding to the number of learners with Down's Syndrome in particular who have successfully participated in IE programmes.

The purpose of this chapter will be to elucidate some of the main aspects of Feuerstein's ideas so that IE can be understood within its proper context. A brief description of IE will then be given, relating it to these ideas and explaining Feuerstein's insistence upon proper training in what he terms 'the mediation process'. A résumé will be provided of some of the more important research studies into the effects of IE carried out across the world and some conclusions will be drawn about the importance of this work for teacher training and classroom practice.

Source: M. J. Coles and W. D. Robinson (eds), *Teaching Thinking*, (Bristol Press, 1989), pp. 71–80.

THE ROOTS OF THE THEORY

Reuven Feuerstein is a Rumanian Jew who was one of the founder members of the Zionist state of Israel after World War II. As one of the people responsible for the education of young people pouring into the new country from all corners of the world, he became aware not only of their culturally different backgrounds but also of the fact that many who were being categorised as mentally retarded because of what he terms 'cultural deprivation' or other reasons were potentially far more capable or 'dynamic' than was being revealed by conventional assessment techniques.

Out of this experience and his later work in Morocco, Feuerstein began to formulate a set of ideas which were quite revolutionary for their time. First, his definition of cultural deprivation is totally different from the once popular and now largely discredited notions of Bernstein and other sociologists of the 1960s. In Feuerstein's terms, culture should be seen as the active process by which knowledge, values and beliefs are transmitted from one generation to the next. Cultural deprivation is described as 'a state of reduced cognitive modifiability of the individual, in response to direct exposure to sources of stimulation' (1980, p. 15) which is the result of a failure on the part of a group to transmit or mediate its culture to the new generation. Further elaboration of Feuerstein's thoughts on culture can be found in one of his key early papers (1982).

The importance of this notion of cultural deprivation and its potential effects later on in life centres upon the fact that the most successful members of society and, for that matter, the most successful societies, are usually those who have access to their own cultures. Furthermore, knowing your own culture – having a sense of dignity and place within it – is surely the prerequisite to being able to adjust to or indeed assimilate another culture without losing your own identity. One of the primary tasks for parents and educators, therefore, must be to make that culture available to the child. Unless they do so, the children will fail educationally and cultures will ultimately die out.

Thus a key issue for parents and teachers is how to teach children to learn how to learn and to understand themselves as learners in this process. For Feuerstein this became a burning question which subsequently led him to attack many strongly entrenched beliefs about human development; it also brought him into direct conflict with two of the most respected psychologists of their time, Jean Piaget and Arthur Jensen.

In his quest to gain a greater understanding of how children learn Feuerstein moved to Geneva to study under Piaget; there he met and became impressed by the ideas of a less well-known psychologist Andre Rey, to whom he has always acknowledged his indebtedness. However, at a time when everything spoken and written by Piaget was being received unquestioningly by most child development scholars, Feuerstein came to believe that far too little emphasis was placed by the Genevan school on the social context of learning. In this he mirrored the, at the time largely unknown, idea of the great Russian psychologist Vygotsky and some of the later work of Jerome Bruner and others.

At the same time the fashionable views of Jensen and his British adherents, Burt and Eysenck, concerning the largely fixed and inherited nature of intelligence, ran counter to Feuerstein's developing views which focused on the difference between intellectual potential and measured performance on IQ tests, and on the possibility of bringing about positive cognitive changes in even the most retarded individuals. On his return to Jerusalem and in his subsequent travels to North America and other parts of the world, Feuerstein began to build up a team of like-minded colleagues who set about funding practical ways of shattering some of these established myths. The most influential and enduring of those collaborators have been Jacov Rand and Mildred Hoffman and, later, Mogens Jensen. With initial funding from a group of Canadian Jewish women, the Hadassah-Wizo Research Institute was set up on the outskirts of Jerusalem and became a centre for teaching, advice and support for teachers, parents and research workers from all over the world.

At a time when he was regularly dismissed as a 'crank' because his ideas were so out of keeping with current psychological dogma, Feuerstein began to travel the world speaking at international conferences about the remarkable changes that he claimed his team's ideas and methods were bringing about in the cognitive performance of individuals previously dismissed as 'unteachable'. To the world at large Feuerstein's growing reputation was only accessible by word of mouth or from brief conference proceedings, and it was not until the publication of two key texts – *The Dynamic Assessment of Retarded Performers* in 1979 and *Instrumental Enrichment* one year later – that his work and ideas became widely accessible. These texts are still essential reading for anyone seeking to understand the primary function of IE and its related assessment technique, the Learning Potential Assessment Device (LPAD).

IMPORTANT ASPECTS OF FEUERSTEIN'S THINKING

Feuerstein emphasises that ideas and theories do not grow out of nothing but are always based on values and belief systems. He sees such belief systems as fundamental to effective action and argues that without a belief in an almost limitless human potential, artificial barriers will always remain to prevent change. Thus he begins with the belief that all humans of any age, however severely disabled for whatever cause, can become fully effective learners. He is not prepared to compromise on this. This view is clearly at odds with the still often held view that children with learning difficulties are coming to the classroom as static learners with fundamental disabilities which prevent any real access to change in their learning. Feuerstein views all humans as potentially dynamic; hence his belief in their potential for change. Given these arguments might it not be possible that we, in special education in particular and indeed in education generally, have severely under-taught generations of children by traditionally presuming that their ultimate ability to change is limited by their condition?

Once one is 'freed' by adopting such a belief system, a number of logical consequences automatically follow. Perhaps the key consequence for Feuerstein is his notion of 'structural cognitive modifiability' which is his way of saying that even the cognitive structure of the brain can be changed by enabling people to learn how to learn, in that learning becomes cumulative and in turn affects performance over one's lifespan. This, of course, runs counter to other traditional dogmas that we become less effective learners as we grow older. Feuerstein himself argues:

> The essential feature of this approach is that it is directed not merely at the remediation of specific behaviours and skills but at changes of a structural nature that alter the course and direction of cognitive development ... 'structural changes' refer ... to the organism's manner of interacting with, that is, acting on and responding to, sources of information. Thus a structural change, once set in motion, will determine the future course of an individual's development (1980, p. 9).

The key to learning to learn lies in the notion of 'mediated learning experience' which is at the heart of Feuerstein's social interactionist theory of learning.

By mediated learning experience (MLE) Feuerstein refers:

> to the way in which stimuli emitted by the environment are transferred by a 'mediating' agent, usually a parent, sibling or other care giver. This mediating agent, guided by his intentions, culture, and emotional investment, selects and organises the world of stimuli for the child ... Through this process of mediation, the cognitive structure of the child is affected (1980, pp. 15–16).

Much of the 'theory building' at the Jerusalem research institute has been directed towards explicating what is meant by mediation and where and how it occurs. In some ways it is the most fundamentally important aspect of Feuerstein's work but the least widely understood and acknowledged. Without mediation IE becomes just another thinking skills 'package' and the LPAD becomes an interesting set of diagnostic materials. Understanding these views is critical to using and evaluating Feuerstein's work in the classroom. Both of the present writers have been trained in using these materials and it becomes increasingly clear with experience in using them that the concept and process of mediation in general and the teacher's role as mediator in particular are fundamental to producing a classroom culture of positive support to which all group members belong.

The three essential aspects of any proper mediation of a learning experience by a parent, teacher or care giver are that:

1 the mediator should be aware of, make known and ensure that the learner has understood what s/he is going to do (intentionality and reciprocity);

2 the mediator should explain why s/he is going to do it (investment of meaning); and

3 the act should be conveyed as having value beyond the here and now (transcendence).

In describing the process of mediation Feuerstein suggests that:

An interaction that provides mediated learning must include an intention, on the part of the mediator, to transcend the immediate needs or concerns of the recipient of the mediation by venturing beyond the here and now in space and time. Indeed it is the intentional transcendent nature of the interaction that is the defining characteristic of a mediated interaction (1980, p. 20).

A useful example of such intentional transcendence might be the scenario of two parties on the top level of a double decker bus, each party comprising one child and a parent. Looking out of the window child A says to parent A, 'Look, mummy/daddy, what's that?' Parent A looks up from reading a newspaper and says impatiently, 'It's a cow. Don't they teach you anything at that nursery school?' Further down the bus, however, child B asks the same question of parent B but gets the reply 'What does it look like? Tell me things about it. What colour is it? What is it doing?' Finally, after exhausting the immediate information about 'cow', the parent proceeds to elaborate and extend the child's knowledge beyond the immediate by discussing aspects of farming, milk and butter production, etc. The important differences are that child B has had a mediated learning experience within which she has been an active and dynamic participant. Child A on the other hand is little wiser to the concept of 'cow' than prior to the interaction.

The implications of intentional transcendence for children with special educational needs are clear if one accepts that all children bring a kaleidoscope of their own successful learning strategies with them to the classroom. All too often, however, the teacher fails to match what the child brings with what is required, thus preventing the child from sharing familiar aspects and concepts of her own culture within the learning situation of the classroom. It is this denial of cultural sharing which ultimately impedes the child in making sense of what is going on, thus causing difficulties in learning.

Other important aspects of mediation are as follows:

- mediation of feeling of competence;
- mediation, regulation and control of behaviour;
- mediated sharing behaviour;
- mediated individuation and psychological differentiation;
- mediation of goal seeking, goal setting and goal achieving planning behaviour;
- mediation of challenge: the search of novelty and complexity;
- mediation of an awareness of the human as a changing entity.

Only when all of these become an integral part of the teacher's repertoire and are used constantly and appropriately can true mediation be said to be occurring.

Bearing this in mind, it becomes clear that the effectiveness of any instigated IE programme will be largely dependent upon the quality of mediation – more even than the 'Instruments' themselves, although these are not unimportant. Any proper evaluation of IE should therefore concentrate as much upon the quality of the mediation process as upon pupil-centred outcomes. This also explains why Feuerstein is adamant that IE should not become a cheap and freely available 'package' but must be accompanied by intensive training and ongoing teacher support.

The final important foundation stone of both Instrumental Enrichment and the Learning Potential Assessment Device is Feuerstein's notion of the cognitive map. Basically, what this does is to identify the most important elements involved in the completion of any mental act. Seven key features are proposed:

1 the universe of content around which the act is centred;
2 the modality or language in which the act is expressed;
3 the phase of the cognitive functions required by the mental act;
4 the cognitive operations required by the mental act;
5 level of complexity (including novelty and familiarity);
6 level of abstraction;
7 the level of efficiency with which the mental act is performed.

The construction of both the LPAD and IE was directly related to each of these elements in a step-wise progression. Particular reference is made to the phase element within which the notion of deficient cognitive functions is introduced. It is argued here that in order to function effectively on any cognitive task information has to be gathered in an efficient manner (input), worked upon cognitively (elaboration), and any proposed solution must be expressed appropriately (output). A number of important ways have been identified in which these processes are disrupted or inefficiently performed. At the input level, for example, a person may act impulsively or in an unsystematic way or may lack the necessary verbal tools or spatial skills. At the elaboration level s/he may not see the need to pursue logical evidence, may lack strategies for hypothesis testing or may only have an episodic grasp of reality. At the output level s/he may only be able to communicate in an egocentric manner or again may not possess the necessary verbal tools to communicate adequately elaborated responses.

It follows that in identifying missing or inappropriate learning strategies in this way, we can also identify the kinds of behaviours that will foster learning. One of the most important functions of the LPAD is to identify a person's deficient cognitive strategies; one of the main purposes of IE, on the other hand, is to teach appropriate learning strategies and correct deficient cognitive functions. IE also aims to teach the concepts, operations and vocabulary necessary for successful problem-solving, to develop motivation, to produce insight into reasons for success and failure, to foster successful work habits that will become both spontaneous and automatic, and to turn passive recipients into active generators of knowledge.

THE INSTRUMENTAL ENRICHMENT PROGRAMME

The term Instrumental Enrichment was deliberately chosen to represent the instrumental way in which the various activities are designed to enrich the cognitive abilities of retarded performers by means of appropriate mediation. The 'Instruments' can thus be seen as content-limited 'hooks' by which the teacher can introduce mediated learning experiences which can be generalised (or 'bridged') into academic or real-life problem situations. There are fourteen Instruments in all, which are usually incorporated into a lesson plan involving an introductory session setting out the aims of the lesson, a period of independent work on one Instrument, and a discussion period aimed at developing insight and principles for generalisation.

The Instruments are usually taught two or three times a week for 40–60 minutes per lesson over two years. It is common for two Instruments to be taught at any one time in consecutive lessons. The programme always begins with the Instrument known as Organisation of Dots which sets the scene for much of what is to follow. This Instrument is the most content-limited of all and often poses teachers a considerable challenge for this very reason. It is usually taught in conjunction with the first of the two Instruments devoted to spatial orientation. These are followed in the first year by Analytic Perception, Comparisons, Illustrations, Family Relations and Orientation in Space II. In the second year the Instruments become increasingly complex and abstract. Categorisation builds upon the work begun in the Comparison Instrument and is followed by Temporal Relations, Instructions, Numerical Progression, Syllogisms, Transitive Relations and Representational Stencil Designs. Examples of each of these Instruments are given in Howard Sharron's introductory text *Changing Children's Minds*, and are described in full in Feuerstein's 1980 text.

DOES IE WORK?

There are now more than 100 reported studies into the effects of IE, carried out in several countries across the world and with a variety of different populations. The interested reader is referred to Burden (1987) for a review of this literature and discussion of some of the major difficulties faced by researchers in attempting to evaluate something as complex as IE with all its attendant aspects. A number of these studies show conclusively that performance in IQ tests is significantly affected by exposure to IE programmes. This has been found for educable mentally retarded, learning disabled, behaviourally disturbed, culturally deprived, deaf, brain-injured and disaffected students from the age of twelve upwards. Whereas most studies have tended to concentrate upon simple measures of student-centred learning outcomes such as IQ or attainment test scores, it should, however, be apparent to the reader that a far wider set of issues is involved. The quality of mediated learning experiences offered by the teacher, for example, will be absolutely crucial to any specific, or indeed general, learning outcome, yet this is rarely even mentioned. Significantly, both present authors have been involved in the organisation and delivery of a number of UK training courses in IE. What has consistently emerged from these courses is the qualitative change over time in teaching style produced in the IE trained teachers. As a result of these experiences IE awareness sessions are now incorporated in both initial and in-service courses presently directed by both writers.

Other important factors about which far too little is yet known are the cumulative effect of IE over time, the minimum amount of input required to bring about change, the relative effect of various instruments and the most effective way of 'bridging' into mainstream curriculum areas. (An excellent 'Mediation Manual' devoted to this issue of bridging has been prepared by Ilg and Fisher at the Father Flanagan High School, Omaha, Nebraska.) Some studies have also shown positive effects on educational attainments, but it is clear that the quality of the bridging process plays a very important part here. Less striking are the measured improvements on self-concept tests, but interviews and observer ratings show clearly that students consider themselves to have benefited greatly from IE and that teachers who stick with it feel that their professional skills develop and that they enjoy teaching more.

CLASSROOM IMPLICATIONS OF IE

In this chapter we have argued that Feuerstein's concept of mediation has a central role to play in promoting the active involvement of children in their own learning. The process of mediation promotes an acknowledgment of the fundamental dignity of the child within the learning situation. 'Bridging' enables the teacher to make sense of and extend what is happening in the classroom, thus enabling the children to participate in the lesson on their own terms of understanding rather than the teacher's. Thus, the learners concerned become interactive participants in the lesson, and in the process learn to reflect, hypothesise, seek information, listen to others, share in decisions and knowledge, and perhaps most importantly learn to acknowledge the individual differences which, far from dividing them, can be individually used to contribute to the collective wisdom of them all.

This process acknowledges a central role for the teacher as a dynamic filter for the new experiences that confront and confound children daily within the classroom environment. In this process the change in teaching style from transmission to mediation supports the development of a classroom culture based upon engagement and dignity within learning, rather than disaffection and fear of failure – a feature of schools that has, for far too long, been part of the daily curriculum diet of children experiencing difficulties in learning.

REFERENCES

Burden, R. L. (1987) 'Feuerstein's Instrumental Enrichment Programme: important issues in research and evaluation', *European Journal of Psychology of Education*, 2(1), 3–16.

Feuerstein, R., Rand, Y. and Hoffman, M. B. (1979) *The Dynamic Assessment of Retarded Performers*. Baltimore: University Park Press.

Feuerstein, R., Rand, Y., Hoffmann, M. B. and Miller, R. (1980) *Instrumental Enrichment: An Intervention Programme for Cognitive Modifiability*. Baltimore: University Park Press.

Feuerstein, R. and Hoffmann, M. B. (1982) 'Intergenerational conflict of rights: cultural imposition and self realization', *Journal of School Education, Indiana University*, 58(1), 44–63.

Ilg, J. and Fisher, M. B. (1987) *FIE Mediation Manual*. Omaha, Nebraska: Father Flanagan High School.

Sharron, H. (1987) *Changing Children's Minds*. London: Souvenir Press.

THE STORY OF STORIES: AN ENQUIRY INTO CHILDREN'S NARRATIVE THOUGHT

3.4

MICHAEL ARMSTRONG

My purpose is to present to you a fragment of the thought and action of five children. But I will begin with a few general remarks by way of preface.

I have grown impatient with the concept of 'research'. In the context of a study of education, it has acquired too narrow a connotation, especially in regard to criteria of rigour, evidence and validity. I prefer the word 'enquiry': 'the action of seeking', according to the Shorter OED, 'especially (now always) for truth, knowledge or information concerning something; search, research, investigation, examination'. In presenting the episode that is to follow I am seeking to define, in the only appropriate way as it seems to me, that is to say through example, a particular form of critical enquiry into children's learning.

The form of enquiry which I have in mind is grounded in the experience of teaching, and in particular in that practice of sustained observation which is inseparable from good teaching, at least, and especially, within what, for want of a better term and despite the misconceptions that cluster around it, I still prefer to call the 'progressive' mode. In one of the extraordinary series of essays which he wrote on the subject between 1859 and 1862, Tolstoy defined education as 'the study of the ways in which people form themselves and cooperation with this free process of formation'.[1] Study and cooperation intertwine in the form of enquiry I seek to define. In the best of daily practice they are probably inseparable; it is only in the interstices of a teaching life that they can be held distinct.

For a first general characterisation of the kind of observation that concerns me I turn to two remarks of Goethe's. First from the preface to his *Theory of Colours* – 'For merely looking at an object cannot be of any use to us. All looking goes over into an observing, all observing into a reflecting, all reflecting into a connecting, and so one can say that with every attentive look we cast into the world we are already theorising'.[2] Then from his *Maxims and Reflections* as quoted in translation by John Berger, following Walter Benjamin, in an essay on the photography of August Sander: 'There is a delicate form of the empirical which identifies itself so intimately with its object that it thereby becomes theory'.[3] An 'attentive look' that is 'already theorising': such is my aim. Description is too often and too easily set against theory. It is regarded as illustrative, illuminative, at worst little more than local colour,[4] at best paving the way for theory, experiment or test.

Source: *Curriculum* (1983), 4, 5–13.

For reasons which I do not have space to elaborate here, I believe this to be a mistake. At any rate, the theoretical significance of what I have to say is, for the most part, embedded within the descriptions which I am about to offer. But a further reason for citing Goethe is this: that the quality of observation, identified by Goethe, which is required of us as teachers to understand our pupils' learning, is in essence the same quality which is displayed by those pupils themselves in the best of their learning. That is to say, the method by which we study learning is also the method by which the objects, or rather the subjects, of our study learn.

Thus in presenting the episode that follows I shall be seeking to define at once a method of enquiry and a particular theory of children's learning. (It might be better to call it a theory of children's understanding.) My example deals with children's narratives and is designed to evoke the range and quality of their narrative interests and to establish the seriousness, often a playful seriousness, of their narrative purposes. As such it represents a small part of a wider theoretical claim, outlined, again through description, in my book *Closely Observed Children*. In the broadest terms, my claim is that children operate as it were on the inside of what Paul Hirst and Richard Peters call the 'public modes of experience', almost from their first encounters with them.[5] In *Closely Observed Children* I expressed this claim in terms of the concept of appropriation, the taking or turning of knowledge to one's own use.

> From their earliest acquaintance [I wrote] with the various traditions of human thought, with literature, art, mathematics, science and the like, [children] struggle to make use of these several traditions, of the constraints which they impose as well as the opportunities which they present, to examine, extend and express in a fitting form their own experience and understanding.[6]

I argued further that 'intellectual growth can properly be seen as a product or consequence of children's successive attempts at appropriation from task to task over the course of weeks, months and years'.[7] The manner of this progress, as of its origins in children's earliest acts of appropriation, is a matter about which I understand as yet little. A fuller understanding depends above all, in my view, upon a programme of naturalistic enquiry sustained over many years. But that is not the issue of the moment. The task I have set myself here is the simpler one of defining the act of appropriation as it is manifested in five children's narrative thought, and it is to this that I now turn.

The five children are members of my present class, a class of 33 children between the ages of nine and eleven, the oldest children in a primary school of 110 pupils in the village of Harwell on the southern boundary of Oxfordshire. Harwell is scarcely a rural village, sandwiched as it is between Didcot Power Station, a mile or so away to one side, and the Atomic Energy Research Establishment, a mile or so away to the other side. Few of the parents of Harwell's primary schoolchildren work on the land; few have lived in the village all their lives. Half the children in my class come from one of three council estates built in the village since 1945; the rest live either in the old village houses along the main street and around the church, or in the newer private houses built after the coming of 'The Atomic' shortly after the war, or along the roads beyond the village towards Didcot or Wantage. Their parents work in the power station, at AERE, or in the nearby towns as far as Oxford.

Like all four classes in the school, my class is informal in its organisation, with myself as its only teacher. Towards the beginning of each week I am inclined to suggest to the class a particular theme for writing – for a story, a poem or an anecdote. On one particular occasion, last autumn, I gathered the class together in the carpeted area to one side of our classroom space and read them a short story by Tolstoy which was to serve as a possible model for a story of their own, a stimulus, as I hoped, to their own imaginations. The story, one of Tolstoy's many *Stories for Children* written for his *ABC Book* in the 1870s, ran as follows:

THE LITTLE GIRL AND THE MUSHROOMS

Two little girls were going home with baskets full of mushrooms. On the way they had to cross the railway.

They thought the engine was far away and climbed the embankment to cross the tracks.

Suddenly they heard the engine. The bigger girl ran back, but the smaller one ran straight across the tracks.

'Don't run back!' screamed the bigger girl to her sister.

But the engine was so near and making so much noise that the little girl did not hear her right and thought she was told to run back. So back she ran across the tracks, stumbled, spilled her mushrooms, and began picking them up and putting them in the basket, one by one.

The engine was near now and the driver blew his whistle as hard as he could.

'Drop the mushrooms!' screamed the older girl. But the little one thought she was being told to gather them well, and crawled between the tracks on her hands and knees.

The engine-driver could not hold back his engine. He blew the whistle as hard as he could, but the engine rolled over the little girl.

When the train passed, everybody saw her lying very still between the tracks with her face down.

Then, when the train had moved on a way, she raised her head, sprang to her knees, gathered her mushrooms, and ran to her sister.

After I had read the story I spoke briefly to the children about Tolstoy and then, without further discussion of the story, I suggested that during the week in question, if they were looking for a subject for a story, they should try to write a story about danger along the lines of the story which I had read them. We talked for a minute or two, no longer, about what they might write. I remember mentioning the possibility that the story might be about themselves and take place in the village.

The children knew that they did not have to write on this subject if there was something else which they preferred to write about. Nor did they have to set to work on the story right away. In the end 21 of them responded to my suggestion some time that week, though some of them chose as their model a second story of Tolstoy's which I read them, about a boy who was chased by a shark. I did not record, nor closely observe, how they set about their task, how long it took them, how single-mindedly or spasmodically they worked at it. Nor did I, at the time, discuss their stories with them. My reflection on their work is therefore decidedly incomplete. Above all it is based on what, rather than how, they wrote; on product rather than process (though I confess that I doubt whether an analysis of the process of composition would have led me to different conclusions).

On reading and later copying their stories my first response was to the variety of ways in which they seemed to have appropriated Tolstoy's story to their own distinctive purposes. Later I began to appreciate the way in which these brief stories cast light on certain distinctive features of children's narrative styles and concerns as a whole. Later still, in discussions with other teachers, I came to understand how well, also, the stories illustrated the children's responses to the concept of danger in a variety of its manifestations. I believe that a fuller analysis of these stories, even without the availability of evidence as to precisely how the children had set about their task or how later they felt about what they had written, would show us a great deal about a child's handling of narrative and understanding of literary form. For the moment however I have set myself a more limited objective: to present and discuss, more or less tentatively, just five of the stories which the children wrote.[8]

I will begin with a story which seems to me to have remained relatively faithful to the spirit of the Tolstoyan model. It was written by Lesley, who is the oldest child in the class, a fluent writer, at her best perhaps in the anecdote, often based on something that has happened to her in 'real life', although she is equally fond of adventure stories or fairy tales. Her most successful narratives tend to be short, often no more than a page of handwriting, and sometimes, as on this occasion, considerably less. Here is her story:

THE SHEEP

One day as I was walking down by the railway track with Tina and Lynn down Townsend a sheep ran in front of us. It had a cut leg, it ran towards the railway track. Lynn shouted 'I can hear a train coming, get that sheep off the track'. So Lesley ran to the sheep. It lay on the track exhausted. The train was getting nearer all the time. Lesley grabbed the sheep and ran. The sheep struggled and made Lesley fall over and cut her knees and face. She got back up and limped off the track just as the train come.

It is the quality of singlemindedness that links this miniature story to its model. In a bare 103 words Lesley achieves the same compression, the same narrow intensity of focus, as Tolstoy in his somewhat larger narrative. The incident of the sheep is everything; there is no background beyond the simple reference to place, 'down Townsend', and no explanation. But the circumstances of the two writers' respective achievements could scarcely be more violently contrasted. For Tolstoy, the compression represents a calculated contraction of the literary means available to him and within his command; for Lesley, compression is a necessity, forced on her by the unavoidable limitations of her present literary circumstances and skills. Lesley is writing at the full stretch of her resources, whereas Tolstoy, who had already composed *War and Peace* by the time he wrote his *ABC Book*, is engaged in an act of literary self-denial. Nevertheless I wish to emphasise *not* the constraints imposed upon Lesley by virtue of her literary inexperience, but, rather, the manner in which she turns these constraints to her own literary advantage. For in the narrowness of its compass this story is a fine example of the characteristic suggestiveness of children's written narratives, where a single word, circumstance or detail embraces – has to embrace – a wealth of meaning. (Incidentally this characteristic was described, in incomparable detail, by Tolstoy himself, in an essay on children's writing published in 1861 under the title 'Should we teach the peasant children to write or should they teach us?'. The present paper is in effect no more than a gloss on Tolstoy's astonishing essay.)[9]

I will cite just three instances of the suggestiveness of Lesley's brief narrative. First the matter-of-fact precision with which two juxtaposed circumstances, baldly asserted, herald the approaching crisis: 'It had a cut leg, it ran towards the railway track.' Then, the powerful resonance of individual words, in particular of the words that are expressive of effort and violent action; 'exhausted', 'grabbed', 'struggled', 'limped'. Finally the psychological conviction implicit in the action – and it is *only* the action that is described: the sense of alarm conveyed by this frantic effort after the menacing words 'the train was getting nearer all the time'.

Although Lesley's story opens, as Tolstoy's does not, with the conventional preface 'one day', it ends abruptly, more abruptly and with less dramatic contrivance than Tolstoy's story, breaking off at the very moment that danger is averted. The abruptness of children's narratives, which may at first seem somewhat disconcerting to an adult reader, more particularly to a teacher, is a matter of some importance.[10] In an essay entitled 'The Storyteller', Walter Benjamin distinguishes the traditional art of storytelling, whether oral or written, from 'information' – that 'new form of communication', characteristic of the press, which emerges in a fully developed capitalism and threatens the existence both of the story and of other written forms.

If the art of story telling has become rare [he writes] the dissemination of information has had a decisive share in this state of affairs. Every morning brings us the news of the globe and yet we are poor in newsworthy stories. This is because no event any longer comes to us without already being shot through with explanation. In other words, by now almost nothing that happens benefits storytelling; almost everything benefits information. Actually, it is half the art of storytelling to keep a story free from explanation as one reproduces it . . . The most extraordinary things, marvellous things, are related with the greatest accuracy, but the psychological connection of the events is not forced on the reader. It is left up to him to interpret things the way he understands them, and thus the narrative achieves an amplitude that information lacks.[11]

I want to suggest that the quality of 'amplitude' which Benjamin picks out in this passage is precisely characteristic of the best of young children's written narratives. As far as children's writing is concerned, what Benjamin calls 'the chaste compactness which precludes psychological analysis'[12] has its source not so much in the broad economic and social considerations advanced by Benjamin in the essay in question as in the psychological and social constraints within which children come to learn how to write. The effect however is strikingly similar to that which Benjamin describes. Like Herodotus's story of Psammenitus, which Benjamin uses as his model, a story such as Lesley's 'offers no explanations', 'does not expend itself', but 'preserves and concentrates its strength'. It is, I want to say, in the nature of children's literary thought – indeed, more generally, of child art as a whole – that this should be so.

The 'chaste compactness' of Lesley's story was nevertheless somewhat unusual, at least among the stories written by my class in response to the Tolstoy story, in its narrow focus. Other stories on this occasion, though equally compact, displayed a more centrifugal amplitude, which is perhaps more typical of children's narratives. Take, for example, the story written by Lesley's friend Lynn, a girl who, like Lesley, was among the oldest children in the class, and perhaps of all of them the most socially mature, certainly the most self-consciously grown up. Her most characteristic stories tended to be realistic, homely, almost documentary, scenes as of her own life.

THE RAILWAY

One day Tina rang Lynn up and said 'Would you like to come down the railway with Lesley, Emma and Melanie?' 'But the boys will be down there, I have seen them. It is Lewis, Jason and Gordon and they are bringing their friends from Didcot Boys', said Lynn. 'But we don't have to be with them. We can meet up the bus stop in fifteen minutes.' So Tina got on her boots and jacket and went to the bus stop. Melanie, Emma and Lesley were at the bus stop. When the two girls got there they could hear the boys from the end of the road and it sounded like they were playing on the old broken bridge. Suddenly there was a scream. The girls ran to the railway and they could see that a train was coming. Gordon was lying on the railway track unconscious. The girls ran to get Gordon out and so did the boys. The train was about 100 yards away, it was coming nearer and nearer fast. It was about three feet away and the girls and boys just snatched Gordon away from the train's reach. The two girls Lynn and Tina between them carried Gordon to the bus stop with the help of the boys. Then a bus pulled in and they all got on. There, sitting on the bus, was Gordon's mum. When she saw Gordon she nearly fainted. Then they told her what had happened and his mum took him home. He had a broken collar bone but they went round to see him the next day and they all wrote their names on the plaster and he thanked them all very much for saving his life.

Once again the scene is set on the railway track, yet apart from that there is in some respects little in common between Lynn's story and Lesley's. The focus of the story is no longer so intently on the single incident. On the contrary, what is most striking in Lynn's story is the manner in which a particular adventure opens out, by way of the context in which it is so painstakingly set, into a portrait of a particular form of life. The narrative has become circumstantial.

Consider the opening dialogue, how readily it suggests the world of late childhood, bordering upon adolescence, a world, exciting and anxious, of older boys, gangs, uncertain encounters. (Lewis, Jason and Gordon are all names of boys who left the village school last year for Didcot Boys', the local comprehensive two miles away in the nearby town.) Later we are introduced to another kind of anxiety, the reciprocal anxiety of parents, in the figure of the mother who nearly fainted on catching sight of her injured son being carried on to the bus. Anxiety finally relieved – for Gordon had suffered no more than a broken collar bone – the story closes with the traditional ritual of inscribing the plaster cast, a further insight into this late childhood world which also serves to enliven what might otherwise seem a somewhat tame, routine ending. As in Lesley's story, the psychological suggestiveness of Lynn's narrative is conveyed without any attempt at explanation or any explicit account of feeling, solely by means of the narrated events themselves. But if the 'psychological connection of the events is not forced on the reader', the way is opened for a wide-ranging interpretation, for any amount of observing, reflecting and connecting on the part of an attentive reader.

For psychological connection of another order, directed towards the anxieties of the inner world of older children, I turn to a third story, by Tina, the friend both of Lynn and of Lesley, who has already appeared, by name at least, in the first two stories. I have implied that in certain respects both Lesley's and Lynn's stories were characteristic of *them*, as well as of children's narratives as a whole. The same may now be said of Tina's story, which is one of several that she has written around the same theme over the course of the present school year. It is a theme which seems to fascinate her, perhaps because it reflects something of the apparent contrast in her own personality between the confidence with which she moves among her peers and the tentativeness of her relationship with adults and the world of adult concerns.

The day I nearly got run over

One day I was just going down the shop for my mum when I noticed this car following me very slowly. As I crossed the road a car drove into the car park next to Dearloves. Inside the car was a man with short black hair with a beard. I went into the shop, bought my mum's shopping, and went out. I looked for the car but it wasn't there. I began to walk along the path. I got to the last house before the road called Jennings Lane, then I crossed the road. A car shot out of Jennings Lane, it missed me by about a yard. I ran home as fast as I could. I told my mum but I don't think my mum believed me. But I never saw that man again.

We are here further still from the Tolstoyan model. Tina has taken over the bare detail of a person being run over and assimilated it into the pattern of her own narrative concerns. The most noteworthy feature of her story, aside once again from the use that is made of such significant details as 'a man with short black hair with a beard', is its air of uncertainty and mystery, the lack of any plausible explanation of events, together with the sense, nonetheless, of a sinister motivation. How many cars are there or are they all one and the same? What is to be believed and whom? Can you trust your mother or your feeling that she doesn't believe you? Can you even trust your own senses? Was, indeed, anything seen at all: 'But I never saw that man again'.

There is a powerful contrast in Tina's story between the exact and substantial physical detail and the prevailing mood of uncertainty. Consider such phrases as 'the car park next to Dearloves', or 'the last house before the road called Jennings Lane'. Objects, places and events are precisely located; the setting is altogether palpable. Not so the significance of what takes place. There, nothing is certain, precision is unattainable, a vague disquiet is all.

I have suggested that Lynn's story is open to interpretation inasmuch as it evokes a particular world, the world within which the described adventure is set. Tina's story has a different effect; it is itself *about* interpretation, about the mystery behind the substantial appearances. Reality and fantasy, fiction and fact, are the subject matter of the narrative; the story is self-referential.

I want to add a reflection on the frame in which Tina sets her story: 'One day . . . But I never saw that man again'. Tina has played many variations on this particular ending, in itself conventional enough, in her recent stories. For example, another mysterious adventure, this time like a fairy tale, closes with the sentence 'When at last he got home he told his wife all about it but all she said was "I think you'd better go and see a doctor"'. In 'The day I nearly got run over' the conventional ending has, as I have already hinted, a double significance. It casts doubt on the narrative itself, confirming the story's mystery. But like all such frames it also serves to mark the narrative off as a fiction. Most of the children in my class still seem to require such markers, at least as far as their own fictions are concerned. The conventional frame offers them ready points of departure and arrival, helping them quickly to get into their stories and quickly out. Even in response to a model story which almost self-consciously avoids such a frame, a majority of the class added it. But then such conventions have their idiosyncratic and ulterior uses too as Tina's story shows. The way in which gradually the conventional frame drops away from children's stories would be an interesting study in itself, always assuming that the frame has not been forced out by the pressure of teachers' demands.

I come now to two stories which seem more self-consciously stylish than those I have considered so far. They are stylish in a way which Tolstoy in his own story deliberately seeks to avoid but which the children who wrote these particular stories evidently relish. There is something almost pretentious about their writing. But these are the pretensions of those who delight in displaying their literary skill and in experimenting with the literary means available to them.

First a story from Teresa, a vivacious writer, especially in the comic mode, fond of witty phrases, absurd names, verbal jokes of all kinds. The story in question, however, is one of her comparatively rare serious pieces, which at a first reading, led me to misconstrue it.

DANGER

One misty morning Kara and her younger sister Jenny were walking home from their grandmas. On the way, like their mother told them to, they stopped and bought some pomegranates. Kara and Jenny went in. Kara stood on tiptoe (in order to see over the counter). She bought what they wanted. Then they made their way home, playing and mucking around. It was a long way home so they stopped to play in the park. Kara dreaded the main road. 'Come on Jenny.' Jenny came. Soon they turned the corner, the very same corner that revealed the main road. Kara turned to put her bag down. Jenny ran across the road. She stopped to go back and get her bag. It was too late. It was wet. The car couldn't stop. She was dead.

When I first read this story I was disconcerted by its manner, delicately poised as it seemed to be between realistic adventure and fairy tale. I went so far as to suggest to Teresa that the ending was too suddenly shocking; the tone of the piece, I implied, was at odds with the final tragedy. Teresa was scornful; Jenny had to be killed and that was that. Now, after many subsequent readings, I would be ready to concede her point. The elements of fairy tale at the opening of the story – the pomegranates, the misty morning – no longer bother me. It is out of the idyll of this low homeward stroll through the mist 'playing and mucking around', that Teresa fashions her narrative's sense of foreboding, while the shock of the final sentence challenges the convention of a happy ending, as exploited for example by Tolstoy in the story that served Teresa and her classmates as a model.

There is indeed a remarkable degree of contrivance in Teresa's story. How beautifully, for example, Teresa reconstructs the opening convention: 'One misty morning'. Not that this phrase is merely a lovely conceit; it is this mistiness that will later become the wetness that prevents the car from stopping in time. Or consider how deftly Teresa introduces the parenthesis in the story's fourth sentence: 'Kara stood on tiptoe (in order to see over the counter).' The sentence in itself does not require the brackets which Teresa, whose punctuation elsewhere was somewhat casual, was careful to include here, but the brackets modify the sense, drawing attention both to the presence of the narrator, explaining her characters' actions, and to the explanation itself which is suggestive not just of Kara's size but also, maybe, of her inquisitiveness and of the character of the village shop which evokes such inquisitiveness. Imagine the sentence without the brackets; its effect is at once diminished.

Throughout her brief narrative Teresa's handling of sentence structure is especially assured. Her sentences are in general more varied and more elaborately constructed than those of a majority of her classmates, on this as on other occasions. Subordinate clauses are used to considerable effect in sentences such as the second – 'On the way, *like their mother told them to*, they stopped and bought some pomegranates' – or later – 'Soon they turned the corner, *the very same corner that revealed the main road*' – where the second half of the sentence is carefully designed to reinforce the foreboding already aroused three sentences earlier in the words 'Kara dreaded the main road'. At the climaxes of the narrative, however, the sentences are staccato. '"Come on Jenny." Jenny came': how little is said, how much implied. As for the catastrophic ending, the sentences are here cut fiercely short: 'It was too late. It was wet. The car couldn't stop. She was dead.' (It is not clear from her own punctuation whether Teresa regarded these words as four sentences or as a single sentence composed of four curt, coordinate clauses. The effect is similar, if not perhaps quite the same, either way.) The suddenness and decisiveness of the accident is further marked by Teresa's handling of tense in these last sentences with the implication that it is already all over.

I have suggested that in young children's stories individual words almost of necessity come to possess an amplitude that opens out possibilities beyond what is actually written. Children have to do a great deal with small means. In Teresa's story, however, this characteristic feature of children's writing seems to have been turned into a distinctive literary device, the occasion for more or less self-conscious literary play. It is impossible to be unaware of the lacuna between the words 'Kara dreaded the main road' and the words '"Come on Jenny." Jenny came,' or of the manner, almost in passing, in which the car is introduced in the penultimate sentence. The reader is asked, expected, to fill in the spaces. What is *not* said is required to complete the sense of what *is*. The story makes a virtue of its omissions, the writer of her limitations.

So to my last story. Tom, who wrote it, is the most obviously, characteristically, intellectual child in the class, slight of build, bespectacled, well-spoken. He does not however stand apart from his classmates; on the contrary, in his play and in his chatter he is typical of his group. To adults nevertheless he tends to convey, at least at school, an impression of unusual self-control; an impression that at times amounts to coldness. It seems hard to follow his emotions, except when he is hurt, when the effort to stifle his tears contorts his face into an expression of violent shame, embarrassment and chagrin. His imagination thrives on the worlds of space and technology: on science fiction, stories of motor racing, wartime adventures. Like Teresa he writes slowly, both physically and mentally as it were, and like her too he often writes quite long and complex narratives. But whereas Teresa's narratives tend to be comic fantasies, Tom's fantasies are for the most part serious, even earnest. On this occasion the setting was a motor racing track, which he knows and has visited. Except for the presence of a threatening vehicle, the world which Tom describes in this story could scarcely be more different from the world of Tolstoy's tale: there seem more than a hundred odd years between Tom's race track and Tolstoy's railway line. The story's emotional force is wholly different too. Tom is at the centre of his narrative world in a way in which Tolstoy decidedly is not.

DANGER!

I was at Thruxton motor racing track. I was watching the saloon racing. For once a Capri or a Rover wasn't winning but a Division Two Volkswagen Golf. As I drunk the last of my Ribena I wondered if I should buy a Talbot patch or a Renault patch or a Lotus patch with the rest of my money. When I arrived at the stalls I discovered that the Lotus patch cost too much. The Talbot patch would look good on my jacket but then the Renault patch would look good on my new cap. I bought the Renault patch and started to go back. The footbridge had lots of shouts coming from it so I went to investigate. I asked a man. He replied 'A girl has fallen down the steps. No one knows if she's hurt.' I thanked the man and walked back to the grandstand. When the saloon racing had finished the Minis came onto the starting grid. The fuss in the footbridge still hadn't cleared yet. Then I saw a boy climb over the crash barrier. The Mini race started. I ran to see if I could stop him running across. The boy tripped. He got up. 'A good Dangerboy that boy is', I thought to myself. A Mini came round the corner. SCREECH . . . splat! Dangerboy had been run over. As I sat in the grandstand I watched cars exit over the bloodstained track.

Tom's story, like Lynn's, brings a particular world to living form, the world of the race track as seen through the eyes of a young boy. Indeed almost half the story is taken up in establishing this world, through the accumulation of precise, if not pedantic, detail: the naming of cars, drink and patches; the pocket money, the gear, the stalls. Other readers of this story have sometimes felt that the setting of the scene takes up altogether too much space, as if, perhaps, by the time he had exhausted his supply of circumstantial detail Tom found himself with insufficient energy for the narrative paper. Certainly that is a not uncommon occurrence in children's writing, though I believe that it is rarely by itself sufficient explanation of a story's drift. In Tom's story, however, the apparent inconsequentiality of all this preliminary fussing over what patch to buy is in keeping with the inconclusive character of the subsequent plot. For there are two accidents that happen in the course of the story. The first, the affair of the footbridge, takes place almost in a corner of the narrative, like the fall of Icarus in Breugel's painting. The man who answers the narrator's question tells him that no one knows if the girl who has fallen down the steps is hurt. Nor do we ever know; this first accident is never clarified. Not that the absence of clarification is accidental. On the contrary, the narrative draws particular attention to it: 'The fuss in the footbridge still hadn't cleared yet.' That, however, is all we learn, for at once the narrative moves on to the second accident as the narrator's attention is distracted by the boy who climbs over the crash barrier.

The vagaries of Tom's narrative have a double significance. They represent, in extreme form, that openness which I have claimed to be characteristic of children's use of narrative. Incompleteness has here become indeterminacy. 'No one knows if she's hurt' – and we shall never know. Readers can choose to accept the uncertainty or resolve it as they will. But this indeterminacy seems neither careless nor idly formal, in the context of a motor race with its crowds, its noise, its side shows and its confused and uncertain excitements. Cars flash by and disappear, accidents take place around the corner or on the other side of the track, a spectator catches no more than periodic glimpses of the main action. In circumstances such as these the indeterminacy of Tom's narrative is surely an altogether appropriate form.

Tom's story was the only one to dispense entirely with the conventional frame. In this, if in little else, it resembled Tolstoy's story. The ending, like Tolstoy's, is highly contrived but to the opposite effect. Tolstoy leads us to expect the worst and then, at the last, relieves us of anxiety, in the manner of a conjuror's trick. Tom's narrator, more realistically perhaps, is relieved of his anxiety only to discover that the worst has happened after all. The ruthlessness of the concluding sentence is more pretentious than any other sentence in the five stories I have discussed. We seem to have come a long way from the simple directness of Lesley's ending to the story with which my analysis began.

For all that, I think we may regard all five stories as variations on a single theme. Here, as I see it, are five children grappling, more or less self-consciously – and I acknowledge the problematic character of that more or less – with literary form, within the constraints of their present experience and skill. These constraints present them with opportunities as well as imposing limitations: above all with the opportunity to make a few words go a long way. The 'chaste compactness' of their narratives brings them, in one crucial respect, remarkably close to what, in the essay already cited, Walter Benjamin defines as the essence of storytelling. And this, I have sought to show, is no accident.

According to the prevailing twentieth-century view, at least among intellectuals in any way sympathetic to children, child art in all its forms is as Ernst Gombrich describes it, in relation to children's paintings, in the last of three essays published in the *Listener* under the title 'The Primitive and its Value in Art': 'spontaneous, happy go lucky, even slapdash, especially since modern schools rightly encourage inventiveness and originality at the expense of manual skill. It has often been observed', Gombrich goes on, that this carefree stage comes to an end with puberty and the growing self-consciousness of the adult.'[13] The conclusion which I would draw from reflection on such examples as the five stories discussed in this paper is entirely otherwise. It seems clear from such instances that child art is neither uncontrolled nor pre-rational, but displays in a striking, even irresistible manner, the early life of reason. In particular it displays, as in the case of these five stories, a consciousness of form, and of content enlivened by and enlivening form. And what of the consequences for teaching and learning, for pedagogy and the sciences of development, for schools and classrooms, for research? You may think that I have only now reached the nub of the matter. But as it happens I want to end here. Even to begin to sketch an answer to this question would require another chapter, more likely several. Besides, I am not at all sure how to answer it except in a form that might well appear utopian. Consider for a moment, in the light of my argument, the way in which we choose to mark, examine, evaluate children's writing, let alone how we set about teaching them how to write. And then consider the present climate of educational opinion.

Or of educational research?

Notes

1 Alan Pinch and Michael Armstrong (eds) (1982) *Tolstoy on Education*. Athlone Press, p. 294.

2 I am grateful to Prof. Edmund Pabst of Southampton University for pointing out and translating for me this passage from Goethe's *Theory of Colours*.

3 John Berger (1980) *About Looking*. Writers and Readers, 1980, p. 28.

4 See, for example, the 'case study' of a 'high gain informal classroom' in Neville Bennett's *Teaching Styles and Pupil Progress*, Open Books, 1976, pp. 97–9.

5 Paul Hirst and Richard Peters (1970) *The Logic of Education*, RKP, p. 32.

6 *Closely Observed Children*, p. 129.

7 *Closely Observed Children*, p. 131.

8 I have tried to present these five stories in such a way as to encourage others to supplement and revise the particular interpretations which I offer. It is a necessary condition for the success of the method of inquiry which I propose that the presented material should be thus open to a variety of interpretations.

9 *Tolstoy on Education*, pp. 222–71.

10 For the following argument, including the reference to the work of Walter Benjamin, I am indebted to Monroe Engel of Harvard University.

11 Walter Benjamin (1973) *Illuminations*. Fontana, p. 89.

12 *Illuminations*, p. 91.

13 *The Listener*, 8 March 1979, p. 348.

Index

NOTE: All names listed in this index refer to people whose work is discussed in the text, rather than merely to references.